Recent Advances in Embedded Computing, Intelligence and Applications

Recent Advances in Embedded Computing, Intelligence and Applications

Editors

Jorge Portilla
Andres Otero
Gabriel Mujica

MDPI • Basel • Beijing • Wuhan • Barcelona • Belgrade • Manchester • Tokyo • Cluj • Tianjin

Editors
Jorge Portilla
Universidad Politécnica de Madrid
Spain

Andres Otero
Universidad Politécnica de Madrid
Spain

Gabriel Mujica
Universidad Politécnica de Madrid
Spain

Editorial Office
MDPI
St. Alban-Anlage 66
4052 Basel, Switzerland

This is a reprint of articles from the Special Issue published online in the open access journal *Electronics* (ISSN 2079-9292) (available at: https://www.mdpi.com/journal/electronics/special_issues/embedded_computing).

For citation purposes, cite each article independently as indicated on the article page online and as indicated below:

LastName, A.A.; LastName, B.B.; LastName, C.C. Article Title. *Journal Name* **Year**, *Volume Number*, Page Range.

ISBN 978-3-0365-4246-1 (Hbk)
ISBN 978-3-0365-4245-4 (PDF)

© 2022 by the authors. Articles in this book are Open Access and distributed under the Creative Commons Attribution (CC BY) license, which allows users to download, copy and build upon published articles, as long as the author and publisher are properly credited, which ensures maximum dissemination and a wider impact of our publications.

The book as a whole is distributed by MDPI under the terms and conditions of the Creative Commons license CC BY-NC-ND.

Contents

About the Editors vii

Preface to "Recent Advances in Embedded Computing, Intelligence and Applications" ix

Martin Ferianc, Hongxiang Fan, Divyansh Manocha, Hongyu Zhou, Shuanglong Liu, Xinyu Niu, Wayne Luk
Improving Performance Estimation for Design Space Exploration for Convolutional Neural Network Accelerators
Reprinted from: *Electronics* **2021**, *10*, 520, doi:10.3390/electronics10040520 1

Robert Stewart, Andrew Nowlan, Pascal Bacchus, Quentin Ducasse, Ekaterina Komendantskaya
Optimising Hardware Accelerated Neural Networks with Quantisation and a Knowledge Distillation Evolutionary Algorithm
Reprinted from: *Electronics* **2021**, *10*, 396, doi:10.3390/electronics10040396 15

Markos Losada, Ainhoa Cortés, Andoni Irizar, Javier Cejudo and Alejandro Pérez
A Flexible Fog Computing Design for Low-Power Consumption and Low Latency Applications
Reprinted from: *Electronics* **2021**, *10*, 57, doi:10.3390/electronics10010057 37

Pablo Merino, Gabriel Mujica, Jaime Señor, and Jorge Portilla
A Modular IoT Hardware Platform for Distributed and Secured Extreme Edge Computing
Reprinted from: *Electronics* **2020**, *9*, 538, doi:10.3390/electronics9030538 59

Minseon Kang, Yongseok Lee and Moonju Park
Energy Efficiency of Machine Learning in Embedded Systems Using Neuromorphic Hardware
Reprinted from: *Electronics* **2020**, *9*, 1069, doi:10.3390/electronics9071069 85

Alberto García, Rafael Zamacola, Andrés Otero and Eduardo de la Torre
A Dynamically Reconfigurable BbNN Architecture for Scalable Neuroevolution in Hardware
Reprinted from: *Electronics* **2020**, *9*, 803, doi:10.3390/electronics9050803 95

Francisco Pajuelo-Holguera, Juan A. Gómez-Pulido and Fernando Ortega
Performance of Two Approaches of Embedded Recommender Systems
Reprinted from: *Electronics* **2020**, *9*, 546, doi:10.3390/electronics9040546 131

Abelardo Baez, Himar Fabelo, Samuel Ortega, Giordana Florimbi, Emanuele Torti, Abian Hernandez, Francesco Leporati, Giovanni Danese, Gustavo M. Callico and Roberto Sarmiento
High-Level Synthesis of Multiclass SVM Using Code Refactoring to Classify Brain Cancer from Hyperspectral Images
Reprinted from: *Electronics* **2019**, *8*, 1494, doi:10.3390/electronics8121494 147

Hyun Woo Oh, Ji Kwang Kim, Gwan Beom Hwang and Seung Eun Lee
The Design of a 2D Graphics Accelerator for Embedded Systems
Reprinted from: *Electronics* **2021**, *10*, 469, doi:10.3390/electronics10040469 165

About the Editors

Jorge Portilla

Jorge Portilla received his M.Sc. in Physics from the Universidad Complutense de Madrid, Spain, in 2003, and Ph.D. in Electronic Engineering from Universidad Politécnica de Madrid (UPM), Spain, in 2010. He is currently an Associate Professor at UPM and researcher within the Centro de Electrónica Industrial, belonging to the UPM. His research interests are focused on Wireless Sensor Networks, Internet of Things, Digital Embedded Systems and Reconfigurable FPGA-based embedded systems. He has participated in more than 30 funded research projects, including European and national funded projects, as well as private industry funded projects, mainly related to WSN and IoT. He was a visiting researcher with the Industrial Technology Research Institute (ITRI), Hsinchu Taiwan, in 2008 and with the National Taipei University of Technology (Taipei Tech), Taiwan, in 2018. He has authored numerous publications in prestigious international conferences and journals with good impact factors.

Andres Otero

Andrés Otero received his M.Sc. degree in Telecommunication Engineering from the University of Vigo, where he graduated with honors in 2007. He received his Master of Research and Ph.D. degrees in Industrial Electronics from Universidad Politécnica de Madrid (UPM), in 2009 and 2014, respectively. He is currently an Assistant Professor of electronics with the UPM, as well as a researcher in the Centro de Electrónica Industrial (CEI). His current research interests are focused on Embedded System Design, Reconfigurable Systems on FPGAs, Evolvable Hardware and Embedded Machine Learning. Over recent years, he has been involved in different research projects in these areas, and he is the author of more than 30 papers published in international conferences and journals. He has served as a program committee member of different international conferences in the field of reconfigurable systems, such as FPL, SAMOS, ReConFig, DASIP and ReCoSoC.

Gabriel Mujica

Gabriel Mujica received his Ph.D. degree in Industrial Electronics engineering from Universidad Politécnica de Madrid and he is an Assistant Professor and Research Member in the Center of Industrial Electronics, belonging to UPM, where he is mainly involved in the areas of Internet of Things, Networked Embedded Systems and Wireless Sensor Networks (WSN). He has participated in different national and European research projects (including Horizon 2020 projects), related to the development and optimization of WSN under real deployment contexts. He has authored more than 30 contributions in high-impact international conferences and journals. He has collaborated in the organization of research tutorials, seminars, and acted as a reviewer and guest editor in international conferences and indexed journals. Moreover, his visiting research stay at Trinity College Dublin strengthened the vision and applicability of IoT technologies in the research center for smart and sustainable cities.

Preface to "Recent Advances in Embedded Computing, Intelligence and Applications"

The latest proliferation of Internet of Things deployments and edge computing combined with artificial intelligence has led to new exciting application scenarios, where embedded digital devices are essential enablers. Moreover, new powerful and efficient devices are appearing to cope with workloads formerly reserved for the cloud, such as deep learning. These devices allow processing close to where data are generated, avoiding bottlenecks due to communication limitations. The efficient integration of hardware, software and artificial intelligence capabilities deployed in real sensing contexts empowers the edge intelligence paradigm, which will ultimately contribute to the fostering of the offloading processing functionalities to the edge.

In this book, researchers have contributed nine peer-reviewed papers covering a wide range of topics in the area of edge intelligence. Among them are hardware-accelerated implementations of deep neural networks, IoT platforms for extreme edge computing, neuro-evolvable and neuromorphic machine learning, and embedded recommender systems. In chapters 1 and 2, the importance of speeding up the design space exploration and the optimization of reconfigurable accelerations for neural networks is introduced to the readers and addressed by proposing a novel method for improving the performance estimation of key metrics during the design space exploration, as well as the evaluation of multi-objective evolutionary algorithms with quantization in real hardware acceleration platforms.

Moreover, in chapters 3, 4, and 5, the topic of low power design for the Fog, Edge and Extreme Edge layers is presented to the readers from three main perspectives: low-latency wireless communication considering energy management strategies on hardware platforms; the modularity and flexibility of the sensor nodes for resource-constrained distributed computing with enhanced security; and energy-aware machine learning strategies through neuromorphic hardware. Chapter 6 reinforces the idea of scalable neuroevolution in hardware by proposing a dynamically reconfigurable block-based neural network model integrated with an evolutionary algorithm implemented in hardware.

Finally, chapters 7, 8, and 9 show three exciting and diverse investigations where embedded systems and embedded intelligence techniques are applied to recommender systems, hyperspectral image processing for brain cancer classification, and 2D graphic accelerators embedded in hardware platforms. This way, the benefits of using hardware acceleration techniques close to the data sources are presented to the readers.

The guest editors would like to thank all the authors who contributed to the Special Issue for their very high-quality research works in embedded computing, intelligence, and applications. The underlying advances and actual implementations allow significant progress to be made in the related application domains.

Jorge Portilla, Andres Otero, and Gabriel Mujica
Editors

Article

Improving Performance Estimation for Design Space Exploration for Convolutional Neural Network Accelerators [†]

Martin Ferianc [1,*,‡], Hongxiang Fan [2,‡], Divyansh Manocha [3], Hongyu Zhou [4], Shuanglong Liu [5], Xinyu Niu [6] and Wayne Luk [2]

1. Department of Electronic and Electrical Engineering, University College London, London WC1E 7JE, UK
2. Department of Computing, Imperial College London, London SW7 2AZ, UK; h.fan17@imperial.ac.uk (H.F.); w.luk@imperial.ac.uk (W.L.)
3. Independent Researcher, Cambridge CB23 7UE, UK; divyanshmanocha@gmail.com
4. Independent Researcher, Changsha 410081, China; hongyu.hyzhou@gmail.com
5. School of Physics and Electronics, Hunan Normal University, Changsha 410081, China; liu.shuanglong@hunnu.edu.cn
6. Corerain Technologies Ltd., Shanghai 201203, China; xinyu.niu@corerain.com
* Correspondence: martin.ferianc.19@ucl.ac.uk
† This paper is an extended version of our paper published in Lecture Notes in Computer Science, vol. 12083. Springer, Cham.
‡ These authors contributed equally to this work.

Abstract: Contemporary advances in neural networks (NNs) have demonstrated their potential in different applications such as in image classification, object detection or natural language processing. In particular, reconfigurable accelerators have been widely used for the acceleration of NNs due to their reconfigurability and efficiency in specific application instances. To determine the configuration of the accelerator, it is necessary to conduct design space exploration to optimize the performance. However, the process of design space exploration is time consuming because of the slow performance evaluation for different configurations. Therefore, there is a demand for an accurate and fast performance prediction method to speed up design space exploration. This work introduces a novel method for fast and accurate estimation of different metrics that are of importance when performing design space exploration. The method is based on a Gaussian process regression model parametrised by the features of the accelerator and the target NN to be accelerated. We evaluate the proposed method together with other popular machine learning based methods in estimating the latency and energy consumption of our implemented accelerator on two different hardware platforms targeting convolutional neural networks. We demonstrate improvements in estimation accuracy, without the need for significant implementation effort or tuning.

Keywords: field-programmable gate array; deep learning; neural network; performance estimation; Gaussian process

1. Introduction

Recently, neural networks (NNs) have demonstrated superhuman performance in a multitude of tasks, such as in image classification [1], object detection [2], semantic segmentation [3] or natural language processing [4]. NNs are also making their way into real-life practical applications, such as in medical diagnostics [5], autonomous driving [6] or aviation [7–9]. While in medicine, the applications of NNs are primarily limited by their algorithmic performance, in other practical scenarios such as in autonomous driving, their hardware performance needs to also be considered in addition to their decision making capabilities. The hardware performance is usually considered in terms of latency or energy efficiency, which is especially crucial when aiming at real-time response rates. While it is indeed possible to run NNs on stock hardware platforms such as central processing units (CPUs) or graphical processing units (GPUs), to achieve peak hardware performance, it is also necessary to consider reconfigurable hardware accelerators [10]. Considering the rapid pace of NN architecture design, accelerators need to be partially reconfigurable such that they are adaptable to the new generation of NN designs, while still achieving favourable hardware performance.

Therefore, to fully utilise the performance capabilities of a reconfigurable accelerator, it is necessary to perform design space exploration (DSE) [11] to determine the optimal hardware configuration of the accelerator, given the desired NN architectures. The search space when performing DSE is determined by the available accelerator's configuration domains which can, for example, be determined by the levels of implementable parallelism [10]. Naively, DSE is conducted by systematically synthesising different configurations of a given accelerator on the hardware platform and measuring the real-world performance of the desired NNs on the accelerator. Given a large search space, consisting of different configurations of the accelerator, the time and resource costs of actually implementing the accelerator on the target hardware platform limit the speed of DSE. Practically, it is therefore necessary to accurately estimate the hardware performance during DSE with respect to multiple different hardware specifications, to enable the fast exploration and exploitation of the available configurations for the given NNs.

There are several performance estimation frameworks for reconfigurable accelerators [12–14]; however, estimating the performance without knowing the run-time intricacies when running different NNs is still a challenging task. There are two main reasons for this complication: (1) the cost of executing a certain operation on hardware varies by on/off-chip communication, synchronisation, control signals, I/O interruptions, in particular for the NN accelerators, the NN's architecture, complicating the estimation; (2) it is difficult to accurately select the most representative design features for all hardware specifications during performance estimation.

In this work, we propose a novel approach for performance estimation of custom convolutional neural network (CNN) accelerators. The proposed method constitutes a Gaussian process regression model [15] coupled with features that can be readily read off datasheets for the underlying hardware platform or the target algorithm (a tutorial code is available at https://git.io/Jv31c). We evaluate the method for estimating layer-wise latency, as well as network-wise latency and energy consumption. Experiments were conducted with respect to two hardware platforms, the Intel Arria GX 1150 field-programmable gate array (FPGA), as well as a structured application-specific integrated circuit (ASIC) implementation of the targeted accelerator. We compared the proposed approach to other machine learning-inspired methods such as linear regression (LR), gradient tree boosting (GTB) or a feed-forward fully-connected NN. The proposed approach is simple to implement, fast in providing predictions and more accurate in comparison to the other compared methods in estimating both latency and energy. This article extends our previous work [16] by further evaluation with respect to estimating an additional hardware metric, energy consumption, by benchmarking the proposed method with respect to an additional hardware implementation platform (ASIC) and by supportive software experiments. The further experimentation proves that the Gaussian process is an accurate estimator that can be used to estimate the hardware performance for running CNNs.

In Section 2, we discuss the background on NN design and the related work on performance estimation. Then, in Section 3, we introduce the proposed method, followed by Section 4, where we describe the implemented hardware design of the benchmarked accelerator. Then, we present the experiments, results and discussion in Section 5. Lastly, we conclude the work in Section 6.

2. Background and Related Work

In this section, we present an overview of NNs and their compute pattern and related work on performance estimation methods.

2.1. Neural Networks

NNs are built by stacking several mathematical operations on top of each other, otherwise known as layers. In this work, we mainly demonstrate our method on an accelerator for CNNs; however, the proposed method is not limited to accelerators for CNNs. The processing of a CNN is usually done in a layer-by-layer fashion; nevertheless, most modern networks [17–19] have residual or concatenative connections between them [17]. Specifically for CNNs, frequently used layers are 2D convolutional, fully-connected or pooling layers interchanged with element-wise applied non-linearities [20]. Convolutional or fully-connected layers aim to learn useful features that can be used to recognise patterns in the input data, while pooling aims to reduce the representation and pool the most important information, while processing the data through the NN. Practically, convolutional and fully-connected layers take up over 90% of the computation and energy consumption in a CNN model [2,21,22]. The algorithm behind 2D convolution is shown in Algorithm 1. The notation used in this paper is presented in Table 1.

Algorithm 1 Convolution.

Input: Input feature map **I** of shape $C \times H_I \times W_I$; weight matrix **W** of shape $F \times C \times K \times K$

Output: Output feature map **O** of shape $F \times H_O \times W_O$

1: for $(f = 0; f < F; f++)$

2:     for $(c = 0; c < C; c++)$

3:         for $(h = 0; h < H_O; h++)$

4:             for $(w = 0; w < W_O; w++)$

5:                 $\mathbf{O}[f][h][w] \mathrel{+}= \sum_{i=1}^{K-1} \sum_{j=1}^{K-1} \mathbf{W}[f][c][i][j] * \mathbf{I}[c][h*s+i][w*s+j]$

Table 1. Notation used in this paper.

H_I	Height of the input feature map	W_I	Width of the input feature map
H_O	Height of the output feature map	W_O	Width of the output feature map
K	Kernel size	F	Number of filters
C	Number of channels	s	Stride in a convolution
W	Weights in a neural network	PF	Parallelism in the filter dimension
PC	Parallelism in the channel dimension	PV	Parallelism in the data vector dimension
M_{CLK} (MHz)	Memory access clock cycle time	L_{CLK} (MHz)	Logic clock cycle time
M_{EFF} (%)	Memory transfer efficiency	S (bits)	Memory transfer size
DW (bits)	Processing data width	M	Number of input features
B	Number of layers in a neural network	N	Number of training samples

As illustrated in Algorithm 1, the convolution accepts a $C \times H_I \times W_I$ sized input feature map, and then, the input is convolved with a kernel with the shape of $F \times C \times K \times K$. Each kernel window with the size of $K \times K$ is applied to one channel of the input $H_I \times W_I$ by sliding the kernel with a stride of s to produce one output feature map $H_O \times W_O$; then, the results of C channels are accumulated to produce one filter of the output. All filters of the output feature maps $F \times H_O \times W_O$ are generated by repeating this process F times. A fully-connected layer can be re-interpreted as a convolution by considering the kernel size $K = 1$. Utilizing this compute pattern, it is then possible to summarize the number of compute operations, as well as the number of memory transfers, as shown in Table 2. At the same time, given the different for-loops in Algorithm 1, it is possible to parallelise the convolution operation in each for-loop dimension: filter, channel, data vector or kernel. In Section 4, we introduce the implemented accelerator, which is capable of taking advantage of this property in multiple dimensions.

Table 2. Number of operations and the data size for a convolution.

Sizes	Number of Operations/Data Size
Number of compute operations	$F \times C \times H_I \times W_I \times K \times K$
Input size	$H_I \times W_I \times C$
Weights size	$F \times C \times K \times K$
Output size	$H_O \times W_O \times F$

2.2. Performance Estimation

As discussed in Section 1, the most accurate and reliable method for determining the performance of a CNN for a specific system configuration is deploying the CNN on the hardware platform and measuring its performance. A significant drawback of this method is that it requires re-implementation for different hardware specifications on the hardware's fabric. Given a large number of potential configurations that might need to be benchmarked during DSE, this approach is too time consuming and resource demanding. Therefore, it is more feasible and practical to perform DSE with respect to an estimate of the performance at the software level, rather than running the CNN for each hardware configuration of different hardware architectures. Considering a complex accelerator for multi-layer CNNs, it is likely that due to the intricacy of the data manipulation or the compute, the performance for the CNNs will need to be estimated on a case-by-case basis. Therefore, this approach is infeasible in general, as it is usually constrained to a single hardware configuration. Nevertheless, there have been a few researchers who have proposed general performance estimation methodologies [12–14].

A performance estimation framework for reconfigurable dataflow platforms was proposed by Yasudo et al. [12], which can analytically determine the number of accelerator units suitable for an application. Dai et al. [13] proposed an estimation method based on a GTB and a high-level synthesis report. However, their method requires a significant amount of data and features from the synthesis report, which might not be available, especially when high-level synthesis is not being used to implement the accelerator. Liu et al. proposed a general heuristic based method [14] for estimating the performance of FPGA based CNN accelerators and that is now used as the standard go-to estimation method. The heuristic analytic approach does not depend on any potentially collected measurements to perform the estimation, and it is simple to implement since it relies only on the variables that can be easily read from the respective datasheets for the hardware platform or the algorithmic configuration. Nevertheless, this general estimation method usually computes the most optimistic estimate, and it does not take into account communication, synchronisation or control. One way to refine the estimation is that we can collect a few runtime data points and use them to improve the estimate.

Therefore, in our work, we propose using a Gaussian process (GP) regression model [23] together with data samples collected by running the CNN on real hardware. GP is a model built on Bayesian probabilistic theory, which can embody prior knowledge into the predictive model and can be used for the regression of real-valued non-linear targets [23].

3. Method

In this section, we motivate and describe the proposed method for performance estimation, which is based on a GP regression model.

Given a dataset $\mathcal{D} = \{(x_i, y_i)\}; i = 1, \ldots, N$ consisting of N observations with inputs and outputs as $x_i \in \mathbb{R}^M$ and $y_i \in \mathbb{R}^1$, respectively, a function f needs to be induced to hypothesise y_* on new, previously unseen, inputs x_*. x represents a vector of M features, while y represents the real-valued target that is to be estimated in this case. As discussed in the previous Section 2.2, there are multiple function classes that can be used to perform this task.

A naive parametric approach would make use of a predictive conditional distribution that can be written as $p(y_*|w, \mathcal{D}, x_*)$. This approach constitutes an LR, using parameters

w, such that the prediction is made as $y = \sum_m^M w_m x_m$. It requires learning the parameters w, which represent one potential function realisation f that fits the data.

Assuming a Gaussian weight prior $p(w) = \mathcal{N}(w|0, \Sigma_w)$, with some pre-defined covariance matrix Σ_w, we can induce a Gaussian distribution on any set of y: $p(y|x) = \mathcal{N}(y|\mu, K)$, where $K \in \mathbb{R}^{N \times N}$ is the covariance matrix characterised by a covariance function and μ represents the mean. This leads to the consideration of a non-parametric predictor, where instead of learning w, the focus is shifted towards inferring an entire distribution of function classes for explaining the data. Specifically, a non-parametric predictor uses a parametric model and integrates the parameters. A prior $p(\theta)$ induces a distribution over plausible functions, where θ is a latent random variable. Using such a probabilistic modelling framework, we can sample plausible data-fitting functions directly. This approach avoids necessitating a decision on which predefined class of function predictors to use, as it considers all of them. The assumption that any set of values specified at an arbitrary point x_i over functions is Gaussian distributed leads to a GP model.

GP is a flexible Bayesian model characterised by a finite collection of Gaussian random variables $[f_1, f_2, \ldots]$, such that for any finite set of plausible inputs X_*, the vector $f_* = f(X_*)$ follows a Gaussian distribution [23]. The stochastic process can be entirely determined by second-order statistics: a mean function $m(.)$ and a kernel (covariance) function $k(.,.)$. The mean function represents the value that the mean across the functions f tends towards. The covariance matrix K is characterised by the kernel function values $[K]_{i,j} = k(x_i, x_j) = \phi(x_i)^T \phi(x_j)$, for some non-linear function $\phi(.)$, which represent the value that the sample covariance for all sampled functions tends towards for the points x_i and x_j. The kernel encodes structural information of the latent function f and must be symmetric and positive semi-definite.

For N Gaussian observations $X_N \in \mathbb{R}^{N \times M}$; $Y_N \in \mathbb{R}^{N \times 1}$, $y_i = f(x_i) + \epsilon_i$ where $\epsilon_i \sim \mathcal{N}(\epsilon_i|0, \sigma^2)$, the posterior for unseen data X_* is defined as in Equations (1) and (2) (for a detailed derivation, please refer to [23]):

$$f_*|y \sim \mathcal{N}(m_{*|N}, K_{*,*|N}) \tag{1}$$

$$m_{*|N} = m(X_N) + K_{*,N}(K_{N,N} + \sigma^2 I)^{-1}(Y_N - m(X_N))$$
$$K_{*,*|N} = K_{*,*} - K_{*,N}(K_{N,N} + \sigma^2 I)^{-1} K_{N,*} \tag{2}$$

Furthermore, training the GP requires finding appropriate latent random variables or hyperparameters θ. Considering the posterior over hyperparameters: $p(\theta|X,y) = \frac{p(y|X,\theta)p(\theta)}{p(y|X)}$, hyperparameters θ^* are obtained through maximising the log of marginal likelihood $\theta^* = \arg\max_\theta \log p(y|X, \theta) + \log p(\theta)$.

In this paper, we propose to use a GP regression model as outlined above to predict the performance of an algorithm realisation on a given accelerator and a hardware platform. We propose to use the characteristics of the accelerator at design time and the target NN as features, as shown in Table 1, with respect to which we can predict the target performance measure (a tutorial code is available at https://git.io/Jv31c). Practically, this means that an input vector x is a vector of M features with algorithmic or hardware properties for one configuration of the system, while y can represent the performance that is to be estimated. The features of the input vector x being used are those that are already known and used in the standard analytic estimation [14], avoiding the need for any additional feature extraction from the dataset or the datasheets. These features consist of characteristics of the CNN to be run, as well as the hardware accelerator. Additionally, it is possible to embody the standard analytic method into the GP based estimator, through using it as the mean function $m(.)$. This model enables us to use any available measurements as training data and does not restrict us to one class of predictors; it considers a plausible family of best fitting models that are characterised by the kernel and the mean function. The proposed method is able to make predictions outside of the observed data samples without collapsing [23]. At the same time, by choosing the features given by the datasheets, the model is more interpretable than an NN or an LR, where the corresponding uninterpretable weights w need to be learned. Moreover, the Gaussian noise assumption can be interpreted as an additive instrumentation error, while collecting measurements. Furthermore, if used during DSE, the GP model can additionally provide an uncertainty estimate for its predictions, which can more precisely guide the exploration and the exploitation of the search space [23]. The overall system diagram, including all the necessary parts of the prediction methodology, is presented in Figure 1. The dashed lines symbolise the fitting of the GP, through providing hardware measurements, along with the characteristic NN and hardware features, to the GP to obtain the $\theta^*, Y_N, K_{N,N}$ to be used during the evaluation. During the evaluation, the features and the fitted GP model are then used for prediction.

For a training set of size N samples, the computational complexity of the training scales in $\sim\mathcal{O}(N^3)$ due to the unavoidable Cholesky factorisation, while the prediction is $\sim\mathcal{O}(N^2)$, and the memory requirements are $\sim\mathcal{O}(NM + N^2)$. Therefore, given a typical number of collected real-world measurements (which is <1000) for different configurations of the accelerator, the method is scalable to be used in practice.

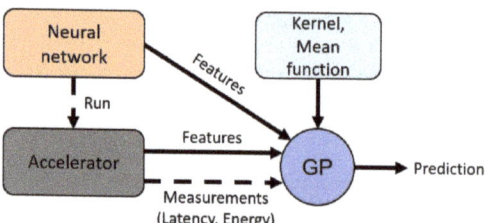

Figure 1. Overview of the proposed prediction methodology based on a Gaussian process (GP).

In the next section, we present the CNN accelerator on which we used the proposed method. We compare our approach with other estimators in predicting layer-wise latency and network-wise latency and energy consumption.

4. Hardware Design

In this section, we detail the accelerator architecture, the performance for multiple different CNN architectures of which we aim to estimate.

4.1. Accelerator's Architecture

The hardware design of our accelerator is illustrated in Figure 2. The design consists of a CNN engine, a central communication interconnect and an off-chip main memory. The weights of the whole network are transferred and stored in the off-chip memory via a central communication interconnect before the processing. The CNN engine is composed of an input buffer, a weight buffer, a convolutional processing engine (PE) and other functional modules including batch normalisation (BN) [24], shortcut (SC) [17], pooling (Pool) and rectified linear unit (ReLU) activation. In order to fully utilise the extensive concurrency exhibited in CNNs and improve the hardware efficiency, we support three types of fine-grained parallelism in our CNN engine: filter parallelism (PF), channel parallelism (PC) and vector parallelism (PV). The accelerator processes each layer in a CNN one-by-one, and the intermediate results between layers are transferred and stored in the off-chip memory, in case the output size is bigger than the available on-chip memory. To achieve higher hardware performance, the accelerator is designed to support 8 bit operations.

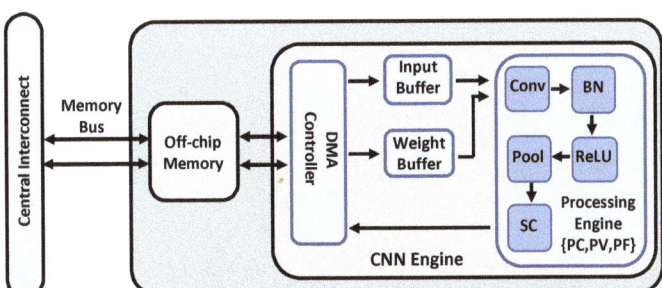

Figure 2. The convolutional neural network accelerator's design. SC, shortcut; PC, channel parallelism; PV, vector parallelism; PF, filter parallelism; DMA, direct memory access.

To avoid large memory consumption on the on-chip memory, we adopt the channel-major computational pattern for convolution, which is illustrated in Algorithm 2. In our channel-major PE, the computation required along the channel dimension in each filter is finished first. In this way, the on-chip memory only needs to cache the intermediate results for one filter, which largely decreases the memory usage.

In this paper, we used this accelerator design to perform the benchmarking of our proposed estimator method in estimating layer-wise latency, network-wise latency and energy consumption.

Algorithm 2 Channel-major computational pattern.

Input: Input feature map **I** of shape $C \times H_I \times W_I$; weight matrix **W** of shape $F \times C \times K \times K$

Output: Output feature map **O** of shape $F \times H_O \times W_O$

1: for $(f = 0; f < \frac{F}{PF}; f++)$
2:   for $(h = 0; h < H_O; h++)$
3:     for $(w = 0; w < \frac{W_O}{PV}; w++)$
4:       for $(c = 0; c < \frac{C}{PC}; c++)$
5:         $\mathbf{O}[f][h][w] \mathrel{+}= \sum_{i=1}^{K-1}\sum_{j=1}^{K-1}\mathbf{W}[f][c][i][j] * \mathbf{I}[c][h*s+i][w*s+j]$

4.2. Standard Analytical Latency Model

In this section, we outline the layer-wise processing latency model for the proposed accelerator, which constitutes the standard method as proposed in [14] for comparison.

The simplest form of a heuristic that estimates layer-wise latency on a hardware accelerator consists of partitioning the overall processing time to individual layers, T_i, corresponding to the time to perform one convolution in a feed-forward CNN consisting of B convolutions/layers. The per-layer latency of an implemented CNN accelerator consists of three parts: (1) time for loading the input; (2) computation time; (3) time for storing the results.

The complete input has to be loaded into the on-chip memory only once for the first layer, while the partial results that do not fit into the on-chip memory are off-loaded to the off-chip memory. Nevertheless, the time spent on this memory transfer is assumed to be negligible.

The size of the weights and the input/output for convolution is shown in Table 2, following the notation defined in Table 1. The per-layer latency T_i for a single convolutional layer $i; i = 1, \ldots, B$ of a CNN with B layers is shown in Equations (3)–(5) as follows:

1. Loading time, i.e., the time to load the input into the on-chip memory. Note that the loading of the data is in parallel with respect to the channel parallelism PC:

$$T_{weights_i} = \frac{K_i \times K_i \times F_i \times C_i \times DW}{PC \times PV \times M_{CLK} \times S \times M_{EFF}}$$

$$T_{data_i} = \frac{H_{I_i} \times W_{I_i} \times C_i \times DW}{PC \times PV \times M_{CLK} \times S \times M_{EFF}}$$

$$T_{load_i} = T_{weights_i} + T_{data_i} \qquad (3)$$

2. Computation time, i.e., the time to compute $PF \times PC$ parallel filters and channels, respectively:

$$T_{compute_i} = \frac{F_i \times C_i \times H_{I_i} \times W_{I_i} \times K_i \times K_i}{PF \times PC \times L_{CLK}} \qquad (4)$$

3. Storing time, i.e., the time to store the output back to the off-chip memory. Note that similar to the input loading time, the storage time is divided by the channel parallelism PC:

$$T_{store_i} = \frac{H_{O_i} \times W_{O_i} \times F_i \times DW}{PC \times PV \times M_{CLK} \times S \times M_{EFF}} \qquad (5)$$

Therefore, the time required to process a single convolutional layer can be written as in Equation (6) below:

$$T_i = \begin{cases} T_{i=1} &= T_{load_i} + T_{compute_i} \\ T_{i \neq 1 \vee N} &= max(T_{weights_i}, T_{compute_i}) \\ T_{i=N} &= max(T_{weights_i}, T_{compute_i}) + T_{store_i} \end{cases} \qquad (6)$$

Note the *max* operations, which are present due to pipelining of the design, result in a latency determined by the slowest operation.

5. Experiments

In this section, we present the experimental settings, as well as the results with respect to both latency and energy estimation on different CNN architectures on the implemented accelerator (Section 4). The experiments were performed on an FPGA, as well as a custom ASIC. The networks were quantized into 8 bits [25], such that $DW = 8$ bits.

5.1. Evaluation for FPGA Design

This section describes the accelerator on an Intel Arria GX 1150 FPGA, and we evaluate the proposed GP based method with respect to layer-wise latency estimation, while running CNNs on the accelerator. The fixed hardware parameters used for the FPGA implementation are such that the filter, channel and data parallelism were set as $PF = 64, PC = 64, PV = 1$. At the same time, the memory and logic clock frequencies were $M_{CLK} = 200$ MHz and $L_{CLK} = 200$ MHz. The memory efficiency was assumed to be $M_{EFF} = 70\%$, and the communicating data-width size was $S = 64$ bits. The evaluation dataset comprised of several different configurations of convolutional layers, which were the building blocks of three different CNNs, namely SSD [18] with 24 convolutions, Yolo [19] with 75 convolutions and ResNet-50 [17] with 57 convolutions. The characteristics of the dataset from a software perspective are shown in Table 3. These networks were chosen because their algorithmic structures present challenges to the accelerator design, its control and its scheduling. In particular, SSD and Yolo are characteristic by their irregularities, which result in the output being produced at different times, while ResNet is known for its residual blocks, which require implementing additional control in hardware.

Table 3. Dataset for the evaluation of the layer-wise latency on an FPGA.

Parameter	Min	Mean	Max
H_I/W_I	1	42	418
H_O/W_O	1	37	416
K	1	2	7
C	3	360	2048
F	64	371	2048
Latency (ms)	0.018	0.841	11.727

In total, the dataset for layer-wise latency estimation for each layer i consisted of $N = 156$ training samples, and the input feature size M was 15, corresponding to: $H_{I_i}, W_{I_i}, H_{O_i}, W_{O_i}, K_i, F_i, C_i, PF, PC, PV, M_{CLK}, L_{CLK}, M_{EFF}, S$ and DW. The recorded latency per convolution represents the targets y. Due to the limited size of the dataset, leave-one-out cross-validation (LOOCV) with respect to the mean absolute error (MAE) was used to compare the estimators. LOOCV is a particular case of leave-k-out cross-validation where $k = 1$, which means that a model is trained on all samples except one, on which the performance is then evaluated. Although potentially more expensive to implement, it provides a less biased estimate of the test errors. In this instance, the performance of the predictor is measured by the absolute error between the prediction and the target value. The error is accumulated for all samples from which the mean is then calculated by dividing the total summed error by the number of samples.

In the evaluation, the proposed method is compared with the standard analytical method, including LR, GTB and a fully-connected multi-layer NN. Due to the few data samples, we used the layer-wise latency model as presented in Section 4.2 as the mean function $m(.)$ of the GP model. We considered several hyperparameters for the proposed GP based method such as the learning rate, ranging from 0.1 to 0.000001 on a logarithmic scale, and the kernel, ranging from linear, Gaussian to Matérn kernels [23], and their combinations. The best parameters were found by a grid search with respect to the LOOCV MAE. For GTB and NN, we needed to determine the most influential parameters such as the learning rate, ranging from 0.01 to 0.0001 on a logarithmic scale, or for the GTB, the number of trees or the tree depth determined by gradual pruning. For the NN, we needed to decide the number of hidden nodes, between [10, 1], [10, 10, 1] and [10, 10, 10, 1], and for the activation function, we considered tanh, ReLU and sigmoid. The hyperparameters were similarly found through a grid search with respect to the LOOCV MAE. For the standard method and LR, it was not necessary to determine any hyperparameters. The results for latency estimation are presented in Table 4.

Table 4. Evaluation of layer-wise latency estimation for different methods on the convolutional neural network accelerator on an FPGA.

Methods	Layer-Wise Latency LOOCV MAE (ms)	Implementation and Optimiser	Properties
Standard method	0.450	None	None
Linear regression	0.450	Sklearn [26]	Default
Gradient tree boosting	0.607	Sklearn [26]; AdaBoost [27]	Learning rate: 0.1 Number of trees: 10 Maximum depth: 3
Neural network	1.257	TensorFlow [28]; Adam [29]	Batch size: 8 Learning rate: 0.1 Regulariser: L2, 0.001 Number of nodes: 10,10,1 Activations: ReLU
Our method	0.312	GPFlow [30]; Adam [29]	Mean function: T_i Learning rate: 0.001 Kernel: Matérn 3/2

Overall, the best method proved to be the combination of the standard method as the mean function for the GP and the collected data. In comparison to other approaches, the proposed method achieved approximately a 30.7% improvement in LOOCV with respect to MAE, decreasing to 0.312 ms in comparison with the second best-performing methods, which were LR and the standard method with a 0.450 ms MAE.

5.2. Evaluation on the ASIC Design

In this section, we implement the outlined hardware accelerator using 28 nm eASIC [31] technology on the Intel N3XS platform with 8GB DDR3 installed as an off-chip memory. The whole design was clocked at $M_{CLK}, L_{CLK} = 333$ MHz, and the PF, PC and PV were set as 64, 64 and 1, respectively. The example design we used in this experiment kept the same parallelism configuration for the entire CNN model. Other designs, such as the streaming design [32], can support layer-wise configurable parallelism. However, the layer-wise instantiation of a modern deep CNN requires extensive hardware resources, which are often not available.

Before the evaluation of our GP based estimation, we compare both the FPGA and eASIC implementations in terms of latency and power efficiency (frames per second per Watt (FPS/W)) on four CNN models including SSD, ResNet-50, Yolo and VGG-16. It can be clearly seen from Table 5 that the eASIC design achieved higher energy efficiency and smaller latency than the FPGA implementation on all four CNN models.

Table 5. Hardware performance comparison between the FPGA and eASIC design.

	SSD [18]		ResNet-50 [17]		Yolo [19]		VGG-16 [33]	
	Latency (ms)	FPS/W	Latency (ms)	FPS/W	Latency (ms)	FPS/W	Latency (ms)	FPS/W
FPGA	3.24	7.01	4.62	4.92	41.22	0.55	23.18	0.98
eASIC	2.39	22.02	3.06	17.20	31.55	1.67	15.35	3.43

Next, we evaluated the GP based estimation for the eASIC design with respect to latency and energy consumption. Instead of estimating per-layer latency, this experiment aimed at validating the GP based estimation of a whole NN for both latency and energy consumption. We ran ResNet-50 [17] using different network configurations with respect to energy and latency to form the evaluation and training datasets, which is illustrated in Figure 3.

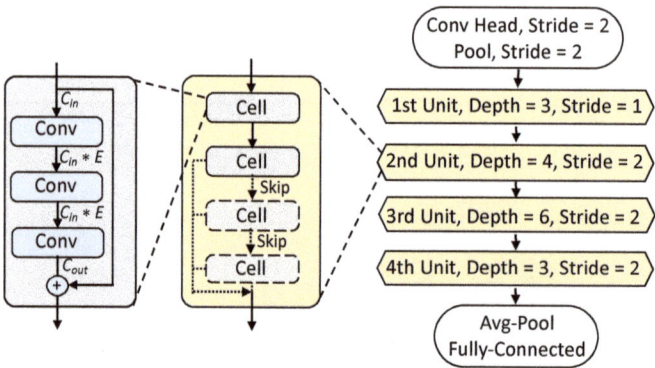

Figure 3. ResNet-50 with different depths, channel numbers and expansion ratios.

The network contains three parts: head part, middle part and tail part. The head part includes a convolutional layer and a pooling layer with stride-2, while the tail part consists of an average pooling layer followed by a fully-connected layer. We fixed the head and tail parts while changing the network configurations for the middle part that contains four residual blocks with a gradually reduced feature map size and increased channel numbers. In each residual block, the depth ranges from two to D_i, where D_i denotes the maximal depth in the ith block. In each cell of the residual block, the expansion ratio (E) was chosen from [0.5, 0.75, 1.0]. For regression, as the hardware properties are fixed for the eASIC design, we only needed to encode the network configurations as a 13-dimensional vector, which represents the expansion ratio used in the 13 cells, giving $M = 13$. The expansion ratio was zero, if this cell was skipped. We randomly sampled 800 different network configurations and evaluated these networks on our eASIC designs with respect to latency and energy consumption. We used 600 samples for training and 200 samples for evaluation. Therefore, even though the hardware configuration remained fixed, we benchmarked the methodology with respect to changing various software parameters.

To demonstrate the advantages of GP based estimation compared with other regression techniques, we also compared it with LR, GTB and NN, which is illustrated in Table 6. In this instance we used a zero mean function, such that the methods should rely more on data, instead of any bias that could have been potentially induced by inaccurate analytical approximation. All methods used the same hyperparameters as in Section 5.1, to demonstrate the flexibility and simplicity of the implementation of the proposed GP regression model. It can be seen that our method achieved a smaller MAE on both latency and energy estimation, when compared with the other methods. In comparison to LR, which is a simple and widely adopted estimator, the performance can be improved by approximately two times with respect to both latency and energy estimates.

Table 6. Evaluation of network-wise latency and energy estimation for different methods on the convolutional neural network accelerator on an eASIC.

Methods	Latency MAE (ms)	Energy MAE (W)	Implementation and Optimiser	Properties
Linear regression	0.177	0.272	Sklearn [26]	Default
Gradient tree boosting	0.476	0.501	Sklearn [26]; AdaBoost [27]	Learning rate: 0.1 Number of trees: 10 Maximum depth: 3
Neural network	0.108	0.241	TensorFlow [28]; Adam [29]	Batch size: 8 Learning rate: 0.1 Regulariser: L2, 0.001 Number of nodes: 10,10,1 Activations: ReLU
Our method	0.079	0.151	GPFlow [30]; Adam [29]	Mean function: 0 Learning rate: 0.001 Kernel: Matérn 3/2

Furthermore, in Figure 4, we show the advantages of GP over the aforementioned methods on smaller datasets by varying the training dataset size and number of features as the input of the models with respect to the overall prediction latency and energy consumption on the eASIC. Each experiment was repeated three times varying the number of available data points or features to evaluate the robustness of the compared methods. It can be observed that the GP is more accurate and also more robust as the standard deviation is consistently smaller in comparison to the other methods in all experiments.

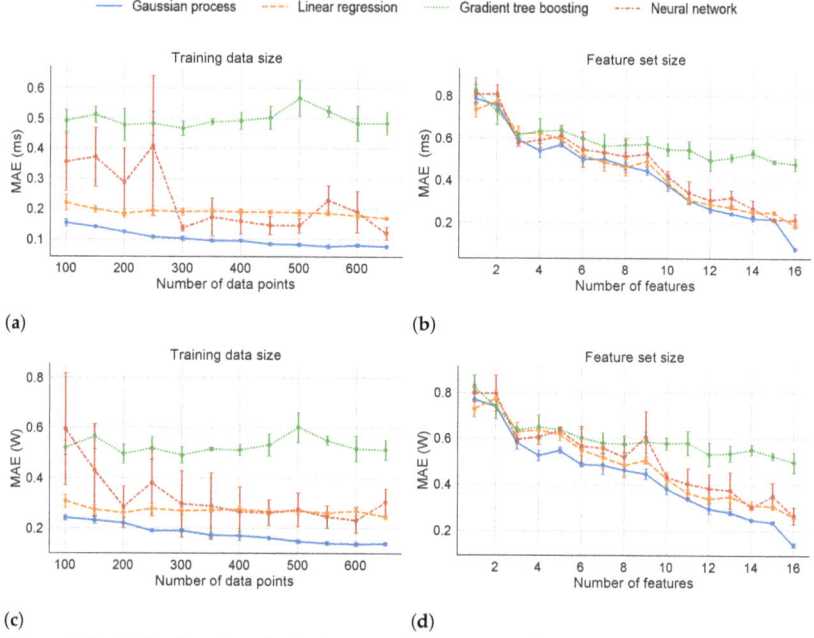

Figure 4. Prediction benchmarks for latency with respect to changing training data size (**a**) and feature set size (**b**). Benchmarks for energy with respect to changing training data size (**c**) and feature set size (**d**).

The main advantage of the proposed method lays in its implementation simplicity, as it reuses those variables that can be commonly found in hardware or algorithmic datasheets and commonly used in DSE, combined with recorded measurements. The method can be improved by recording more measurements and simple fine-tuning of the hyperparameters related to the kernel K. Nevertheless, as demonstrated in Sections 5.1 and 5.2, the method is capable of estimating the performance even with respect to few collected data samples.

A potential limitation of this method, as was eluded to in Section 3, stems from the kernel computation, which scales with the complexity of $\mathcal{O}(N^3)$. This means that the inference time can be prolonged if there are many training samples. One possible solution to overcome this problem is to use variational inference to determine the k most important points that have to be included in the kernel computation [34]. Nevertheless, the inference time is much less than the time needed for synthesis and then running the design on hardware.

6. Conclusions

In this paper, we propose an accurate method for estimating the performance of an accelerator for convolutional neural networks and compare it with the standard method, linear regression, gradient tree boosting and an artificial neural network. Moreover, we evaluate our method with respect to two hardware platforms on which we accurately predict the overall latency or energy consumption of the given convolutional neural networks. The evaluation demonstrates that the innovative Gaussian process method paired with collected data can provide an accuracy improvement with respect to the other compared methods. Future work includes providing tools to automate our approach, and extending it to cover applications beyond machine learning designs.

Author Contributions: Conceptualization, M.F., H.F. and D.M.; data curation, M.F. and H.F.; investigation, M.F. and H.F.; resources, S.L. and X.N.; supervision, W.L.; validation, M.F. and H.F.;

writing—original draft, M.F., H.F. and D.M.; writing—review and editing, M.F., H.F., D.M., H.Z., S.L. and X.N. All authors read and agreed to the published version of the manuscript.

Funding: The support of the U.K. EPSRC (EP/L016796/1, EP/N031768/1, EP/P010040/1 and EP/S030069/1), Corerain, Intel and Xilinx is gratefully acknowledged.

Data Availability Statement: The data presented in this study are available on request from the corresponding author.

Acknowledgments: We thank Yann Herklotz, Alexander Montgomerie-Corcoran, the ARC'20 and Electronics reviewers for insightful suggestions.

Conflicts of Interest: The authors declare no conflict of interest. The funders had no role in the design of the study; in the collection, analyses, or interpretation of data; in the writing of the manuscript; nor in the decision to publish the results.

Abbreviations

The following abbreviations are used in this manuscript:

ASIC	Application-specific integrated circuit
CPU	Central processing unit
CNN	Convolutional neural network
DSE	Design space exploration
FPGA	Field-programmable gate array
GP	Gaussian process
GPU	Graphical processing unit
GTB	Gradient tree boosting
LOOCV	Leave-one-out cross-validation
LR	Linear regression
MAE	Mean absolute error
NN	Neural network

References

1. Ferianc, M.; Fan, H.; Rodrigues, M. VINNAS: Variational Inference based Neural Network Architecture Search. *arXiv* **2020**, arXiv:2007.06103.
2. Fan, H.; Liu, S.; Ferianc, M.; Ng, H.C.; Que, Z.; Liu, S.; Niu, X.; Luk, W. A Real-Time Object Detection Accelerator with Compressed SSDLite on FPGA. In Proceedings of the 2018 International Conference on Field-Programmable Technology (FPT), Naha Okinawa, Japan, 11–15 December 2018; pp. 14–21.
3. Liu, S.; Luk, W. Towards an Efficient Accelerator for DNN-Based Remote Sensing Image Segmentation on FPGAs. In Proceedings of the 2019 29th International Conference on Field Programmable Logic and Applications (FPL), Barcelona, Spain, 8–12 September 2019; pp. 187–193.
4. Brown, T.B.; Mann, B.; Ryder, N.; Subbiah, M.; Kaplan, J.; Dhariwal, P.; Neelakantan, A.; Shyam, P.; Sastry, G.; Askell, A.; et al. Language models are few-shot learners. *arXiv* **2020**, arXiv:2005.14165.
5. Kwon, Y.; Won, J.H.; Kim, B.J.; Paik, M.C. Uncertainty quantification using Bayesian neural networks in classification: Application to biomedical image segmentation. *Comput. Stat. Data Anal.* **2020**, *142*, 106816. [CrossRef]
6. McAllister, R.; Gal, Y.; Kendall, A.; Van Der Wilk, M.; Shah, A.; Cipolla, R.; Weller, A. Concrete Problems for Autonomous Vehicle Safety: Advantages of Bayesian Deep Learning. In Proceedings of the 26th International Joint Conference on Artificial Intelligence (IJCAI'17), Buenos Aires, Argentina, 25–31 July 2017; pp. 4745–4753.
7. Xuan-Mung, N.; Hong, S.K. Barometric altitude measurement fault diagnosis for the improvement of quadcopter altitude control. In Proceedings of the 2019 19th International Conference on Control, Automation and Systems (ICCAS), Jeju, Korea, 15–18 October 2019; pp. 1359–1364.
8. Park, D.; Yu, H.; Xuan-Mung, N.; Lee, J.; Hong, S.K. Multicopter PID Attitude Controller Gain Auto-tuning through Reinforcement Learning Neural Networks. In Proceedings of the 2019 2nd International Conference on Control and Robot Technology, Phuket, Thailand, 25–27 October 2019; pp. 80–84.
9. Nguyen, N.P.; Mung, N.X.; Thanh Ha, L.N.N.; Huynh, T.T.; Hong, S.K. Finite-Time Attitude Fault Tolerant Control of Quadcopter System via Neural Networks. *Mathematics* **2020**, *8*, 1541. [CrossRef]
10. Mittal, S. A survey of FPGA based accelerators for convolutional neural networks. *Neural Comput. Appl.* **2020**, *32*, 1109–1139. [CrossRef]

11. Rahman, A.; Oh, S.; Lee, J.; Choi, K. Design space exploration of FPGA accelerators for convolutional neural networks. In Proceedings of the Design, Automation & Test in Europe Conference & Exhibition (DATE), Lausanne, Switzerland, 27–31 March 2017; pp. 1147–1152.
12. Yasudo, R.; Coutinho, J.; Varbanescu, A.; Luk, W.; Amano, H.; Becker, T. Performance Estimation for Exascale Reconfigurable Dataflow Platforms. In Proceedings of the 2018 International Conference on Field-Programmable Technology (FPT), Naha Okinawa, Japan, 11–15 December 2018; pp. 314–317.
13. Dai, S.; Zhou, Y.; Zhang, H.; Ustun, E.; Young, E.F.; Zhang, Z. Fast and accurate estimation of quality of results in high-level synthesis with machine learning. In Proceedings of the 2018 IEEE 26th Annual International Symposium on Field-Programmable Custom Computing Machines (FCCM), Boulder, CO, USA, 29 April–1 May 2018; pp. 129–132.
14. Liu, S.; Fan, H.; Niu, X.; Ng, H.C.; Chu, Y.; Luk, W. Optimizing CNN based Segmentation with Deeply Customized Convolutional and Deconvolutional Architectures on FPGA. *ACM Trans. Reconfig. Technol. Syst.* **2018**, *11*, 1–22. [CrossRef]
15. Williams, C.K.; Rasmussen, C.E. Gaussian processes for regression. *Adv. Neural Inf. Process. Syst.* **1996**, *8*, 514–520.
16. Ferianc, M.; Fan, H.; Chu, R.S.; Stano, J.; Luk, W. Improving Performance Estimation for FPGA-Based Accelerators for Convolutional Neural Networks. In *International Symposium on Applied Reconfigurable Computing*; Springer: Berlin, Germany, 2020; pp. 3–13.
17. He, K.; Zhang, X.; Ren, S.; Sun, J. Deep Residual Learning for Image Recognition. In Proceedings of the 2016 IEEE Conference on Computer Vision and Pattern Recognition (CVPR), Las Vegas, NV, USA, 27–30 June 2016; Volume 2016, pp. 770–778.
18. Liu, W.; Anguelov, D.; Erhan, D.; Szegedy, C.; Reed, S.; Fu, C.Y.; Berg, A. SSD: Single shot multibox detector. In *Lecture Notes in Computer Science (Including Subseries Lecture Notes in Artificial Intelligence and Lecture Notes in Bioinformatics)*; Springer: Berlin, Germany, 2016; Volume 9905, pp. 21–37.
19. Redmon, J.; Divvala, S.; Girshick, R.; Farhadi, A. You Only Look Once: Unified, Real-Time Object Detection. In Proceedings of the 2016 IEEE Conference on Computer Vision and Pattern Recognition (CVPR), Las Vegas, NV, USA, 27–30 June 2016; Volume 3, pp. 779–788.
20. LeCun, Y.; Boser, B.; Denker, J.S.; Henderson, D.; Howard, R.E.; Hubbard, W.; Jackel, L.D. Backpropagation applied to handwritten zip code recognition. *Neural Comput.* **1989**, *1*, 541–551. [CrossRef]
21. Fan, H.; Luo, C.; Zeng, C.; Ferianc, M.; Que, Z.; Liu, S.; Niu, X.; Luk, W. F-E3D: FPGA based Acceleration of an Efficient 3D Convolutional Neural Network for Human Action Recognition. In Proceedings of the 2019 IEEE 30th International Conference on Application-specific Systems, Architectures and Processors (ASAP), New York, NY, USA, 15–17 July 2019; Volume 2160, pp. 1–8.
22. Venieris, S.; Kouris, A.; Bouganis, C.S. *Toolflows for Mapping Convolutional Neural Networks on FPGAs: A Survey and Future Directions*; ACM: New York, NY, USA, 2018; Volume 51, pp. 1–39.
23. Rasmussen, C.E. *Gaussian Processes in Machine Learning*; The MIT Press: Cambridge, MA, USA, 2005.
24. Ioffe, S.; Szegedy, C. Batch normalization: Accelerating deep network training by reducing internal covariate shift. *arXiv* **2015**, arXiv:1502.03167.
25. Jacob, B.; Kligys, S.; Chen, B.; Zhu, M.; Tang, M.; Howard, A.; Adam, H.; Kalenichenko, D. Quantization and training of neural networks for efficient integer-arithmetic-only inference. In Proceedings of the IEEE Conference on Computer Vision and Pattern Recognition, Salt Lake City, UT, USA, 18–23 June 2018; pp. 2704–2713.
26. Pedregosa, F.; Varoquaux, G.; Gramfort, A.; Michel, V.; Thirion, B.; Grisel, O.; Blondel, M.; Prettenhofer, P.; Weiss, R.; Dubourg, V.; et al. Scikit-learn: Machine Learning in Python. *J. Mach. Learn. Res.* **2011**, *12*, 2825–2830.
27. Friedman, J.H. Stochastic gradient boosting. In *Computational Statistics & Data Analysis*; Elsevier: Amsterdam, The Netherlands, 2002; Volume 38, pp. 367–378.
28. Abadi, M.; Agarwal, A.; Barham, P.; Brevdo, E.; Chen, Z.; Citro, C.; Davis, A.; Dean, J.; Devin, M.; Ghemawat, S.; et al. TensorFlow: Large-Scale Machine Learning on Heterogeneous Systems. 2015. Available online: https://www.tensorflow.org/ (accessed on 14 December 2020).
29. Kingma, D.P.; Ba, J. Adam: A method for stochastic optimization. *arXiv* **2014**, arXiv:1412.6980.
30. Matthews, D.G.; Alexander, G.; Van Der Wilk, M.; Nickson, T.; Fujii, K.; Boukouvalas, A.; León-Villagrá, P.; Ghahramani, Z.; Hensman, J. GPflow: A Gaussian process library using TensorFlow. *J. Mach. Learn. Res.* **2017**, *18*, 1299–1304.
31. Intel Corporation. eASIC Technology. 2018. Available online: https://www.intel.co.uk/content/www/uk/en/products/programmable/asic/easic-devices.html (accessed on 2 December 2020).
32. Venieris, S.I.; Bouganis, C.S. fpgaConvNet: A framework for mapping convolutional neural networks on FPGAs. In Proceedings of the 2016 IEEE 24th Annual International Symposium on Field-Programmable Custom Computing Machines (FCCM), Washington, DC, USA, 1–3 May 2016; pp. 40–47.
33. Simonyan, K.; Zisserman, A. Very deep convolutional networks for large-scale image recognition. *arXiv* **2014**, arXiv:1409.1556.
34. Titsias, M. Variational learning of inducing variables in sparse Gaussian processes. In Proceedings of the Twelfth International Conference on Artificial Intelligence and Statistics (AISTATS), Clearwater Beach, FL, USA, 16–18 April 2009; pp. 567–574.

Article

Optimising Hardware Accelerated Neural Networks with Quantisation and a Knowledge Distillation Evolutionary Algorithm

Robert Stewart [1,*], Andrew Nowlan [1], Pascal Bacchus [2], Quentin Ducasse [3] and Ekaterina Komendantskaya [1]

1. Mathematical and Computer Sciences, Heriot-Watt University, Edinburgh, EH14 4AS, UK; ALloyd.Nowlan@outlook.com (A.N.); E.Komendantskaya@hw.ac.uk (E.K.)
2. Inria Rennes-Bretagne Altlantique Research Centre, 35042 Rennes, France; pascal.bacchus@gmail.com
3. Lab-STICC, École Nationale Supérieure de Techniques Avancées, 29200 Brest, France; quentin.ducasse@ensta-bretagne.org
* Correspondence: R.Stewart@hw.ac.uk

Abstract: This paper compares the latency, accuracy, training time and hardware costs of neural networks compressed with our new multi-objective evolutionary algorithm called NEMOKD, and with quantisation. We evaluate NEMOKD on Intel's Movidius Myriad X VPU processor, and quantisation on Xilinx's programmable Z7020 FPGA hardware. Evolving models with NEMOKD increases inference accuracy by up to 82% at the cost of 38% increased latency, with throughput performance of 100–590 image frames-per-second (FPS). Quantisation identifies a sweet spot of 3 bit precision in the trade-off between latency, hardware requirements, training time and accuracy. Parallelising FPGA implementations of 2 and 3 bit quantised neural networks increases throughput from 6 k FPS to 373 k FPS, a 62× speedup.

Keywords: quantisation; evolutionary algorithm; neural network; FPGA; Movidius VPU

1. Introduction

Neural networks have proved successful for many domains including image recognition, autonomous systems and language processing. State-of-the-art models have an enormous number of parameters, making them highly computationally and memory intensive. For example, AlexNet [1] is a Convolutional Neural Network (CNN) consisting of 60 million parameters and 650 k neurons with an architecture comprising five convolutional layers, multiple max-pooling layers, three fully-connected layers and a final softmax layer. GPUs are often used to train and use neural networks because they can deliver the highest peak arithmetic performance for 32 bit floating point neural network inference compared with CPUs and FPGAs. At the time when the AlexNet model was proposed (2012), the network was too large to fit on a single GPU. This problem was overcome by distributing the model across two GPUs for training. The use of 200+ Watt GPUs for such purposes over days and weeks is prohibitively expensive [2].

In recent years, a new class of hardware has emerged to significantly improve performance-per-Watt for deep learning. Accelerator devices such as the Intel Movidius Myriad X VPU [3] and the Coral/Google Edge TPU [4] accommodate deep learning workloads because they provide a trade off between compute performance and power consumption. The extreme on the hardware spectrum is programmable hardware like FPGAs, which provide extremely high throughput performance of fixed-point deep learning inference [5]. This is essential for real-time domains with low latency throughput requirements, e.g., remote computer vision and automated stack market trading.

It is widely accepted that neural network models exhibit a high level of redundancy. Most parameters contribute little or nothing to the final output [6], and the precision of arithmetic calculations are unnecessarily precise [7]. Removing redundant bloat offers the opportunity of mapping sophisticated models to energy efficient devices. Methods for compressing neural networks include precision reduction, removing redundant parameters or structure, and transferring knowledge from large models to smaller models [8].

The aim of compression is usually to reduce the hardware footprint of a model to increase its inference throughput (decreasing its inference latency), without overtly affecting inference accuracy.

Compressing neural network can:

- Speed up inference time: The size of neural network models are limited by memory capacity and bandwidth. Training and inference computations switch from compute-bound to memory-bound workloads as model sizes increase. This memory capacity bottleneck limits the practical use of very large models [9].
- Improve energy efficiency: It costs orders-of-magnitude more energy to access off-chip DDR memory compared to on-chip memory e.g., SRAM, BRAM and cache memory. Fitting weights into on-chip memories reduces frequency of energy inefficient off-chip memory accesses. Quantised fixed-point representations can significantly reduce energy costs [10], e.g., less than 5 Watts on FPGAs [11].
- Reduce verification costs: Recent SMT-based verification approaches aim to prove a neural network's robustness against adversarial attacks e.g., [12,13]. SMT solvers generally do not support non-linear arithmetic so activation functions must be linearised. This approximates a model for the purpose verification, rendering verification results unreliable. Quantising activation functions can increase reliability of verifying neural networks robust [14], because it is the same model being verified and deployed. Moreover quantised models can be as robust against adversarial attack as their full precision version, possibly because quantisation acts as a filter of subtle adversarial noise [15].

Neural network models vary hugely in their sizes, i.e., from 60 thousand parameters up to 900 million parameters. Figure 1 shows how compression such as quantisation and knowledge distillation can put relatively large models within reach of high throughput hardware accelerators [16–20].

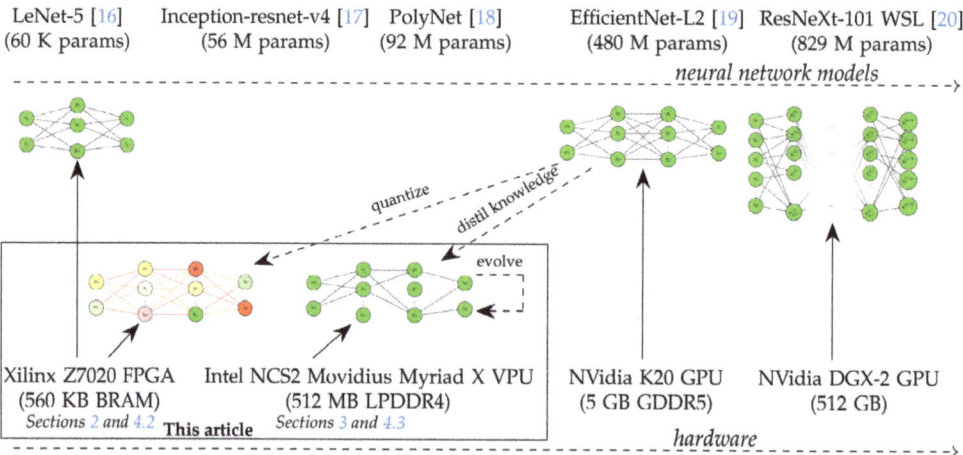

Figure 1. Meeting in the middle: compressing neural networks for acceleration.

This paper evaluates the accuracy, throughput, training time and resource costs of two compression approaches applied to different sized models: (1) an evolutionary algorithm that modifies the structure of 16 bit precision neural networks targeting the Intel Movidius

Myriad X VPU, and (2) 1–8 bit precision quantisation of fixed neural networks targeting the Xilinx Z7020 FPGA.

Contributions

This paper makes the following contributions:

- A new framework called NEMOKD for hardware aware evolution of knowledge-distilled student models (Section 3).
- An evaluation of neural network quantisation by measuring inference accuracy, throughput, hardware requirements and training time, targeting *programmable* FPGA hardware (Section 4.2).
- An evaluation of NEMOKD showing its ability to minimise both latency and accuracy loss on Intel's *fixed* Movidius Myriad X VPU architecture (Section 4.3).
- A comparison of NEMOKD and quantisation performance on these architectures (Section 4.4).

2. Quantisation Methodology

2.1. Quantisation for FPGAs

Floating point precision permits individual neural network parameters a range of exponent values. Higher precision values (larger exponents) can induce more computational overhead, leading to higher power consumption and longer compute times. Fixed-point quantised models use (usually smaller) fixed exponent values for all network parameters. This imposed restriction brings a range of benefits such as faster and more power efficient mathematical operations but can also potentially impact a model's accuracy [21].

Quantisation [22] shifts values from 32 bit floating point continuous values to reduced bit discrete values. In a neural network, weights between neurons and activation functions can be quantised.

Binarisation [23] is a special case of quantisation that represents weights and/or activation function outputs with a single bit. These methods replace arithmetic operation with bit-wise operations, reducing the energy consumption and memory requirements.

Quantised neural networks can significantly outperform binarised neural networks and can compete with the accuracy of full precision models [22].

2.2. FINN Framework

Section 4.2 evaluates very low precision neural networks, quantising precision from 32 bits to 1–8 bits to fit within the resource constraints of FPGAs. Xilinx's FINN quantisation framework and FPGA backend is used in these experiments. FINN initially supported binarised neural networks [7], then was extended for quantised networks [24] and Long-Short Term Memory Neural Networks (LSTM) [25]. Our experiments in Section 4.2 use FINN functionality from [24].

FINN employs quantisation aware training at the Python level, before generating synthesisable C++ for hardware. The weights and activation functions during training in Python operate on floating point values but Python functions simulate quantisation to limit weights and activation function outputs to discrete values permitted by the chosen quantisation configuration. When generating hardware, the arithmetic precision of weights and activation functions in the C++ match the quantised bit widths simulated during training.

2.3. Weight Quantisation for Training

FINN discretises the range of full precision values by rounding to a close neighbour to fixed point quantised values for weights. The *min* and *max* values for the quantisation range are related to the quantisation precision n, they are defined as:

$$max = 2 - \frac{1}{2^{n-2}} \qquad min = -2 + \frac{1}{2^{n-2}}$$

The quantisation formula for $x \in [min; max]$ is shown in Equation (1).

$$QuantiseWeights(x) = \frac{\lfloor 2^n x + 2^{n-1} - 1 \rfloor}{2^{n-2}} - 2 + \frac{1}{2^{n-2}} \quad (1)$$

Table 1 shows examples of quantised values with $min = -2$ and $max = 2$ with $2^n - 1$ values in this interval. The values are all strictly positive but the quantisation range is symmetric. The step between each quantised value is $\frac{1}{2^{n-2}}$. When n increases, the number of quantised values increase and we can obtain values close to the upper and lower bound of the interval.

Table 1. Quantised weight values between 0.136 and 2 with $min = -2$ and $max = 2$.

Value	Precision (bits)							
	1	2	3	4	5	6	7	8
0.136	1	0	0	0.25	0.125	0.125	0.125	0.140625
0.357	1	0	0.5	0.25	0.375	0.375	0.34375	0.359375
0.639	1	1	0.5	0.75	0.625	0.625	0.625	0.640625
1.135	1	1	1	1.25	1.125	1.125	1.125	1.140625
2	1	1	1.5	1.75	1.875	1.9375	1.96875	1.984375

2.4. Activation Function Quantisation for Training

The quantisation of activation functions works similarly to weight quantisation. For the quantised hyperbolic tangent function $tanh(x) = \frac{e^x - e^{-x}}{e^x + e^{-x}}$, the range of values in Table 1 is optimal because the function has two asymptotes towards -1 and 1, e.g., $tanh(2) = 0.964$. The saturation plateau of the activation function is almost attained. Figure 2 shows the shape of $tanh$ for different quantisation precisions.

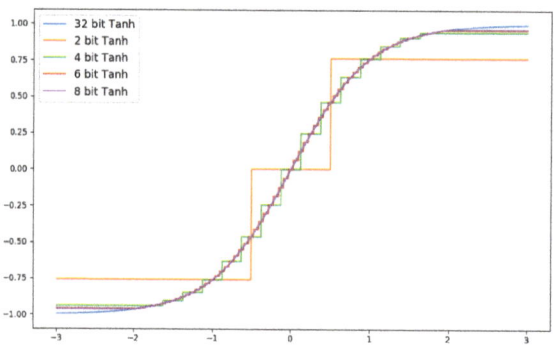

Figure 2. Hyperbolic tangent with different quantisation configuration.

3. NEMOKD: Knowledge Distillation and Multi-Objective Optimisation of Neural Networks

This section presents our new NEMOKD framework. Its aim is to produce accurate neural networks small enough to fit onto hardware accelerators to achieve high throughput. Section 3.2 describes its knowledge distillation based training. Section 3.3 shows its multi-objective optimisation that evolves encoded neural network hyper-parameters to find optimal trade-offs between accuracy and throughput. Section 3.4 presents the NEMOKD methodology for hardware-aware optimisation, which measures inference latency *on the intended target device* to feed into the evaluation of evolved CNN architectures.

3.1. Evolutionary Algorithms

Evolutionary deep learning approaches [26] have been proposed as an alternative training approach to stochastic gradient descent. However, due to the enormity of the search space for state-of-the-art neural networks that comprise millions of parameters, evolutionary algorithms often fail to discover optimal solutions.

Recent neuro-evolution techniques retain stochastic gradient descent and back propagation for training, before using evolutionary algorithms to search for optimal architectural configurations. Device-aware Progressive Search for Pareto-Optimal Neural Architectures [27] is a method of neural architecture search that has been shown to simultaneously optimise device-related objectives such as inference time and device-agnostic objectives such as accuracy. This search algorithm uses progressive search and mutation operators to explore the trade-offs between these objectives. Applying this algorithm to problems on a range of different hardware devices from a NVIDIA Titan X GPU to a mobile phone with an ARM Cortex-A35, the authors of [27] were able to obtain higher accuracy and shorter inference times compared to the state-of- the-art CondenseNet [28].

Neural-Evolution with Multi-Objective Optimisation (NEMO) [29] is a neural network optimisation algorithm. It is a machine learning technique that uses multi-objective evolutionary algorithms to simultaneously optimise both accuracy and inference time of neural networks by evolving their architecture.

3.2. Knowledge Distillation

Neural networks often have a softmax output layer that produce probabilities of given inputs belonging to each class. The cross entropy loss function measures the similarity of the softmax output vector against a ground truth vector defined by the training set. Given ground truth label vector **y**, N classes in the vector, and a softmax prediction vector **p**, the cross entropy loss is:

$$\mathcal{H}(\mathbf{y}, \mathbf{p}) = -\sum_{i}^{N} y_i \ln(p_i) \qquad (2)$$

Knowledge distillation incorporates an additional hyper-parameter, *temperature* (T), into this softmax calculation. Softer probability distributions over classes are obtained by using higher temperatures [8]. Knowledge distillation employs a loss function that uses two weighted objective functions:

1. **Student loss:** cross entropy of the student's standard softmax output ($T = 1$) with the ground truth vector.
2. **Distillation loss:** cross entropy of the teacher's high temperature ($T = \tau$) output with the students high temperature output.

The loss function for knowledge distillation (from [30]) is:

$$\mathcal{L}(\mathbf{x}; \mathbf{W}) = \underbrace{\alpha \, \mathcal{H}(\mathbf{y}, \sigma(\mathbf{z_s}; T=1))}_{\text{Student Loss}} + \underbrace{\beta \, \mathcal{H}(\sigma(\mathbf{z_t}; T=\tau), \sigma(\mathbf{z_s}; T=\tau))}_{\text{Distillation Loss}} \qquad (3)$$

where **x** is an input, **W** are the parameters of the student network, **y** the ground truth vector and $\sigma(\mathbf{z}; T = \tau)$ is the softmax function applied to logit vector **z** and temperature $T = \tau$. The student and teacher logit vectors are s and t, and hyper-parameters α and β are arbitrary constants.

In the NEMOKD methodology (Section 3.4), student models in the initial CNN architecture population are partially trained using knowledge distillation.

3.3. Multi-Objective Optimisation

Multi-Objective Optimisation solves optimisation problems with at least two conflicting objectives. For a solution space **A** that contains all permissible neural networks configurations, the two objectives of NEMOKD are (1) minimise inference latency (*latency*) and (2) minimising accuracy loss (*error*):

$$min_{a \in \mathbf{A}} (latency(a), error(a)) \qquad (4)$$

NEMOKD generates this solution space **A** by encoding and evolving hyper-parameters of student models (Section 3.3.1) then evolving these to optimise for Equation 4 (Section 3.3.2).

3.3.1. Encoding Student Models for Evolution

The evaluation of NEMOKD in Section 4.3 uses two baseline student architectures: FlexStudent and Resnet8x4. We encode certain features of these model into genotypes to evolve their hyper-parameters.

We encode the FlexStudent model with 11 genes. Genes 1 and 2 determine the number of convolutional and fully connected layers respectively. Genes 3–7 determine the number of output channels in convolutional layers. Genes 8–11 encode the number of fully connected layers. Figure 3 shows how NEMOKD decodes the genotype representation of the baseline FlexStudent model into a CNN architecture.

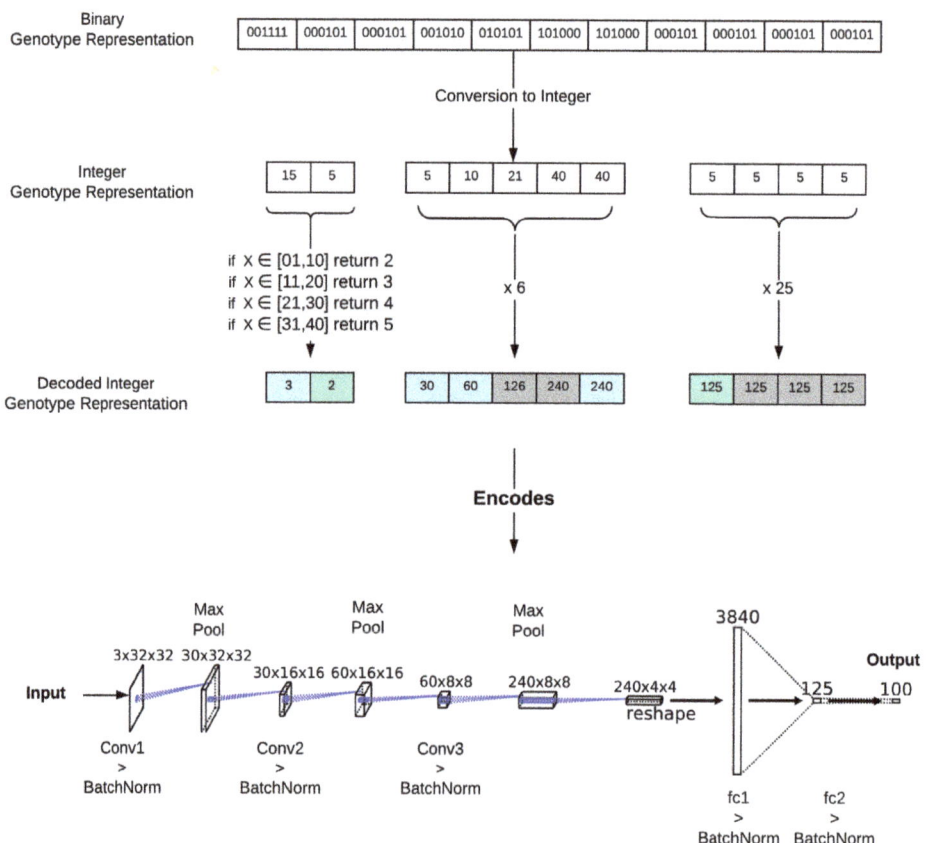

Figure 3. Decoding the genotype representation of the baseline FlexStudent.

For the Resnet8x4 student we encode hyper-parameters to evolve the number of layers in the output channels from convolutional layers. The number of layers are fixed.

3.3.2. Multi-Objective Evolution

We employ the Non-Dominated Sorting Genetic Algorithm version II (NSGAII) [31] to facilitate evolutionary multi-objective optimisation, starting from the baseline architecture trained with knowledge distillation. Model mutations with NSGAII are both fine and coarse grained. Mutation in our NEMOKD framework modifies four hyper-parameters:

1. The number of convolutional layers.
2. The number of Fully Connect layers.
3. The number of output channels.
4. The number of Fully-Connected neurons.

NEMOKD uses NSGAII to generate a set of CNN architecture solutions from one population member. Student models (either FlexStudent or Resnet8x4) are first encoded into a genotype sequence (Figure 3). The evolutionary process then happens in two steps: (1) crossover generates a new solution by combining genotypes of two parents; (2) ranking and selection chooses the fittest members of the population, based on the best trade-off between accuracy and latency when evaluated on the VPU. For every solution, mutation alters one or more genes at random.

For the two objectives of minimising latency (f_1) and error (f_2), a solution a dominates solution b if it outperforms for one of these objectives and is not worse in the other:

$$\forall i \in [1,2], \exists j \in [1,2] : f_i(a) \leq f_i(b) \text{ and } f_j(a) < f_j(b) \tag{5}$$

NEMOKD uses NSGAII to search for Pareto optimal solutions. A CNN architecture solution a is Pareto optimal if it is not dominated by any other solution in a solution space **A**:

$$\forall b \in \mathbf{A}, \forall i \in [1,2], \exists j \in [1,2] : f_i(a) \leq f_i(b) \text{ and } f_j(a) < f_j(b) \text{ and } a \neq b \tag{6}$$

The final output from NEMOKD is a population of evolved models, which includes those in the Pareto optimal set.

3.4. NEMOKD Methodology

The NEMOKD methodology combines knowledge distillation and the multi-objective evolutionary algorithm above. The methodology comprises two phases:

Phase 1: Knowledge Distillation: A baseline model is trained with knowledge distillation to provide a comparison for NEMOKD performance. NEMOKD uses that baseline architecture as a starting point to generate variants using evolutionary multi-objective optimisation.

Phase 2: Model Evolution: Each generation produces 10–20 variations of the baseline model, each then trained using knowledge distillation. The two objectives, *minimising latency* and *minimising error*, are measured for each model on the VPU device. The Pareto optimal models are retained to form part of the next generation. The other models are discarded. This process repeats for a specified number of generations. In our NEMOKD evaluation (Section 4.3), generations range from 14 to 27.

The NEMOKD methodology is shown in Figure 4. A population N is initialised. Each member of this population is a genotype that represents a CNN student architecture in the solution space (Section 3.3.1). To increase the chance of finding comparable or better solutions in a small number of generations, random perturbations are then applied to half the population to encourage more diverse solutions.

First, each genotype is decoded to construct a CNN model. These are then partially trained with knowledge distillation and are then converted to the ONNX format and finally a half-precision Intermediate Representation for VPU deployment. The fitness of each individual genotype is then assessed on the VPU device based on accuracy and latency performance. Genotype evaluation results are passed to NSGAII for evolution of student model hyper-parameters (Section 3.3.2).

NSGAII selects genotypes based on their fitness values to add new members. Crossover and mutation are applied to this member set, to add to the overall population. This evolve/decode/select process repeats until a specified number of NEMOKD generations. The algorithm outputs the final population including the Pareto optimal set (Equation (6)). This set of solutions provides optimal trade-offs between the two objectives in the objective space.

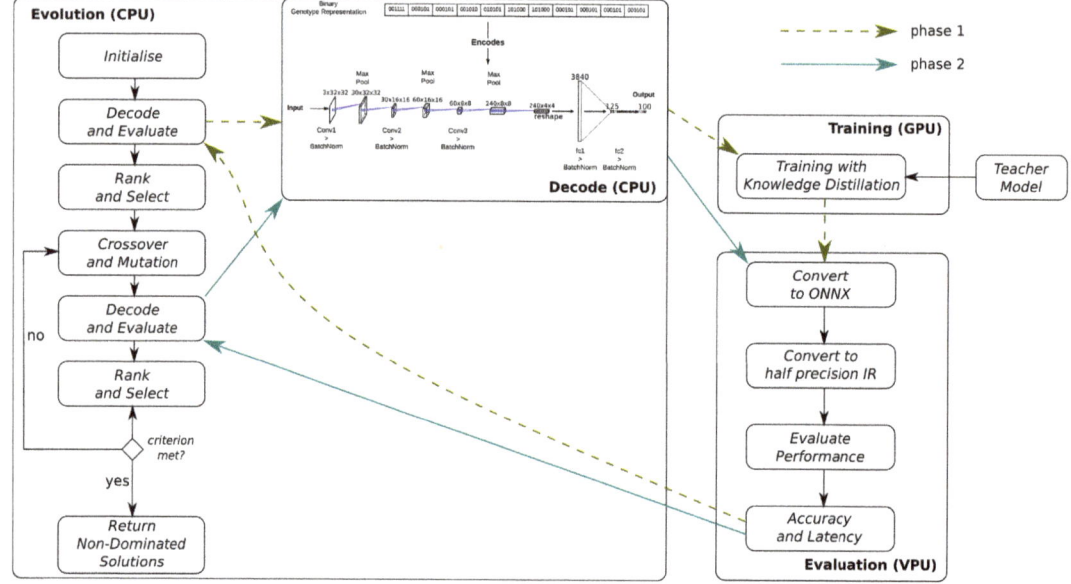

Figure 4. NEMOKD methodology.

3.5. NEMOKD versus NEMO

Our NEMOKD methodology extends NEMO [29] in three ways:

1. Knowledge distillation replaces standard training in the learning phase of the evaluation procedure.
2. To conserve time and computational resources in the learning phase, *partial* training is provided with only 30 epochs (in phase 1) as opposed to fully training each member of initial population.
3. Latency and accuracy is measured on the VPU device to asses the fitness of population members. This evaluation data is fed into the evolutionary NSGAII algorithm.

Accuracy after 30 epochs is indicative of performance should full training later be performed. Therefore to save time and energy costs of fully training all evolving student variants, a developer might select a fully evolved partially trained model that meets latency requirements, then subject it to more training with 200+ epochs.

We say NEMOKD's evolutionary optimisation is *hardware-aware*, because fitness is measured on the processor architecture (Intel's Movidius VPU) intended for deploying the model. This is based on the idea that a model's latency performance depends on the processor architecture used, and that optimising a model for one architecture may be ineffective if deploying to another [27].

4. Evaluation

4.1. Hardware Platforms

This section evaluates quantisation for programmable hardware, and our NEMOKD evolutionary algorithm for the fixed VPU architecture. The dataset and neural network model for the experiments are shown in Table 2.

For the *programmable hardware* experiments we target the mid-range Xilinx Zynq Z7020 140 mm × 87 mm FPGA on the Xilinx PYNQ-Z2 development board which uses ≈13.8 W energy. This FPGA has 53 k Lookup Tables (LUT), 106 k Flip Flops (FF) and 560 KB of Block RAM (BRAM) memory. Of the 64 quantised neural networks in Section 4.2, only four fit on this FPGA. This validates the need for aggressive compression approaches such as quantisation, on small to medium sized FPGA devices.

Table 2. Quantisation and model evolution experiments

Device	Model		Dataset	Section
Xilinx Z7020 FPGA	3 layer fully connected MLP		MNIST	Sections 4.2.1 and 4.2.2
(quantisation)	3 layer fully connected MLP		FASHION-MNIST	Section 4.2.3
Intel Movidius Myriad X VPU	*Teacher*	*Student*		
(model evolution)	MobileNetV2	FlexStudent	CIFAR10	Section 4.3
	Resnet32x4	FlexStudent	CIFAR100	Section 4.3
	Resnet32x4	Resnet8x4	CIFAR100	Section 4.3

For the *fixed hardware* experiments we use a USB-based Intel Neural Compute Stick 2 (NCS2) accelerator using a 72.5 mm × 27 mm Intel Movidius Myriad X Visual Processing Unit (VPU) which uses ≈1.5 W energy. The NCS2 comprises dedicated accelerators with the 16 programmable 128-bit VLIW Vector Processors optimised for processing highly parallel workloads. The device can compute up to 1 Tera Operation Per Second (TOPS). The centralised 2.5 MB of on chip memory facilitated by the intelligent memory fabric enables memory access latencies of 400 GB/s and reduces the requirements for more costly off-chip data transfer. The NCS2 device has 512 MB of LPDDR4 memory [3].

4.2. Quantisation Results

This section investigates the design space granted by FINN's ability to independently quantise weights and activation functions of a Multilayer Perceptron (MLP) network with three Fully-Connected (FC) layers. We created 64 quantised models from a baseline model by independently and exhaustively varying the bit-widths of weights and activation functions from 1 to 8. For 64 neural network quantisation configurations, the evaluation in this section measured:

1. *Absolute* accuracy and hardware resource costs of the 64quantised neural networks (Section 4.2.1).
2. *Relative* performance comparison of accuracy and hardware resource costs, compared with the other 63 quantised models (Section 4.2.2).

The training was done using 50,000 images from the MNIST dataset. A validation dataset of 10,000 images was then used to minimise overfitting. Accuracy was measured using a testing dataset, to test how well the model generalised to new data. FINN's backend converted the model to a binary weight file and a synthesisable C++ implementation for hardware.

4.2.1. Absolute Performance

Absolute Accuracy Performance

Each of the 64 neural networks was labelled with a quantised weight W-X and quantised activation function A-Y with $X, Y \in [1; 8]$. Accuracy is measured after 10, 20, 30, 50 and 100 epochs.

Figure 5 plots the inference error rate for each of the 64 quantised neural networks after training with 10, 20, 30, 50 and 100 epochs. Using 1–3 bits weights had a noticeable effect on accuracy, i.e., between 3.9–4.7% dropping down to below 3.7% using 4 bits or more. Training further with 40–100 epochs shifted the noticeable accuracy boundary to just 1 bit weight, meaning that with enough training, 2 bit weights achieved almost the same inference accuracy as 3–8 bit weights. The quantisation of activation functions had a steady impact on accuracy, i.e., higher precision activation functions result in better accuracy, however, this was not as dramatic as the impact that quantised weight precision has on accuracy. With increased training time, the accuracy performance flattened, where absolute difference in accuracy between the best and worst quantisation configuration greatly diminished. Additionally, we observed a major gap between 1 and 2 bit weights versus 3–8 bit weights, especially for 10 and 20 epochs. Training beyond 40 epochs allowed weights to be quantised from 3 to 2 bits without noticeable accuracy loss.

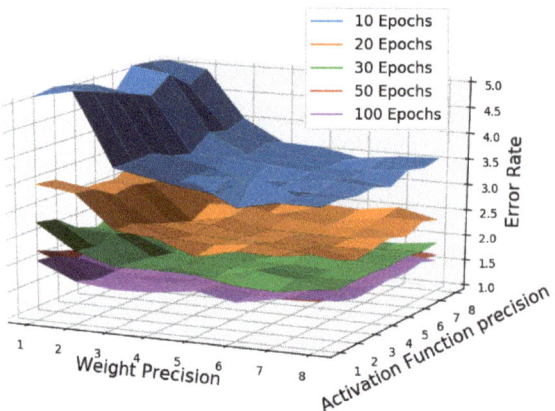

Figure 5. Accuracy of Quantised Neural Networks (QNN) with increasing training

Absolute Resource Utilisation Performance

Figure 6 shows the trade-off between quantised precision and hardware resource use. The X axis is the number of bits for weights, the Y axis is the number of bits for the activation functions. The colour in the heat maps represents the relative measurement of the respective performance metric compared to the other 63 models.

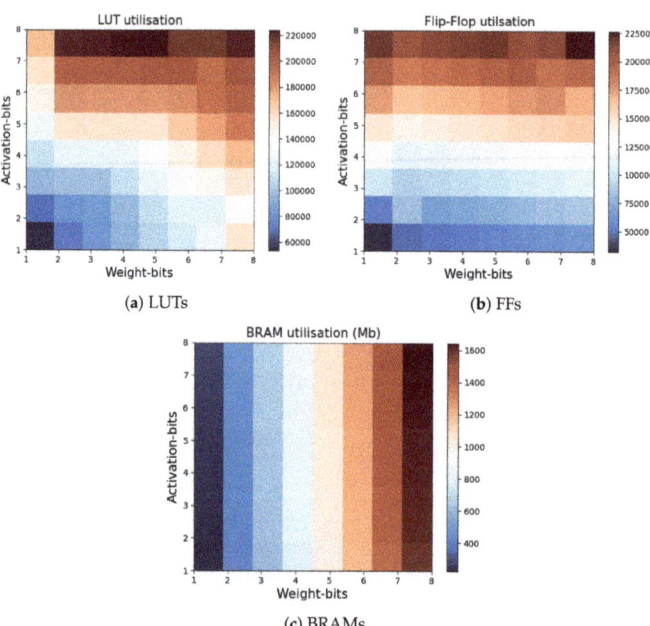

Figure 6. Hardware resources required for 64 quantised neural networks.

Figure 6a shows that both weight precision and activation function precision contributed evenly to LUTs costs. Figure 6b shows that the precision of activation functions determined FF costs. While FFs and LUTs could store small amounts of data, BRAMs had greater storage capacity and were used by hardware synthesis tools for larger data structures such as arrays. Figure 6c shows that BRAM consumption was determined exclusively by weight precision.

4.2.2. Relative Performance

Table 3 gives the best and worst relative performance numbers for the 64 quantised neural networks. The three radar plots in Figure 7 represents different quantised neural network configurations, comparing accuracy and resource use (LUTs, FFs and BRAMs) performance relative to the best and values in Table 3. Each metric defines one branch in a radar chart. The three precision variations in Figure 7 are:

1. Weight oriented distribution (Figure 7a) increased the weight precision and kept the activation function constant at 4 bits, i.e., W1–A4, W3–A4, W6–A4 and W8–A4.
2. Activation oriented distribution (Figure 7b) increased the activation function precision and kept the weight precision constant at 4 bits, i.e., W4–A1, W4–A3, W4–A6 and W4–A8.
3. Linear distribution (Figure 7c) increased both the weight and activation function precision across the diagonal from the heat maps in Figure 6, i.e., W1–A1, W2–A2, W4–A4 and W7–A7.

Table 3. Relative performance for radar plots in Figure 7.

Metric	Relative Performance	
	Worst	Best
Accuracy loss	2.07%	1.52%
BRAM	1643	224
Flip Flops	226,282	31,954
Look Up Tables	223,910	53,336

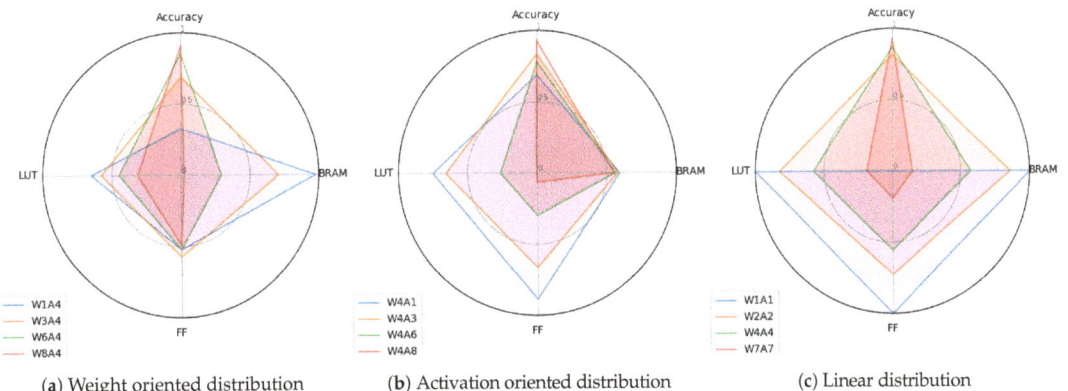

(a) Weight oriented distribution (b) Activation oriented distribution (c) Linear distribution

Figure 7. Radar charts for different quantisation configurations

The radar plots compare the relative performance of these quantisation configurations. The models were ranked on LUT, BRAM and FF requirements (fewer was better), and their accuracy (higher was better). These scores were then normalised between 0 and 1. For example the model with the highest accuracy had a score of 1 and was plotted outermost in the radar plot in the *Accuracy* dimension, whereas the model with lowest accuracy was plotted at the centre point. Likewise for hardware requirements, e.g., the neural network requiring the fewest BRAMs was plotted outermost in the BRAM dimension.

When activation functions were set to 3 bits, increasing weights from W1 to W3 caused the greatest relative accuracy score improvement (Figure 7a). When weights were fixed at 4 bits, all accuracy scores were in the top half, with increases of activation function precision costing significantly more LUT and FF resources, with BRAM costed largely the same (Figure 7b). Scaling both precision linearly had an equal impact on FF, LUT and BRAM scores, yet their accuracy score were all in the top quartile when weights were 2–8 bits (Figure 7c). In summary if top-half relative accuracy performance was the goal, the most important constraint was 2+ bits for representing weights.

The importance of the trade-offs is highlighted by the fact that most of the neural networks did not fit on the target device (Xilinx Zynq Z7020). It had 280 BRAMs and only seven of the networks met this constraint, and 106,400 FFs with 22 of the networks within this constraint.

4.2.3. Parallel Speedups

FINN supports parallelisation on a layer-by-layer basis. The amount of parallel hardware resources used to implement each layer of a neural network is user definable. Parallelism is controlled with two settings: (1) the number of hardware processing elements (PE) to process each output channel, and (2) the number of input channels processed within one clock cycle (SIMD) [24]. Using more parallel hardware for a layer shortens the layer's clock cycle latency, at the cost of increased hardware requirements. If the layer is on the critical path, i.e., is has the highest latency cost, then parallelisation of that layer should shorten overall latency thereby increasing throughput.

Our throughput evaluation used a multi-layer perceptron with three fully connected layers with the FASHION-MNIST dataset. Each quantised model was tested for accuracy and throughput on the Xilinx Z7020 FPGA on the PYNQ-Z2 board. Each model was trained with 40 epochs. The results compared:

1. Inference accuracy.
2. Frames-Per-Second (FPS) image throughput.
3. Quantisation configurations W2A2, W3A3 and W4A4.
4. The parallelism degree for PE and SIMD for all layers, setting both at 2, 8 then 16.

Figure 8 shows throughput results. The model with 2-bit precision achieved 84.9% accuracy. Increasing parallelism did not affect accuracy because each time it was the same model, just implemented with more parallel hardware. Increasing to 3-bit and 4-bit precision increased accuracy to 85.5% and 85.7%. Setting PE and SIMD to 2 achieved a throughput of 6 k FPS. Increasing these parallelism parameters to 8 and 16 increased throughput to 96 k and 373 k FPS for the 2 and 3 bit models—a 62× speedup. The W4A4 quantised model did not fit within the Xilinx Z7020 FPGA's available resources when PE and SIMD is 16, and hence is not shown in Figure 8.

4.2.4. Quantisation Results Discussion

The sweet spot in the quantisation design space for the MNIST and FASHION-MNIST datasets is about 3 bit weights and 3 bit activation functions. Beyond 3 bit quantisation and with enough training, there is no significant improvement to accuracy performance. This confirms results in [25]. Our methodology for evaluating the trade-off between accuracy, throughput and hardware efficiency is similar to [32]. We extend that work by also measuring the impact of varying training of quantised models, and a more fine grained benchmark suite measuring weight precision independently of activation function precision.

In summary, our quantisation experiments show:

- LUT and FF resources increase with increased activation function precision, because increasing arithmetic calculation complexity increases the number of required processing units.

- BRAM increases with increased weight precision, because weight parameters are stored in BRAM memories.
- Inference accuracy is highest with higher precision, i.e., least aggressive quantisation. The biggest improvement in accuracy with a 1 bit increment is switching from 1 to 2 bits weight precision.
- With enough training beyond 50 epochs, 2 bit precision achieves almost the same inference accuracy as 3–8 bit precision.
- Increasing the parallelisation of hardware neural network implementations significantly increases throughput performance from 6.1 k FPS to 373 k FPS, a 62× speedup.
- The trade-off between precision, throughput and accuracy is the W3A3 model with 16 for PE and SIMD, achieving 373 k FPS and 85.5% accuracy for the FASHION-MNIST dataset.

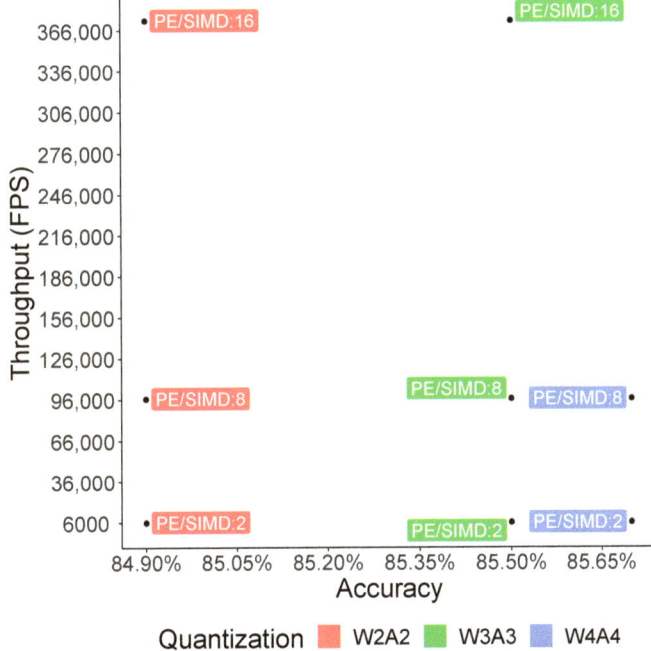

Figure 8. Throughput and accuracy performance of parallel FPGA designs for FASHION-MNIST.

4.3. NEMOKD Results

For the NEMOKD experiments in this section, we used two student models as our solution space for hyper-parameter evolution:

1. FlexStudent , a model that we constructed with a simple five layer model to provide a starting point for the NEMOKD evolution process (Section 3). A similar model performs well as a student architecture on the CIFAR10 dataset [33].
2. A version of the Resnet8x4 architecture, modified to enable the NEMOKD hyper-parameter evolutionary process.

Our NEMOKD framework was measured with three benchmarks:

1. The MobileNetV2 model distilled into a FlexStudent student model with the CIFAR10 dataset.
2. The Resnet32x4 model distilled into a FlexStudent student model with CIFAR100.
3. The Resnet32x4 model distilled into a Resnet8x4 student model with CIFAR100. For this experiment, the number of layers remained fixed.

The experiments used 30 epochs for knowledge distillation and the number of NSGAII generations varies for each experiment, ranging from 14 to 27. For our pruning benchmarks we used Platypus [34] for multi-objective optimisation, RepDistiller [35] for knowledge distillation, and OpenVino's Python API to execute trained exported PyTorch models on the NSC2 device.

4.3.1. Knowledge Distillation Parameter Search

Figure 9 shows knowledge distillation error with 30 epochs. It illustrates how different combinations of knowledge distillation parameters affected the accuracy of the baseline model after 30 epochs. The α value determined how much the distillation loss and student loss contributed to the overall loss e.g., if $\alpha = 0.5$, then both terms in the knowledge distillation loss function were weighted evenly. The softmax function in the distillation loss term was parametrised by the temperature. This softened the output distribution revealing extra information about which classes the model found most alike. The blue surface illustrates the error rate of the baseline model with respect to different combinations of knowledge distillation hyper-parameters. The orange plane indicates the baseline test error performance without knowledge distillation.

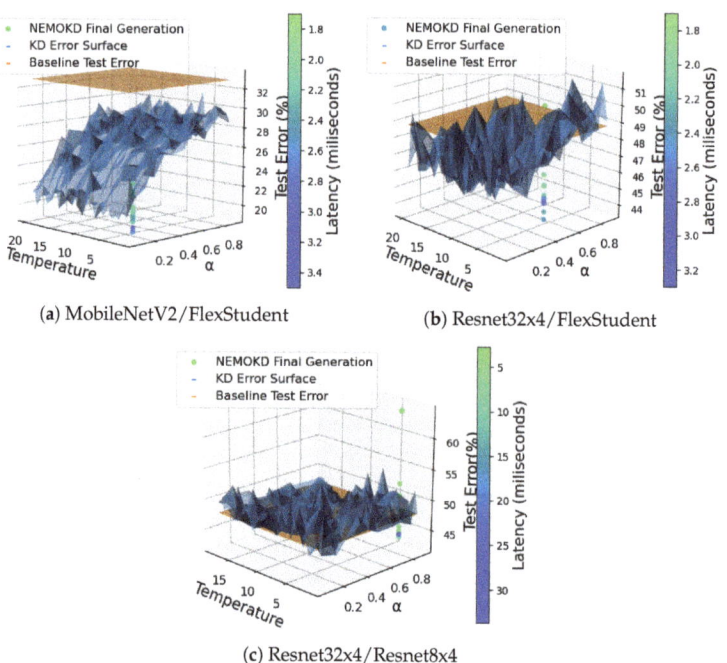

Figure 9. Knowledge distillation parameter search for *Teacher/Student* distillation

For the MobileNetV2 teacher, a FlexStudent student model and CIFAR10 in Figure 9a, any choice of knowledge distillation hyper-parameters provided a significant increase in accuracy over the baseline model.

Figure 9b shows that some combinations of the knowledge distillation parameters had a negative effect on the accuracy of the baseline model. We observed that this method produced better accuracy than could be obtained by distilling knowledge into the baseline model, once again at the expense of latency. The MobileNetV2/FlexStudent experiment in Figure 9a is similar to Figure 9b, but rather than CIFAR100 it used the simpler CIFAR10 dataset. In this case, every combination of knowledge distillation hyper parameters provided significant improvement over baseline.

In Figure 9c, the majority of combinations of knowledge distillation hyper-parameters had a negative impact on the baseline model accuracy, though certain combinations did provide improvements as shown in Figure 9c. In this case, no major trends were observed with respect to the individual hyper-parameters. We observed that this method, once again, produced better accuracy than could be obtained by distilling knowledge into the baseline model with 30 epochs of training.

4.3.2. Efficacy of NEMOKD Evolution

Figure 10 shows the latency and accuracy performance of student models after 30 epochs for student models. It shows the baseline model trained with just knowledge distillation (green diamonds). The red and blue points show performance of the models at intermediate and final generations of student models. As with the quantisation experiments, accuracy was measured using a testing dataset to asses how the models generalised to new unseen data.

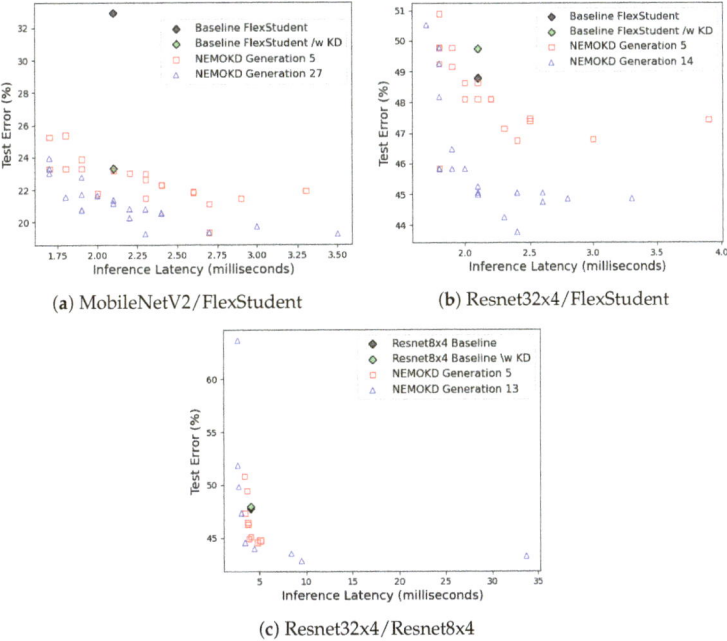

Figure 10. Student latency and accuracy performance for *Teacher/Student* distillation

Figure 10a shows FlexStudent student performance with the MobileNetV2 teacher. The chosen knowledge distillation hyper-parameters for this experiment greatly increased the accuracy of the baseline model. With 30 epochs of training, many students in the final generation evolved to attain a better accuracy than the baseline model but with the same or better latency. The same was also true of the baseline model trained with knowledge distillation. The most accurate students, however, had larger latency values with respect to the baseline model. The best latency/accuracy trade-off for Resnet32x4/FlexStudent distillation with CIFAR10 was an evolved model with five convolutional layers with a relatively small number of output channels and just two fully connected layers. It has a low to moderate number of neurons of about 125–150 neurons.

Figure 10b shows FlexStudent student performance with the larger Resnet32x4 teacher model, for the CIFAR100 dataset. Student models evolved from the same baseline FlexStudent as the experiment in Figure 10a. Figure 10b illustrates the population at two distinct generations of the evolutionary process, in addition to the baseline architecture from which all the students evolved. Interestingly, the combination of knowledge distillation hyper-parameters we chose for this experiment had a negative impact on the accuracy of the baseline model. However, the evolved students appeared to adapt their architecture to accommodate these parameters, resulting in student models with significant accuracy improvements for the same inference latency. The best accuracy produced by the NEMOKD algorithm was obtained by an architecture with a higher latency. In contrast to Figure 10a, every student model in the final generation evolved to have the same layer structure as the baseline model.

Figure 10c shows Resnet8x4 student performance student performance with the Resnet32x4 teacher, for the CIFAR100 dataset. It differs from Figures 10a,b in two ways: (1) a different evolutionary starting point is used for the ResNet8x4 student; and (2) the layers of this student model are fixed, only the output channels of the convolutional layers were modified in the NEMOKD evolutionary process.

4.4. Discussion

4.4.1. Quantisation for FPGAs

Our quantisation experiments (Section 4.2) use the quantisation scheme implemented in Xilinx's FINN framework. Developing compression algorithms for embedded devices is a research area of its own, e.g., a dynamic precision data quantisation algorithm in [36], performed layer-by-layer from a corresponding floating point CNN, with the goal of improving bandwidth and resource utilisation. Other compression approaches are focused on specific goals e.g., reducing power consumption, or target specific hardware e.g., GPUs or FPGAs, or target specific domains or even specific application algorithms.

Device Specific Quantisation

Recent work explores the performance trade-offs between reduced precision of neural networks and their speed on GPUs, e.g., performance aware pruning can lead to 3–10 times speedups [37]. Multi-precision FPGA hardware for neural networks significantly reduces model sizes, which in [38] enables an ImageNet network to fit entirely on-chip for the first time, significantly speeding up throughput. Another recent study [25] measures the hardware cost, power consumption, and throughput for a High Level Synthesis extension of FINN that supports Long Short-Term Memory (LSTM) models on FPGAs. [39] proposes a design flow for constructing low precision, low powered FPGA-based neural networks with a hybrid quantisation scheme. [40] shows that resource-aware model analysis, data quantisation and efficient use of hardware techniques can be combined to jointly map binarised neural networks to FPGAs with dramatically reduced resource requirements whilst maintaining acceptable accuracy.

Domain Specific Quantisation

Some quantisation methods target specific algorithms, e.g., a resource-aware weight quantisation framework for performing object detection in images [41].

4.4.2. NEMO with Knowledge Distillation for the VPU

Knowledge distillation parameters for the NEMOKD experiments (Section 4.3) greatly increase the accuracy of the baseline model. With 30 epochs of training, many students in the final generation evolve to attain a better accuracy than the baseline model but with the same or better latency. The most accurate students, however, have larger latency values with respect to the baseline model. The best trade-off model evolved five convolutional layers with a small number of output channels and just two fully connected layers, with a low to moderate number of neurons of about 125–150 neurons.

Our NEMOKD approach significantly increases inference accuracy at a modest expense of latency. The method consistently provides higher accuracy students than could be obtained through an exhaustive knowledge distillation parameter search with the baseline model, irrespective of the choice of knowledge distillation hyper-parameters. This highlights the importance of the student's architecture in the knowledge distillation process. Evolving students appears to enable models to adapt and accommodate an arbitrary choice of knowledge distillation hyper-parameters, even if the choice was initially detrimental to the accuracy of the baseline model.

4.4.3. Comparing Quantisation and NEMOKD

The quantisation and NEMOKD results are shown in Figure 11. Both compression approaches start from baseline models: ResNet32x4 and MobileNetV2 for NEMOKD, and a 32 bit Multi-Layer Perceptron model for quantisation. Quantisation reduces the arithmetic precision without changing a model's architecture, i.e., the number of hidden layers and number of neurons are unchanged. Training with the FINN framework is quantisation-aware, with performance sweet spots for our benchmarks at around 2–4 bits.

In contrast, the NEMOKD framework changes the model's architecture whilst leaving arithmetic precision unchanged during training. After training, models are converted into the OpenVINO IR format with 16-bit half precision for deployment on the VPU.

Typically, 30 image FPS throughput is considered real-time computer vision performance [42]. Quantisation and the NEMOKD framework both achieve real-time image processing: 590 FPS on the VPU and 373 k FPS on the FPGA.

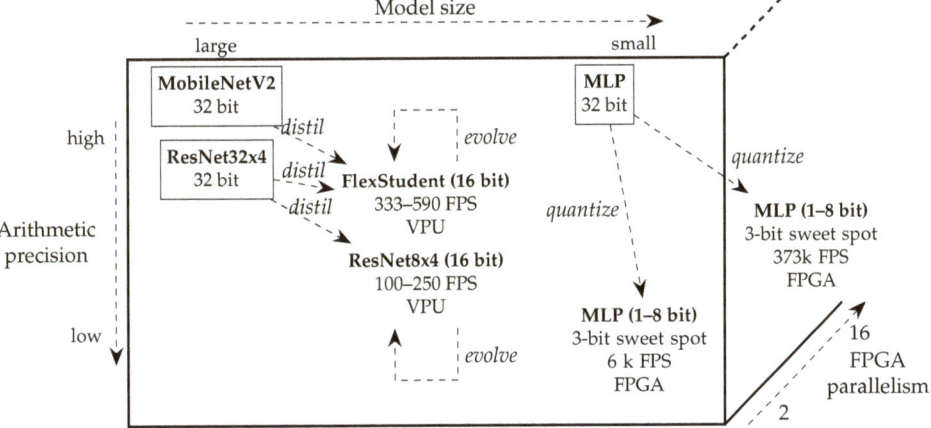

Figure 11. Varying precision and model architectures.

5. Conclusions and Future Work

5.1. Conclusions

This paper explores two optimisation approaches for neural networks for programmable hardware and a fixed AI processor: (1) quantisation precision of fixed models, and (2) evolving hyper-parameters of student models in conjunction with knowledge distillation. There is a sweet spot of 3 bit quantisation in the trade-off between latency, hardware requirements, training time and accuracy. Parallelising hardware implementations of neural networks increases FPS from 6 k to 373 k, a 62× speedup. Evolving student models increases inference accuracy by up to 82% at the cost of 38% increased latency. The lowest inference latencies were 1.7 ms for the FlexStudent model distilled from MobileNetV2, 1.4 ms for FlexStudent distilled from Resnet32x4, and 2 ms for Resnet8x4 distilled from Resnet32x4. This is a throughput of between 100 and 590 FPS.

5.2. Future Work

5.2.1. Larger Datasets and Models

Our experiments use four datasets: MNIST and FASHION-MNIST for quantisation, and CIFAR10 and CIFAR100 for NEMOKD. The quantisation experiments are based on a five layer fully-connected network and the NEMOKD experiments use two student models. More work is required to scale accuracy-preserving compression methods to real world computer vision applications e.g., from 28 × 28 MNIST and FASHION-MNIST images, and 32 × 32 CIFAR10 and CIFAR100 images, to much higher dimensions such as 400 × 150 road lane detection images for autonomous driving [43]. Scaling compressing experiments to (1) deeper models with tens/hundreds of hidden layers, and (2) datasets with thousands of classes e.g., ImageNet, would be an intermediate step in that direction.

5.2.2. Profile Guided Automating Compression

Our quantisation benchmarks were exhaustive in the design space of 1–8 bits for activation functions and weight values. The quantisation was homogeneous across the entire network each time, i.e., each quantisation configuration applied to all parameters. Combining layer-specific dataflow optimisation and layer-specific quantisation allows models to fit entirely in on-chip BRAM, thereby removing off-chip memory accesses which improves throughput performance [44]. In [45], mixed precision quantisation scheme applies layer-wise priority in inverse order of their layer depth, based on findings that binarising different layers has a widely-varied effect on accuracy loss. FINN supports per-layer activation function and weights precision, as well as layer-by-layer clock cycle profiling and accuracy testing. This opens up the opportunity for automating *profile guided* layer-by-layer quantisation methodologies in simulation i.e., without having to run models on hardware, to find the optimal trade-off between throughput and accuracy for each combination of model and dataset.

When using evolutionary algorithms with knowledge distillation for larger datasets and models, enabling more parameters to be the subject of mutation throughout the evolutionary process could prove beneficial in automating search for optimal compressed models. Recent teacher-student methods [35] outperform knowledge distillation in a wide range of problems. Designing a flexible student model that accommodates both evolution and more complex distillation methods would be considerably more challenging, but given the positive results we report for NEMOKD we believe this would be important future work.

5.2.3. Performance Portability of Compressed Models

The two compression methods in this paper were tested on one hardware platform each. Our NEMOKD approach is hardware-aware, since the multi-objective optimisation phase is measured on the Intel Movidius VPU device. Evolving the same initial model with the goal of minimising latency and accuracy loss may produce quite different models for different devices due to different memory latencies, cache size and the number of parallel processing elements on each device. For quantisation, the amount of on-chip BRAM memory ranges from 0.5 to 8 MB for different FPGA devices, meaning aggressive quantisation and binarisation is needed for low-end devices, necessitating auto-tuning of model precision to be device specific.

5.2.4. Combining Knowledge Distillation with Quantisation

Previous work shows that combining compression methods can achieve superior performance compared with using them in isolation, e.g., combining pruning and knowledge distillation [46]. The approach in [47] shows that distilling knowledge to shallower quantised architectures can achieve accuracy comparable with state-of-the-art full-precision models. There are other compression methods such as weight sharing [48] to consider for hybrid compression. A complete study of neural network compression approaches is in [21].

More work is required to evaluate these hybrid neural network compression techniques at the scale of state-of-the-art real world problems. Not only may hybrid methods achieve superior throughput performance and energy efficiency, reducing precision and removing unimportant redundancy at scale may make verification of large real-world deep learning models possible.

Author Contributions: The individual contributions are as follows. R.S.: conceptualisation; funding acquisition; investigation; project administration; resources; supervision; writing—original draft; writing—review and editing. P.B.: software Section 2; data curation Section 4.2; visualisation Section 4.2; formal analysis Section 4.4; writing—original draft preparation Section 2.1 and Section 4.2. Q.D.: software Section 2; data curation Section 4.2.3; visualisation Section 4.2.3; writing—original draft preparation Section 4.2.3. A.N.: conceptualization Section 3; software Section 3; data curation Section 4.3; formal analysis Section 4.3; visualisation Section 4.3; writing—original draft preparation Section 3 and Section 4.3. E.K.: funding acquisition; supervision; writing—review and editing. All authors have read and agreed to the published version of the manuscript.

Funding: This research was funded by EPSRC project "Border Patrol: Improving Smart Device Security through Type-Aware Systems Design (EP/N028201/1)"; EPSRC project "Serious Coding: A Game Approach To Security For The New Code-Citizens (EP/T017511/1)"; National Cyber Security Center, UK, Grant "SecConn-NN: Neural Networks with Security Contracts—towards lightweight, modular security for neural networks"; UK Research Institute in Verified Trustworthy Software Systems research project "CONVENER: Continuous Verification of Neural Networks" (from the "Digital Security Through Verification" call).

Conflicts of Interest: The authors declare no conflict of interest.

References

1. Krizhevsky, A.; Sutskever, I.; Hinton, G.E. ImageNet Classification with Deep Convolutional Neural Networks. In Proceedings of the Advances in Neural Information Processing Systems 25: 26th Annual Conference on Neural Information Processing Systems 2012, Lake Tahoe, NV, USA, 3–6 December 2012; pp. 1106–1114.
2. Lu, D. Creating an AI Can Be Five Times Worse for the Planet Than a Car. New Scientist. 2019. Available online: https://www.newscientist.com/article/2205779-creating-an-ai-can-be-five-times-worse-for-the-planet-than-a-car (accessed on 28 December 2020).
3. Intel. Intel® Movidius™ Vision Processing Units (VPUs). Available online: https://www.intel.com/content/www/us/en/products/processors/movidius-vpu.html (accessed on 28 December 2020).
4. Edge TPU: Google's Purpose-Built ASIC Designed to Run Inference at the Edge. Available online: https://cloud.google.com/edge-tpu (accessed on 28 December 2020).
5. Véstias, M.P.; Neto, H.C. Trends of CPU, GPU and FPGA for high-performance computing. In Proceedings of the 2014 24th International Conference on Field Programmable Logic and Applications (FPL), Munich, Germany, 2–4 September 2014; pp. 1–6.
6. Han, S.; Pool, J.; Tran, J.; Dally, W.J. Learning both Weights and Connections for Efficient Neural Network. In Proceedings of the Advances in Neural Information Processing Systems 28: Annual Conference on Neural Information Processing Systems 2015, Montreal, QC, Canada, 7–12 December 2015; pp. 1135–1143.
7. Umuroglu, Y.; Fraser, N.J.; Gambardella, G.; Blott, M.; Leong, P.H.W.; Jahre, M.; Vissers, K.A. In Proceedings of the FINN: A Framework for Fast, Scalable Binarized Neural Network Inference, Monterey, CA, USA, 22–24 February 2017; pp. 65–74.
8. Hinton, G.E.; Vinyals, O.; Dean, J. Distilling the Knowledge in a Neural Network. *arXiv* **2015**, arXiv:1503.02531.
9. Diamos, G.; Sengupta, S.; Catanzaro, B.; Chrzanowski, M.; Coates, A.; Elsen, E.; Engel, J.H.; Hannun, A.Y.; Satheesh, S. Persistent RNNs: Stashing Recurrent Weights On-Chip. In Proceedings of the 33nd International Conference on Machine Learning (ICML 2016), New York, NY, USA, 19–24 June 2016; Volume 48, pp. 2024–2033.
10. Chen, T.; Du, Z.; Sun, N.; Wang, J.; Wu, C.; Chen, Y.; Temam, O. DianNao: a small-footprint high-throughput accelerator for ubiquitous machine-learning. In Proceedings of the ASPLOS 2014, Salt Lake City, UT, USA, 1–5 March 2014; pp. 269–284.
11. Park, J.; Sung, W. FPGA based implementation of deep neural networks using on-chip memory only. In Proceedings of the ICASSP 2016, Shanghai, China, 20–25 March 2016; pp. 1011–1015.
12. Katz, G.; Barrett, C.W.; Dill, D.L.; Julian, K.; Kochenderfer, M.J. Reluplex: An Efficient SMT Solver for Verifying Deep Neural Networks. In Proceedings of the Computer Aided Verification-29th International Conference (CAV 2017), Heidelberg, Germany, 24–28 July 2017; pp. 97–117.
13. Liu, C.; Arnon, T.; Lazarus, C.; Barrett, C.W.; Kochenderfer, M.J. Algorithms for Verifying Deep Neural Networks. *arXiv* **2019**, arXiv:1903.06758.
14. Kokke, W.; Komendantskaya, E.; Kienitz, D.; Atkey, R.; Aspinall, D. Neural Networks, Secure by Construction: An Exploration of Refinement Types. In *Asian Symposium on Programming Languages and Systems (APLAS), Fukuoka, Japan*; Springer: Berlin/Heidelberg, Germany, 2020.
15. Duncan, K.; Komendantskaya, E.; Stewart, R.; Lones, M.A. Relative Robustness of Quantized Neural Networks against Adversarial Attacks. In Proceedings of the 2020 International Joint Conference on Neural Networks (IJCNN 2020), Glasgow, UK, 19–24 July 2020; pp. 1–8.

16. Lecun, Y.; Bottou, L.; Bengio, Y.; Haffner, P. Gradient-based learning applied to document recognition. *Proc. IEEE* **1998**, *86*, 2278–2324. [CrossRef]
17. Szegedy, C.; Ioffe, S.; Vanhoucke, V.; Alemi, A.A. Inception-v4, Inception-ResNet and the Impact of Residual Connections on Learning. In Proceedings of the Thirty-First AAAI Conference on Artificial Intelligence, San Francisco, CA, USA, 4–9 February 2017; pp. 4278–4284.
18. Zhang, X.; Li, Z.; Loy, C.C.; Lin, D. PolyNet: A Pursuit of Structural Diversity in Very Deep Networks. In Proceedings of the 2017 IEEE Conference on Computer Vision and Pattern Recognition (CVPR 2017), Honolulu, HI, USA, 21–26 July 2017; pp. 3900–3908.
19. Tan, M.; Le, Q.V. EfficientNet: Rethinking Model Scaling for Convolutional Neural Networks. In Proceedings of the 36th International Conference on Machine Learning (ICML 2019), Long Beach, CA, USA, 9–15 June 2019; pp. 6105–6114.
20. Mahajan, D.; Girshick, R.B.; Ramanathan, V.; He, K.; Paluri, M.; Li, Y.; Bharambe, A.; van der Maaten, L. Exploring the Limits of Weakly Supervised Pretraining. *arXiv* **2018**, arXiv:1805.00932.
21. Wang, E.; Davis, J.J.; Zhao, R.; Ng, H.; Niu, X.; Luk, W.; Cheung, P.Y.K.; Constantinides, G.A. Deep Neural Network Approximation for Custom Hardware: Where We've Been, Where We're Going. *ACM Comput. Surv.* **2019**, *52*, 40:1–40:39. [CrossRef]
22. Hubara, I.; Courbariaux, M.; Soudry, D.; El-Yaniv, R.; Bengio, Y. Quantized Neural Networks: Training Neural Networks with Low Precision Weights and Activations. *J. Mach. Learn. Res.* **2017**, *18*, 187:1–187:30.
23. Courbariaux, M.; Bengio, Y. BinaryNet: Training Deep Neural Networks with Weights and Activations Constrained to +1 or −1. *arXiv* **2016**, arXiv:1602.02830.
24. Blott, M.; Preußer, T.B.; Fraser, N.J.; Gambardella, G.; O'Brien, K.; Umuroglu, Y.; Leeser, M.; Vissers, K.A. FINN-R: An End-to-End Deep-Learning Framework for Fast Exploration of Quantized Neural Networks. *TRETS* **2018**, *11*, 16:1–16:23. [CrossRef]
25. Rybalkin, V.; Pappalardo, A.; Ghaffar, M.M.; Gambardella, G.; Wehn, N.; Blott, M. FINN-L: Library Extensions and Design Trade-Off Analysis for Variable Precision LSTM Networks on FPGAs. In Proceedings of the FPL 2018, Dublin, Ireland, 27–31 August 2018; pp. 89–96.
26. Stanley, K.O.; Miikkulainen, R. Evolving Neural Networks through Augmenting Topologies. *Evol. Comput.* **2002**, *10*, 99–127. [CrossRef] [PubMed]
27. Dong, J.; Cheng, A.; Juan, D.; Wei, W.; Sun, M. DPP-Net: Device-Aware Progressive Search for Pareto-Optimal Neural Architectures. In Proceedings of the Computer Vision-ECCV 2018-15th European Conference, Munich, Germany, 8–14 September 2018; pp. 540–555.
28. Huang, G.; Liu, S.; van der Maaten, L.; Weinberger, K.Q. CondenseNet: An Efficient DenseNet Using Learned Group Convolutions. In Proceedings of the 2018 IEEE Conference on Computer Vision and Pattern Recognition, CVPR 2018, Salt Lake City, UT, USA, 18–22 June 2018; pp. 2752–2761.
29. Kim, Y.H.; Reddy, B.; Yun, S.; Seo, C. NEMO: Neuro-Evolution with Multiobjective Optimization of Deep Neural Network for Speed and Accuracy. In Proceedings of the AutoML 2017: Automatic Machine Learning Workshop (ICML 2017), Sydney, Australia, 10 August 2017.
30. Zmora, N.; Jacob, G.; Zlotnik, L.; Elharar, B.; Novik, G. Neural Network Distiller: A Python Package For DNN Compression Research. *arXiv* **2019**, arXiv:1910.12232.
31. Deb, K.; Agrawal, S.; Pratap, A.; Meyarivan, T. A fast and elitist multiobjective genetic algorithm: NSGA-II. *IEEE Trans. Evol. Comput.* **2002**, *6*, 182–197. [CrossRef]
32. Su, J.; Fraser, N.J.; Gambardella, G.; Blott, M.; Durelli, G.; Thomas, D.B.; Leong, P.H.W.; Cheung, P.Y.K. Accuracy to Throughput Trade-Offs for Reduced Precision Neural Networks on Reconfigurable Logic. In Proceedings of the ARC 2018, Santorini, Greece, 2–4 May 2018; pp. 29–42.
33. Exploring Knowledge Distillation of Deep Neural Nets for Efficient Hardware Solutions. CS230 Report. Available online: http://cs230.stanford.edu/files_winter_2018/projects/6940224.pdf (accessed on 28 December 2020).
34. Hadka, D. Platypus: Multiobjective Optimization in Python. Available online: https://platypus.readthedocs.io (accessed on 28 December 2020).
35. Tian, Y.; Krishnan, D.; Isola, P. Contrastive Representation Distillation. In Proceedings of the 8th International Conference on Learning Representations (ICLR 2020), Addis Ababa, Ethiopia, 26–30 April 2020.
36. Qiu, J.; Wang, J.; Yao, S.; Guo, K.; Li, B.; Zhou, E.; Yu, J.; Tang, T.; Xu, N.; Song, S.; et al. Going Deeper with Embedded FPGA Platform for Convolutional Neural Network. In Proceedings of the 2016 ACM/SIGDA International Symposium on Field-Programmable Gate Arrays, Monterey, CA, USA, 21–23 February 2016; pp. 26–35.
37. Radu, V.; Kaszyk, K.; Wen, Y.; Turner, J.; Cano, J.; Crowley, E.J.; Franke, B.; Storkey, A.; O'Boyle, M. Performance Aware Convolutional Neural Network Channel Pruning for Embedded GPUs. In Proceedings of the 2019 IEEE International Symposium on Workload Characterization (IISWC), Orlando, FL, USA, 3–5 November 2019.
38. Zhao, Y.; Gao, X.; Guo, X.; Liu, J.; Wang, E.; Mullins, R.; Cheung, P.Y.K.; Constantinides, G.A.; Xu, C. Automatic Generation of Multi-Precision Multi-Arithmetic CNN Accelerators for FPGAs. In Proceedings of the 2019 International Conference on Field-Programmable Technology (ICFPT), Tianjin, China, 9–13 December 2019; pp. 45–53.
39. Wang, J.; Lou, Q.; Zhang, X.; Zhu, C.; Lin, Y.; Chen, D. Design Flow of Accelerating Hybrid Extremely Low Bit-Width Neural Network in Embedded FPGA. In Proceedings of the FPL 2018, Dublin, Ireland, 27–31 August 2018; pp. 163–169.
40. Liang, S.; Yin, S.; Liu, L.; Luk, W.; Wei, S. FP-BNN: Binarized neural network on FPGA. *Neurocomputing* **2018**, *275*, 1072–1086. [CrossRef]

41. Ding, C.; Wang, S.; Liu, N.; Xu, K.; Wang, Y.; Liang, Y. REQ-YOLO: A Resource-Aware, Efficient Quantization Framework for Object Detection on FPGAs. In Proceedings of the FPGA 2019, Seaside, CA, USA, 24–26 February 2019; pp. 33–42.
42. Gu, Q.; Ishii, I. Review of some advances and applications in real-time high-speed vision: Our views and experiences. *Int. J. Autom. Comput.* **2016**, *13*, 305–318. [CrossRef]
43. Cheng, C.H. Towards Robust Direct Perception Networks for Automated Driving. In Proceedings of the 2020 IEEE Intelligent Vehicles Symposium (IV), Las Vegas, NV, USA, 19 October–13 November 2020.
44. Nguyen, D.T.; Kim, H.; Lee, H. Layer-specific Optimization for Mixed Data Flow with Mixed Precision in FPGA Design for CNN-based Object Detectors. *IEEE Trans. Circuits Syst. Video Technol.* **2020**. [CrossRef]
45. Wang, H.; Xu, Y.; Ni, B.; Zhuang, L.; Xu, H. Flexible Network Binarization with Layer-Wise Priority. In Proceedings of the 2018 25th IEEE International Conference on Image Processing (ICIP), Athens, Greece, 7–10 October 2018; pp. 2346–2350.
46. Turner, J.; Crowley, E.J.; Radu, V.; Cano, J.; Storkey, A.; O'Boyle, M. Distilling with Performance Enhanced Students. *arXiv* **2018**, arXiv:1810.10460.
47. Polino, A.; Pascanu, R.; Alistarh, D. Model compression via distillation and quantization. In Proceedings of the 6th International Conference on Learning Representations (ICLR 2018), Vancouver, BC, Canada, 30 April–3 May 2018.
48. Cheng, Y.; Yu, F.X.; Feris, R.S.; Kumar, S.; Choudhary, A.N.; Chang, S. Fast Neural Networks with Circulant Projections. *arXiv* **2015**, arXiv:1502.03436.

Article

A Flexible Fog Computing Design for Low-Power Consumption and Low Latency Applications

Markos Losada [1,*], Ainhoa Cortés [1,2,*], Andoni Irizar [1,2], Javier Cejudo [1] and Alejandro Pérez [1]

1. CEIT-Basque Research and Technology Alliance (BRTA), Manuel Lardizabal 15, 20018 San Sebastián, Spain; airizar@ceit.es (A.I.); jcejudo@ceit.es (J.C.); aperez@ceit.es (A.P.)
2. Tecnun, Universidad de Navarra, Manuel Lardizabal 13, 20018 San Sebastián, Spain
* Correspondence: mlosada@ceit.es (M.L.); acortes@ceit.es (A.C.); Tel.: +34-943212800 (A.C.)

Abstract: In this paper, we propose a flexible Fog Computing architecture in which the main features are that it allows us to select among two different communication links (WiFi and LoRa) on the fly and offers a low-power solution, thanks to the applied power management strategies at hardware and firmware level. The proposed Fog Computing architecture is formed by sensor nodes and an Internet of Things (IoT) gateway. In the case of LoRa, we have the choice of implementing the LoRaWAN and Application servers on the cloud or on the IoT gateway, avoiding, in this case, to send data to the Cloud. Additionally, we have presented an specific setup and methodology with the aim of measuring the sensor node's power consumption and making sure there is a fair comparison between the different alternatives among the two selected wireless communication links by varying the duty cycle, the size of the payload, and the Spreading Factor (SF). This research work is in the scope of the STARPORTS Interconnecta Project, where we have deployed two sensor nodes in the offshore platform of PLOCAN, which communicate with the IoT gateway located in the PLOCAN premises. In this case, we have used LoRa communications due to the required large distance between the IoT gateway and the nodes in the offshore platform (in the range of kilometers). This deployment demonstrates that the proposed solution operates in a real environment and that it is a low-power and robust approach since it is sending data to the IoT gateway during more than one year and it continues working.

Keywords: harsh environment; fog computing; edge computing; cloud computing; IoT gateway; LoRa; WiFi; low power consumption; low latency; flexible; smart port

Citation: Losada, M.; Cortés, A.; Irizar, A.; Cejudo, J.; Pérez, A. A Flexible Fog Computing Design for Low-Power Consumption and Low Latency Applications. *Electronics* 2021, 10, 57. https://doi.org/10.3390/electronics10010057

Received: 7 December 2020
Accepted: 25 December 2020
Published: 31 December 2020

Publisher's Note: MDPI stays neutral with regard to jurisdictional clai-ms in published maps and institutio-nal affiliations.

Copyright: © 2020 by the authors. Licensee MDPI, Basel, Switzerland. This article is an open access article distributed under the terms and conditions of the Creative Commons Attribution (CC BY) license (https://creativecommons.org/licenses/by/4.0/).

1. Introduction

At the beginning of the new millennium, the increase in users connected to the Internet forced companies to rethink the way they used the Internet to offer their services. The modern wireless communication systems, the infrastructures required by the Internet and the increasing demand for large volumes of data, provided the perfect conditions for Cloud Computing to prosper. Keeping with this trend, computing, control, and data storage has been centralized and moved to the cloud, as was stated years ago in Reference [1]. Cloud Computing allows the possibility of storing and processing data without the need for a specialized HW and/or SW, as long as you have an Internet connection.

Internet of Things (IoT) is a collection of computing devices (specifically things) interconnected through the Internet and intended to offer services aimed at all kinds of applications [2]. Currently, many electronic devices that are part of the IoT are data producers. It is not difficult to think that, a few years from now, that number of devices will be multiplied. By 2025, it is estimated that 30 billion devices will be connected to Internet using Low Power Wide Area (LPWA) networks and proprietary or cellular technologies [3,4]. In this case, the amount of data to be processed in the conventional cloud will make data processing inefficient or even unfeasible.

To alleviate this problem, the concept of Edge Computing emerged. As data is increasingly produced at the edge of the network, it is more efficient to process the data right there. This means that most of the generated data are not transmitted to the cloud, but they are processed at the edge of the network. Several implementations of the Edge Computing principle have been proposed in Reference [5–7], among others: Mobile Cloud Computing (MCC) [8], Cloudlet Computing (CC) [9], and Mobile Edge Computing (MEC) [10]. The different and multiple ways of implementing Edge Computing resulted in new perspectives on the Edge Computing paradigm; hence, the term Fog Computing appeared. Fog Computing represents a complete architecture that distributes resources horizontally and vertically between Cloud-to-Things. As such, it is not just a trivial extension of the cloud, but rather a new actor interacting with cloud and IoT to assist and enhance their interaction [11].

The difference between Fog Computing and Edge Computing is subtle. Furthermore, we have not found in the literature a clear definition to differentiate the Edge Computing term from the Fog Computing term. Due to this ambiguity, we present in this paper how we define these architectures. The main difference between them is where the computational power is located. In Fog Computing, the intelligence is at a node closer to the IoT device. That node can be called IoT gateway. This fits the definition in Reference [12], where Fog Computing is defined as a horizontal, system-level architecture that distributes computing, storage, control, and networking functions closer to the users along a cloud-to-thing continuum. However, in Edge Computing, the edge is the IoT device responsible for the data generation and processing [13], and it is connected to the cloud.

Fog Computing is intended to solve the typical problems of Cloud Computing, such as:

- Unpredictable end-to-end network latencies between the end user and the cloud. Hence, Fog Computing can achieve better time responses, which is important for real-time applications and services.
- Frequent use of Cloud infrastructures. Fog Computing reduces the number of connections with the cloud and, therefore, possible interruptions in the data flow.
- High bandwidth and high energy needs to cope with the intense data traffic. Fog Computing reduces the required bandwidth of the communications with the cloud in a network with a large number of nodes or data since the processing can be distributed at different levels: edge level, gateway level, and cloud level, reducing significantly the quantity of data to be sent to the cloud.

Additionally, Fog Computing offers some advantages with respect to Edge Computing, such as:

- Increasing the security and privacy with the creation of a pre-cloud link to protect the data.
- Reducing the resources at the node to execute complex processes.
- Increasing the autonomy of the edge nodes with a significant reduction of their power consumption.

To our best of knowledge, most of the previous works related to Fog Computing architectures are reviews, surveys, or analysis of the current state of the art [13,14]. Few of them are architectural proposals based on Fog Computing. Furthermore, some implementations presented in the literature propose generic architectures to integrate Fog Computing in IoT-based applications [15] or they present test-bed and simulation results in order to evaluate the viability of the proposals [16]. Reference [17] presents an intra-vehicle resource sharing model with the aim of getting low-latency cloud services. Their motivation is in line with this research. However, they focus on the framework using mobile communications based on 5G technology and not on a low-cost and low-power deployment. In any case, these implementations do not show results in a real use case.

Among the most common technologies used for IoT devices, we can highlight Low Power Wide Area (LPWA). These technologies offer their ability to deliver low-power connectivity to a large number of devices spreading across large geographic areas at an unprecedented low cost. A LoRa-type LPWA network uses a gateway, which can be connected to the cloud. LoRa Tx/Rx has low power consumption and long range compared to other LPWAs. This technology can be operated on sub-gigahertz unlicensed radio bands. Furthermore, with these characteristics, its market penetration and its wide use in the industrial, educational, and amateur community make LPWA LoRa technology ideal for IoT [3,18]. However, the key goal of LoRa technology is to achieve long range with low power consumption and low cost, unlike other technologies that are more appropriate to achieve higher data rates, lower latency, and higher reliability. There are situations where complex processing is required, but the node does not have the necessary resources for that processing. Hence, more data must be sent to the fog or cloud, and a higher data rate communication will be required.

This paper proposes a flexible architecture for IoT based on Fog Computing using LoRa and WiFi communications. This architecture can be easily implemented in many IoT applications. Many of these benefits are inherent to an architecture based on Fog Computing, that is, the Internet connection, security, and privacy and the limitation of resources on the edge, which are characteristics of the own architecture. As well as exploiting the benefits of Fog Computing, the proposed architecture permits us to select the most appropriate wireless connection with the IoT gateway according to the data rate, the payload size, the required range, and the power consumption. Furthermore, the edge nodes contain different sensors with low and medium data sizes, and the data processing can be distributed between the sensor nodes and the IoT gateway as needed. The proposed sensor nodes are ultra-low power solutions, thanks to the power strategies applied to the SW and HW designs. To quantify the benefits of the proposed approach, this paper will present specific results, such as power consumption at the edge node and at the IoT gateway.

The paper is structured as follows. In Section 2, a review of the different IoT applications are introduced. Section 3 provides the description of the case study of this research work. Section 4 presents the implementation of the proposed Fog architecture. In Section 5, the test setup, the measurement methodology, and the experimental results are presented. Finally, the discussions and conclusions obtained from the experimental results are summarized in Section 6.

2. Related Work

As commented in the previous Section, Cloud Computing has played a huge role in IoT applications. Some of these applications have started to demand faster execution in their processes. Hence, the trend has been to take advantage of the capabilities for computing on the edge devices to process data and, among other benefits, reduce the amount of data to be transmitted. More recently, the idea of processing data between the edge and the cloud has reported new benefits, such as an increase in network security and energy-size saving at the end nodes, making possible the implementation of this philosophy for new applications.

Among the applications for IoT reviewed in the literature, we have found several examples in which the rapid response of the system is an essential requirement [19]; therefore, Edge Computing has been used. For example, the increase in security applications, such as fire control, face recognition, or traffic control, have caused video surveillance and video analysis systems to have grown tremendously in recent decades. The algorithms for video analysis require intensive processing and with added privacy, as shown in Reference [20]. In Reference [21], a classification and a review of current architectures for Edge Computing is made, and an experimental analysis is presented for the case of image processing in the field of video games. In this case, Edge Computing performance for a recurse-intensive application is evaluated through different scenarios. Edge Computing satisfies the necessary requirements for these applications to the detriment of the size and consumption of the end nodes. In Reference [17], a vehicular infrastructure model for 5G technology is proposed, taking into account compute intensive applications but providing some kind of cloud assistance and looking for low-latency cloud services. Ref. [7] is more focused on smart cities services at the edge providing security, privacy and protection to exploit edge servers computational, and low network latency capabilities. In spite of the fact that these last approaches look for an optimization of the distribution of the computational complexity for the provided services, none of them are focused on the reduction of the power consumption and cost of the overall architecture.

On the opposite side, there are other IoT applications in which the sensor nodes measure different parameters, and they send the information with the minimum necessary processing. In these applications, the communication of the sensor nodes with the cloud is carried out through low-bandwidth and long-range communications. These nodes are designed to operate for long periods without the need to replace the battery, but they can only work for very low data sizes which permits very small duty cycles. Smart cities are a typical example of IoT in modern infrastructures, which allow, by means of a sensor networks deployment, precise measurements of resources, such as water, electricity, and gas. Architectures, such as those presented in Reference [22–24], have been implemented in these scenarios. However, as has been discussed, the HW implemented in the end nodes is not flexible enough to enlarge the data sizes to be transmitted or to carry out more complex processing. Reference [6] proposes a Reinforcement Learning framework for autonomous energy management focused on mobile user devices. The proposed architecture learns the power-related statistics of the devices, providing a computation environment on the fly but only taking into account the cost of resource usage. As mentioned in Section 1, none of these approaches show results in a real use case.

In summary, we have seen that there are time-sensitive applications with a high computational load, while, in other applications, the fundamental requirement is the low power consumption. For these applications, non-flexible hardware architectures have been designed, i.e., the more efficient in power consumption, the less powerful to process data, or vice versa. Furthermore, remote sensing has opened the doors to new ways of monitoring and controlling a multitude of still unexplored fields, which will lead to the development of new IoT applications; thus, they will demand more flexible architectures. To deal with this problem, new architectures, such as Reference [15,16], have emerged. In these architectures, the computational load has been transferred to an edge gateway near to the end nodes. This edge gateway communicates with an upper gateway by means of LoRa, and this, in turn, communicates with the cloud. A simple HW to achieve a small size and low power consumption characterizes the end nodes. These nodes communicate with the edge gateway through Bluetooth. Hence, when the application requires it, they can send large amounts of data at relatively high speeds. In addition, complex processing is possible at the gateway to respond to the application in the cloud. Thus, these architectures solve certain problems presented in the literature by exploiting the benefits offered by a Fog Computing architecture. However, their approaches are not flexible in terms of the deployment of the end nodes since the gateway must be very close to them. Moreover, their approaches have not been deployed in a real environment and a real use case, which is essential for a system validation to check the applicability and the robustness of this kind of solutions. Furthermore, both communication technologies will always be active at the same time in order to send data to the cloud. This fact entails a re-transmission of the data, thus yielding an extra consumption.

3. System Applicability

The approach presented in this paper provides an efficient architecture for a wide range of applications, such as Smart Buildings, Smart Factories, and Smart Ports. These applications have in common the necessity of deploying low-cost and low-power IoT devices for monitoring the environment and/or the infrastructure degradation using wireless communications to facilitate their own deployment. Our architecture fulfills these costs and power requirements. Furthermore, our solution is capable of changing the wireless link from LoRa to WiFi, and, vice versa, according to the conditions of the specific situation, we can have for one application. As an example, for the Smart Factory application, the IoT gateway could be integrated in an Autonomous Guided Vehicle (AGV) to gather the environmental and degradation data. Hence, the AGV can be capable of getting closer to some sensor nodes, but other ones can be located far away. When the AGV is stopped at the expected control points, our system will be able to receive the data in both scenarios. On the other hand, this will not be the only criterion to select one communication link. The system will be capable of making that decision according to some internal configurations, such as the required data rate and the size of the payload, which will affect the power consumption. These configurations can vary during the operation since one application can have different stages.

Case Study: Smart Ports

This research work is focused on Smart Ports as the case study to prove the efficiency of the proposed architecture. A port is a complex and dynamic environment that includes various activities, such as transportation, logistic, fishing, maintenance, and rescue operations, as well as protection of its environmental impacts [25]. The sensing needs in a port ranges from localization of goods, ships, and infrastructure vehicles (which requires a constant update) to monitor the state of the docks, bollards, cranes, and warehouses, where updatings can be made on a daily or weekly basis. Additionally, ports are subjected to emergency situations (under heavy storms, for example) when it would be desirable to have more frequent updates of the state of the port's infrastructure. Therefore, IoT devices can considerably improve and automate many of these activities to increase the safety and security, as well as reduce the operational delays, of the different processes. However, this scenario also imposes strong conditions in the hardware, software, and network architectures of the IoT deployment. From the end-node perspective, there are two important restrictions: power availability and network access. The first one means that power consumption in the end-node must be drastically reduced in order to last several years without replacing the battery. The second means that the end-node must have some flexibility to access the network infrastructure based on range, power consumption, and data payload.

One of the most important advantages of the proposed architecture is that this design offers a high flexibility in terms of deployment. Hence, this approach can be easily customized to achieve an efficient solution for different applications.

Each application and use case will have different requirements related to latency, privacy, communications coverage, and power consumption. Our approach permits to configure the network on the fly according to these application requirements. In order to do that, the nodes can select the wireless communications to be used (WiFi or LoRa) and can communicate with a local server avoiding the communication with the cloud, if needed. On the other hand, we are capable to increase the computational complexity of the IoT gateway with the aim of reducing the quantity of data sent to the cloud. This fact would reduce the latency, which is a really important factor for real-time applications.

The specific application we have analyzed in this work is the predictive maintenance of critical infrastructures of the port, which can be made by the proposed system remotely and in an unattended manner. Thus, the sensor nodes must be deployed accordingly to measure the structural health of the most critical components or structures identified within the port. The proposed sensor nodes will be able to measure essential parameters to predict the structural health of these structures, such as the temperature, structural movements, corrosion, and pressure. Furthermore, our system is prepared to automatically use the most appropriate wireless connection according to the quantity of data (the size of the payload), the data rate required, and the distance to be covered. Our flexible platform will allow us to embed the IoT gateway into a drone so that, if the drone is capable of flying towards some sensor nodes, and high data rates are required, the WiFi connection will be selected. However, when the sensor nodes are located far away from the drone and over a restricted area where the drone cannot access, LoRa communications will be chosen with the aim of covering large distances. On top of that, there will exist other scenarios and use cases where the criteria to select the communications link will be the efficiency in power consumption, and, for those cases, a further analysis is needed.

Taking into account the requirements of this specific application, the benefits obtained by using our proposed architecture are listed below:

- The aim is to monitor the structure remotely over years. To do so, the sensor nodes, which are deployed and embedded on the structure, must operate using a battery. Our approach applies some low power strategies to comply with this requirement looking for an autonomy of years. On the one hand, the sensor node will stay active when measuring or sending wireless data. On the other hand, the system will manage the wireless communications to be used taking into account the power consumption.
- In the scope of a port, there are critical structures everywhere. Therefore, it is important to cover different distances wirelessly. Our approach can select between WiFi connection when the range is not so long (around 100 m) and LoRa connection when we need higher ranges (in the range of kilometers). Other factor to select the wireless communications is the quantity of data to be sent. Thus, the WiFi connection will be active when large quantity of data are required and/or high data rates are needed but always if we have WiFi coverage (short range). Otherwise, the proposed solution will select between WiFi and LoRa communications according to the power consumption as is evaluated in this paper (see Section 5).
- To predict accurately the state of the critical structures and be able to act in real-time, a reduction of the latency in the communications can be considered as an important benefit. The proposed architecture permits to embed a local server inside the IoT gateway with the corresponding reduction of the overall latency.

This research work has been supported by the STARPORTS Project as is explained in the Funding section. PLOCAN, one of the STARPORTS participants, has an offshore platform very suitable to validate the proposed architecture in a relevant environment but at the same time in a controlled scenario. The offshore platform is 5.7 km from the PLOCAN building, very well suited to test LoRa communications when the IoT gateway is in the PLOCAN premises. Thus, two sensor nodes were deployed in the PLOCAN offshore platform (see Figure 1), and a fixed IoT gateway was installed in the PLOCAN building receiving data through LoRa from the sensor nodes over more than twelve months, working with a Spreading Factor (SF) of 10, in this case (currently the sensor nodes continue working with the same battery keeping good and stable voltage levels).

Figure 1. The sensor nodes deployed in the PLOCAN offshore platform.

4. Design of the Proposed Fog Architecture

The proposed architecture is shown in Figure 2. Note that the red boxes represent the deployed devices such as it is described in the previous Section. In this architecture, the IoT application located in the cloud communicates with the sensor nodes through an IoT gateway with two different wireless communication technologies, which are WiFi and LoRa. This gateway can be fixed or mobile, and it can communicate with each end-node through one of these communication technologies, depending on the demanded data rate, gateway to end-node coverage, or a trade-off between these parameters and power consumption. Cloud communication with the IoT gateway could be done through an Ethernet connection, in the case of a fixed IoT gateway, as in the case of the STARPORTS project, or a 3G/4G connection, in the case of a mobile IoT gateway. Additionally, the IoT gateway is capable of performing complex processes, such as filtering, calibration, correlation, frequency analysis, etc., to alleviate the data load in the cloud or executing safety-critical computation, if needed.

Figure 2. Proposed flexible Fog Computing architecture.

In this architecture, the sensor nodes can be considered low-cost and low-power nodes since an effective power management is applied and the proposed architecture permits not only to alleviate the data load in the cloud but also to distribute in an efficient manner the computational operations between the sensor nodes and the IoT gateway.

The total cost of the sensor node materials is shown in Table 1. In this case, accurate sensors have been used to measure acceleration, temperature, humidity, and corrosion. If the application does not require those measurements, the cost of the sensor node could fall below 30€.

The cost of the IoT gateway materials is shown in Table 2. In our prototype, the IoT gateway has been built using carrier boards. However, we could customize it by designing our own carrier board. In that case, it would only be necessary to acquire the SOM and the LoRa concentrator. Note that the cost of the SOM starts from 54€. The SOM can be customized as a function of the required features; therefore, this cost will depend on the SOM customization level.

Table 1. Total cost of the sensor node materials.

Component	Part Name	Unit Price (€)	×1000 (€)
LoRa Transceiver Module	RN2483	10.81	9.84
Wireless Module	CC3220MODASF12MONR	15.94	10.24
Inductance-to-Digital Converter	LDC1000QPWRQ1	7.73	4.22
Humidity and Pressure Sensor	BME280	5	2.14
MEMS Accelerometer	ADXL355BEZ	40.94	32.71
Real Time Clock	DS1374U-18+	3.15	1.66
Power management ICs		<7	<4
Connectors (UFL, Battery connector)		<2	<1
Other components		<2	<1
PCB	Lab Circuits manufacturer	<10	<5
Total (€)		<93	<65

Table 2. Total cost of the Internet of Things (IoT) gateway.

Component	Part Name	Unit Price (€)
SOM	DART-MX8M	Starting from 54
SOM + Carrier Board	VAR-DT8MCustomBoard	244
LoRa Gateway Concentrator Module	RAK833	80

4.1. The Sensor Nodes

In a Smart Port environment, it would be desirable that the sensor nodes to be deployed work unattended with battery lives of more than 3 years [18]. Other important aspect is the communication range since in that environment you can need short and long range communications. Then, having such flexibility will permit large distances (several kms) but also small distances (<100 m) if a mobile platform is used to gather data from the sensor nodes (using a drone), assuming that the drone is stopped when the system gathers the data. Additionally, in a Smart Port you can have different kind of variables to be measured. Hence, the system must be able to measure from very low sample rate measures to high sample rate variables (∼500 Hz).

The architecture we have developed to fulfill the above features is given in Figure 3. Figure 4 shows a photograph of the sensor node electronics and housing. As can be seen, the node has wireless connectivity with WiFi and LoRa. The main component is the CC3220 micro-controller [26], a Cortex-M4 based device that includes a Network Processor with WiFi Driver, TCP/IP Stack, baseband processor, and complete analog front-end. It also contains a 1MB flash memory that allows storing data and configuration parameters in the node. LoRa connectivity is provided by the RN2483 module [27], which includes LoRaWAN Class A protocol stack). The CC3220 controls the LoRa device using commands via an UART interface.

The node is housing several sensors: 3-axis accelerometer (ADXL355 [28]) with very low noise density (22.5 µg/$\sqrt{Hz}$), a Pressure/Humidity/Temperature sensor (BME280 [29]) and an inductance sensor (LDC1000 [30]) that allows us to measure corrosion levels. All the three sensors can be accessed through a unique SPI interface.

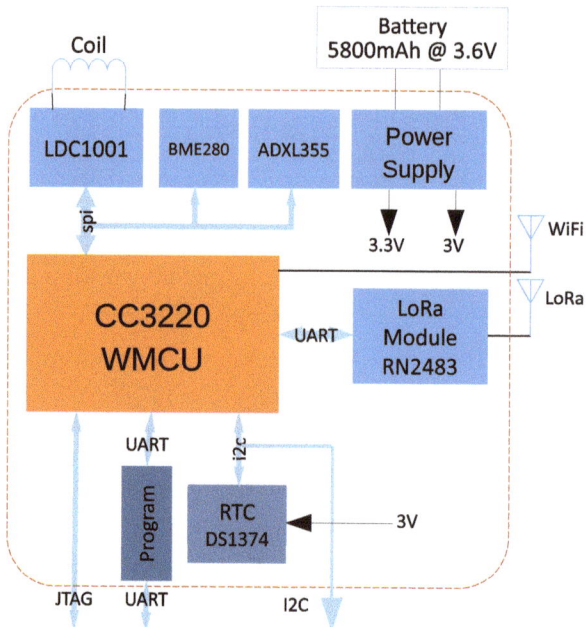

Figure 3. Block diagram of the sensor node.

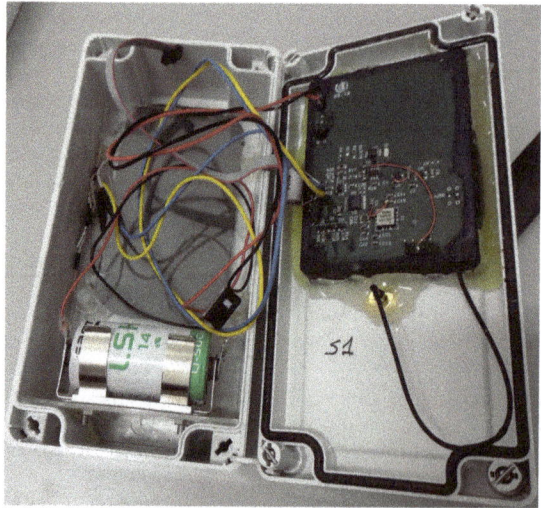

Figure 4. Sensor node.

Low Power Strategies

The power supply is provided by a primary battery of 3.6 V and 5800 mAh. For this battery size and given the required duration, this means the node must draw an average current of less than 250 µA. This value is too small, even for the lowest power micro-controller in the market (∼135 µA/MHz.) Therefore, remote nodes must reduce its power consumption by decreasing its duty cycle. The duty cycle is the relationship between the on-time, the time in which the nodes are working, and the cycle time, which is the total time of one cycle. The off-time is the time in which the nodes are sleeping. The node can modify the duty cycle by configuring the DS1374 RTC device [31] of Figure 3. The node will generate two supply voltages: 3 V for the RTC (see Figure 3) and 3.3 V for the rest of the circuit. The 3 V voltage is always active, but the 3.3 V can be enabled by a switch (first time boot) or by the RTC (generates a pulse that boots the CC3220 after a specified period according to the selected duty cycle). The 3.3 V will be disabled by the CC3220 after all the tasks related to a set of measures. Additionally, each sensor can be individually shutdown from the CC3220 using GPIO signals.

The sensor node has two operational modes: Normal Mode and Storage Mode, for which state machines are given in Figure 5. In Normal mode, the node typically powers up from a RTC pulse (POWER-UP state), loads design parameters from an internal non-volatile memory, takes measures from the sensors (SENSOR state), configures the wireless interface, and sends the data to the IoT gateway (LoRa-WIFI state). The node then waits for the Application server to send new configuration parameters for the next cycle (REMOTE state) and then goes back to the DEEP-SLEEP state by disabling the 3.3 V regulator output. In Storage Mode, the node stores the measures from the sensors in a non-volatile memory and only sends the complete data packet once every several cycles. This Storage Mode can be interesting in the case where we use WiFi communications from a mobile platform, such as a drone. Hence, the sensor node would store the data from areas without WiFi coverage until getting close to the IoT gateway integrated in the drone. On the other hand, both in the case of a fixed and a mobile approach when we need a real-time monitoring for fast processes, the Normal Mode is more suitable.

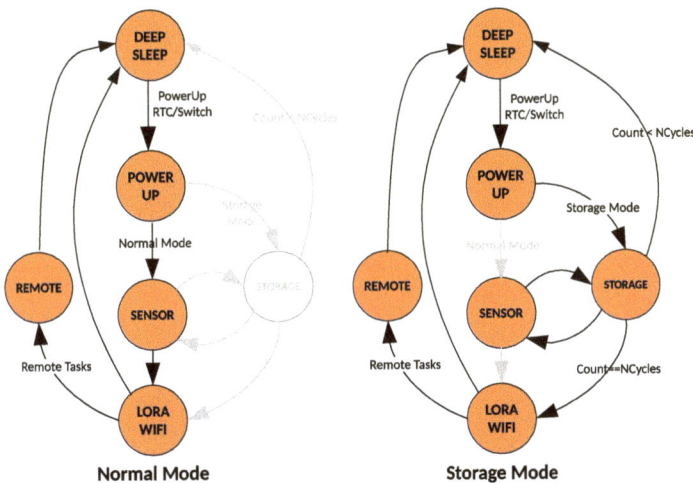

Figure 5. Operational modes and state machine of the sensor node.

LoRa and WiFi are two very different communications systems that complement each other very well in several aspects of a wireless link. Range, bit-rate, and power are the main design variables to consider when selecting a wireless interface. When a decision must be made based on range and bit-rate, the choice can be quite easy. But decisions based on power can be much more difficult because one must consider not only the physical layer of the communication interface but also the upper software layers. For example, from the strict specification of the modulation schemes, WiFi is much more power efficient than LoRa (in terms of nJ/bit, it is around three orders of magnitude more efficient). But, if we take into account the overhead introduced by the protocols and software stacks needed to manage the communications with both methods (much more complex in WiFi than in LoRa), the differences begin to narrow.

Low Power strategies must weight the wireless connection to be used (WiFi or LoRa) depending on the size of the payload, the duty cycle of the sensor node, and the communication range. This is the aim of the experiments carried out in this research work are described in detail in Section 5.

4.2. The IoT Gateway

A block diagram of the IoT gateway is presented in Figure 6. The IoT gateway designed is based on a Variscite DART-MX8M System-on-Module (SOM [32]) based on NXP's i.MX8M with up to 1.8 GHz Quad-core ARM Cortex-A53™, plus 400 MHz Cortex-M4™ real-time processor [33], and works under Debian (stretch) GNU/Linux 9. Although the DART-MX8M contains extensive processing capabilities from its quad-core architecture plus graphics and video processing unit, this SOM is not well suited for running Machine Learning or Artificial Intelligence applications in the gateway. However, our architecture can be easily upgraded to house the DART-MX8M-PLUS, pin-to-pin compatible with the DART-MX8M. The DART-MX8M-PLUS [34] includes the iMX8M-Plus processor [35] that has basically same quad-core Cortex-A53 architecture, plus a Cortex-M7 at 800 MHz and a Digital Signal Processor (DSP) accelerator also at 800 MHz. But, more importantly, it includes a Neural Processing Unit (NPU) that allow the efficient implementation of Machine Learning algorithms in the IoT gateway, reducing power and time consuming data transfers to the cloud.

To include the LoRa connectivity to our IoT gateway we have added a LoRaWAN concentrator [36] that interfaces with the processor through a SPI port. The software that manages the incoming LoRa packets from the concentrator is the Packet Forwarder from Semtech [37]. This software sends the encrypted LoRa packets to the LoRaWAN server of your choice, where they are decrypted by the LoRaWAN and Application servers. For this configuration, we have used The Things Network [38], as is shown in Figure 7. The IoT gateway will also be working as a WiFi Access Point. A software running in the SOM will be responsible for acquiring the data packets from the node.

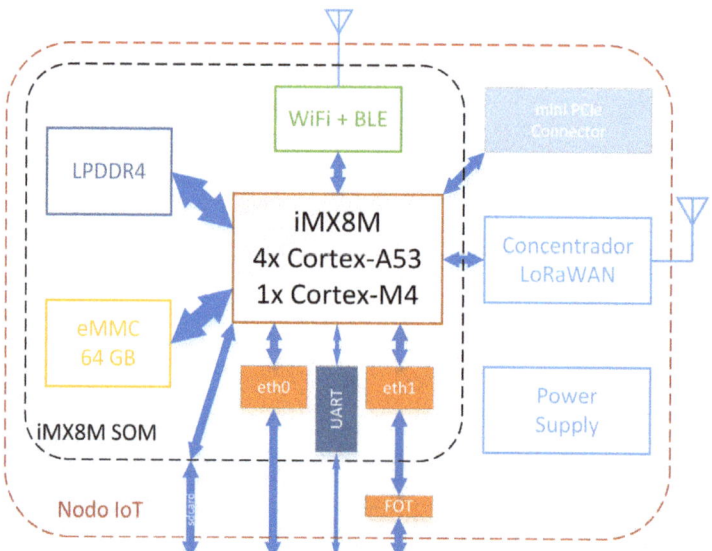

Figure 6. Block diagram of the IoT gateway.

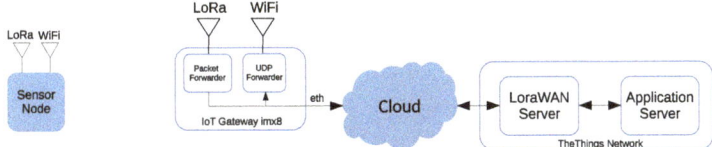

Figure 7. The IoT gateway with the server implemented on the cloud.

The IoT gateway has also the possibility to work, as shown in Figure 8, by installing both the LoRaWAN server and the Application servers in the i.MX8M SOM. As a result, data from the sensors can be processed, normalized, enhanced, and stored at the gateway, reducing the uplink traffic to the cloud. Figure 8 also shows the software architecture of the IoT gateway, an adaptation to the specifications of OpenFog reference architecture [12]. In our case, the physical layers are WiFi and LoRa, and the Protocol Abstraction layers are implemented, in this case, as packet forwarders that respond to the central component of the architecture, i.e., the Node Configuration and Management block. This block has access to the processing and storage resources of the IoT gateway and implements the communications with the cloud infrastructure.

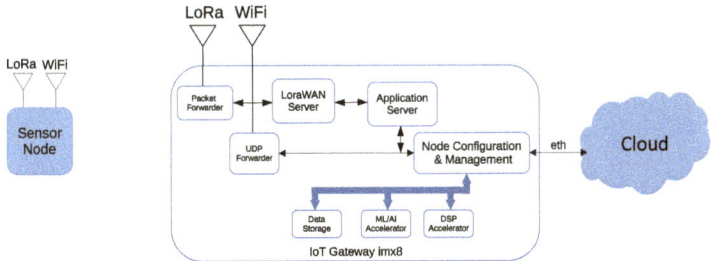

Figure 8. The IoT gateway software architecture with the LoRaWAN server implemented.

5. Results

5.1. Setup and Methodology

The aim of the proposed setup is to measure the energy consumption generated by the sensor node when using WiFi communication or LoRaWAN communication. In order to do that, we have implemented the setup shown in Figure 9. The same setup configuration has been implemented for the both cases, WiFi and LoRa, to carry out parallel tests. The power supply has been set to 3.3 V. The LTC4150 Coulomb counter monitors the current through a precision external resistor between the positive terminal of the source and the power terminal of the sensor node.

A series of pulses are obtained at the output of the Coulomb counter depending on the current consumed by both, the sensor node, and the Coulomb counter. Each pulse corresponds to a quantity of electric charge of 0.307 Coulombs, that is, 0.085 mA/h. A msp430FR2433 [39] micro-controller is responsible for capturing the instant of time in which each pulse was generated. The micro-controller sends the time instant and the number of the pulse to a PC via UART communication for further processing. Note that the micro-controller is powered by the computer; therefore, the consumption generated by itself is not taken into account.

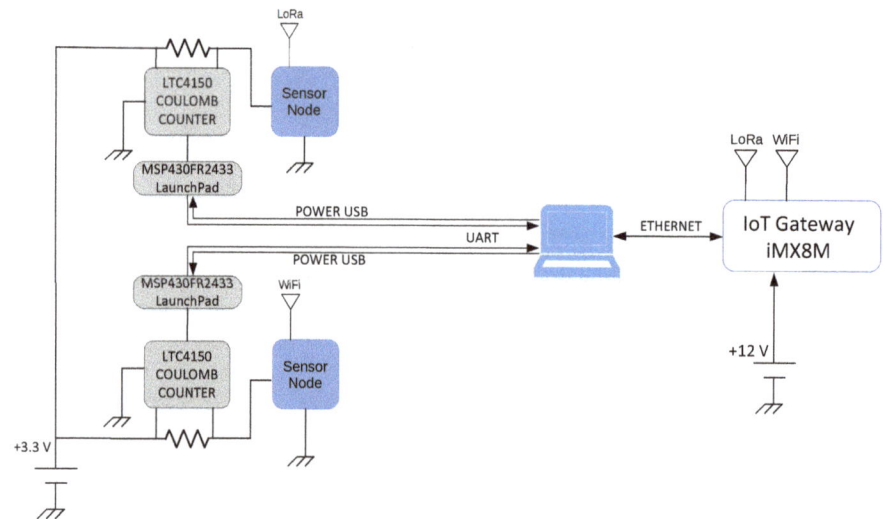

Figure 9. Implemented setup for the energy consumption measurements.

As can be seen in the photogragh of Figure 10, the msp430FR2433 LaunchPad is powered from the PC through the USB connector, whereas the power supply is used to power the sensor nodes and the Coulomb counter at 3.3 V. The LoRa and WiFi gateway have been both implemented in the same Variscite DART-MX8M SOM. A motherboard is used to connect and power the SOM.

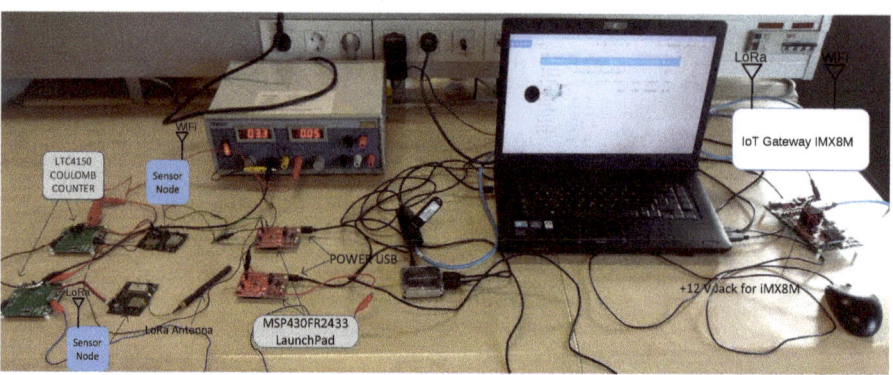

Figure 10. Photogragh of the implemented setup.

5.1.1. Lora and Wifi Gateway Implementation for the Energy Consumption Measurements

- WiFi gateway configuration:
  The WiFi module of the SOM has been configured as an access point, with static IP address and wpa-psk security type. Therefore, the node just needs to connect to the Wifi network generated by the SOM and send its frames.
  In order to receive and manage the received frames, a UDP socket to the WiFi IP address has been created so that every received frame is captured and logged into a file for further analysis.
- LoRa gateway configuration:

As explained in Section 4.2, a RAK833 LoRa concentrator has been used running "LoRa Packet Forwarder". The measured consumption of this LoRa concentrator is 420 mA at 3.3 V. The "LoRa Packet Forwarder" runs on the SOM to forward LoRa packets received by the concentrator to a server through an IP/UDP link. As is shown in Figures 7 and 8, the LoraWAN Server and the Application server can be located on the gateway or on the cloud. For the energy consumption measurements, we have used the configuration mode with the server on the IoT gateway to facilitate the overall setup and the data analysis since The Things Network has several restrictions related to higher data rates and payload sizes according to the SF. That is why we have implemented a Network server stack (Chirpstack) [40] into the SOM to carry out the tests. The Chirpstack LoRa Network Server stack provides open-source components for LoRa networks. Together, they form a ready-to-use solution including an user-friendly web-interface for device management and APIs for integration. The measured consumption of the SOM when Chirpstack is running is 800 mA, supplied at 3.3 V.

5.1.2. Sensor Node Implementation for the Energy Consumption Measurements

The operation of both tested sensor nodes is exactly the same, except that, in one case, it is used WiFi, and, in the other case, LoRa, but both nodes measure, process, and transmit the same number of data, with the same duty cycle and using the same operating modes for further comparison.

To check what communication is more efficient depending on the conditions, different tests have been done with different payloads for every Spreading Factor (SF). Note that different SFs affect mainly the range of LoRa communications.

The software running in both nodes follows the flowchart shown in Figure 11. This flow chart is in line with the normal mode described in Figure 5. As the on-time is not a fixed value due to the communication link, the on-time of each cycle must be measured. Thus, when the node starts a new cycle, it initiates a timer to count the on-time period of the duty cycle. Then, when the serial ports configuration is done, the configuration parameters stored in the flash memory files are read. These parameters are shown in Table 3. After reading the files, the node sets the cycle time in the DS1374 Real Time Clock. Then, the node is configured to use LoRa or WiFi communication based on the mode parameter.

If LoRa mode is active, the node initiates UART interface to communicate with RN2483. The LoRa module is configured with "automatic re-transmit" option and with the SF selected for the test. The frequency plan used is EU863-870. Once the LoRa module configuration is done, the node connects to LoRa network using Activation by Personalization (ABP). The main advantage of this type of connection is that it is not required to join the network in order to send data, that is, the server-side confirmation is not necessary since the session is already manually assigned. It has been preferred over Over the Air Activation (OTAA) because OTAA needs the LoRa module to be active all the time to have the session parameters updated. This means additional power is needed during the end-node's off-time, which can distort the power measurements in our experimental setup.

If WiFi mode is selected, the WiFi network processor subsystem is configured in station mode, with Dynamic Host Configuration Protocol (DHCP), normal power management policy, and auto connection policy. The WiFi standard used is 802.11 b/g/n 2.4 GHz. Once this network processor is configured, the node sets the WiFi network Service Set Identifier (SSID) and connects to it.

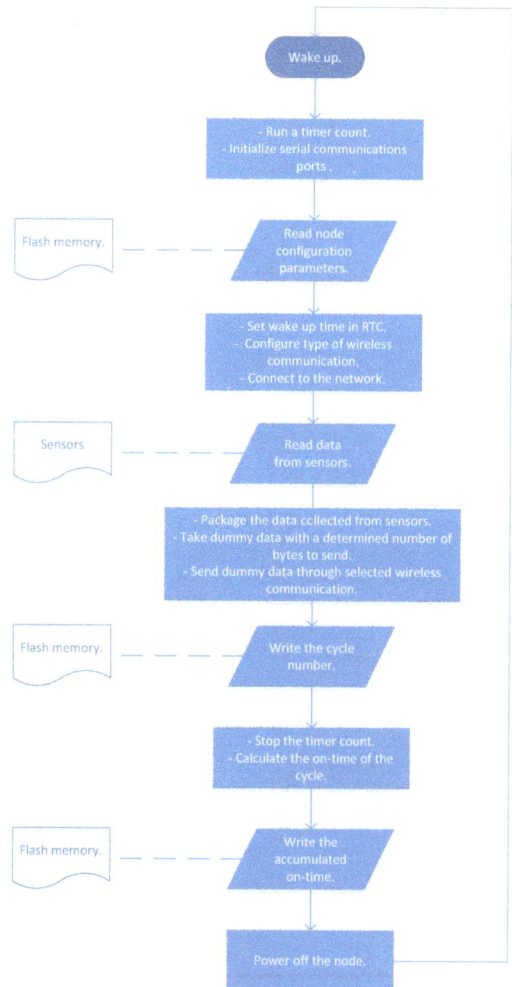

Figure 11. Sensor node software flowchart.

Table 3. Configuration parameters from the flash memory.

Parameter	Description	Value
mode	Selects WiFi or LoRaWAN communication	Variable for each test
ssid	SSID of the WiFi network	STARPORTS
cycle time	The total time of one cycle	20 s
payload	Number of bytes to be sent	Variable for each test
cycles	Number of cycles of the test	4000

When the connection is established, either with the LoRa network or with the WiFi network, the node starts reading data from sensors. The first sensor is an Analog to Digital Converter used to calculate the voltage from battery. The second sensor is ADXL355 accelerometer. After this sensor configuration, the node reads the data from the accelerometer and packages it. The last sensor is BME280, a combined digital humidity, pressure, and temperature sensor. Before getting the data from BME280, some steps are carried out, such as calibrating sensors and compensating measurements. Then, the data obtained from BME280 are packaged.

In order to measure the energy consumption of our approach during the proposed tests, we decided to use the same payload size in each test to compare fairly the consumption results obtained with WiFi and LoRa links. Therefore, the node discards the real data from sensors and takes dummy data with a fixed number of bytes. This fixed payload is configured by reading a payload file from the flash memory according to the payload parameter, described in Table 3, which will select the payload file to be read. The node sends the packet over WiFi or LoRa network depending on the mode configured on the node. Hence, although the data from the sensors are not really sent wirelessly, the measurements done by these sensors have been configured in the same way for all the tests. Thus, we will have the same consumption according to the sensors for each test.

Finally, the cycle number is increased by one and written to a file stored in the flash memory. The timer counter stops and the accumulated on-time of the test is calculated by adding to it the on-time of the cycle, which is written in the internal flash memory. Then, the node goes to the sleep mode until the wake-up time signal from the RTC is received. Once the node completes the total number of cycles as is indicated in Table 3, the test finalizes.

5.2. Energy Consumption Measurements

Figure 12 shows the energy consumed by the sensor node in a 20 s cycle for different Spreading Factors (SF). Note that the SF does not apply to the WiFi technology. Despite this fact, we have evaluated WiFi and LoRa links with parallel tests done at the same time. Hence, as the SF affects LoRa, we have also repeated the WiFi tests for each SF.

In the case of LoRa, it can be seen that the energy consumption increases as the number of bytes to be transmitted or the SF is increased. However, in the case of WiFi, it can be seen that the energy consumption is more stable for different sizes of the payload, that is, the number of data transmitted does not have a great influence on the energy consumption. This effect is closely related to the duty cycle. In the case of LoRa technology, the time the data is at the air is longer than in the case of WiFi technology. Hence, the duty cycle is larger when LoRa is used, which implies a higher energy consumption when we have more bytes or higher SFs. Finally, it can be said that there is a cut-off point between the LoRa and WiFi curves, which, from an energy point of view and depending on the range we need to reach, can help us to determine which technology is more efficient. In this case, we see that, for SF's greater than 10, WiFi technology always consumes less, and, for an SF of 7, LoRa consumes less. For the case of an SF equal to 8, LoRa consumes more than WiFi when more than 140 bytes are transmitted, and, for the case of an SF equal to 9, LoRa consumes more than WiFi when we need to transmit more than 40 bytes.

From the tests carried out, the results have been extrapolated to determine the battery life as a function of the cycle time. Figure 13 shows the duration of a battery with a capacity of 5800 mA/h for different cycle times, different SFs, and different sizes of messages to be transmitted. It can be seen that the cycle time is the parameter that mostly determines the battery life, that is, for a specific SF configuration and data size to be transmitted, the longer the cycle time, the longer the time spent in sleep mode and, therefore, the lower the average energy consumption per cycle.

It can be seen in Figure 14 that, for the STARPORTS use case, with a cycle time of 900 s, sending an average of 32 bytes through LoRa and with an SF of 9, a battery life of 15,720 h (around 1.8 years) is estimated. If we want to extend the battery life up to 3 years, keeping the same range and data size, we should increase the cycle time to 1950 s. In the case of configuring the node with an SF of 12 in order to achieve a higher range, we should increase the cycle time up to 3160 s to get a battery life of 3 years. Otherwise, by using an SF of 7 for short range, we should set the cycle time to 1725 s.

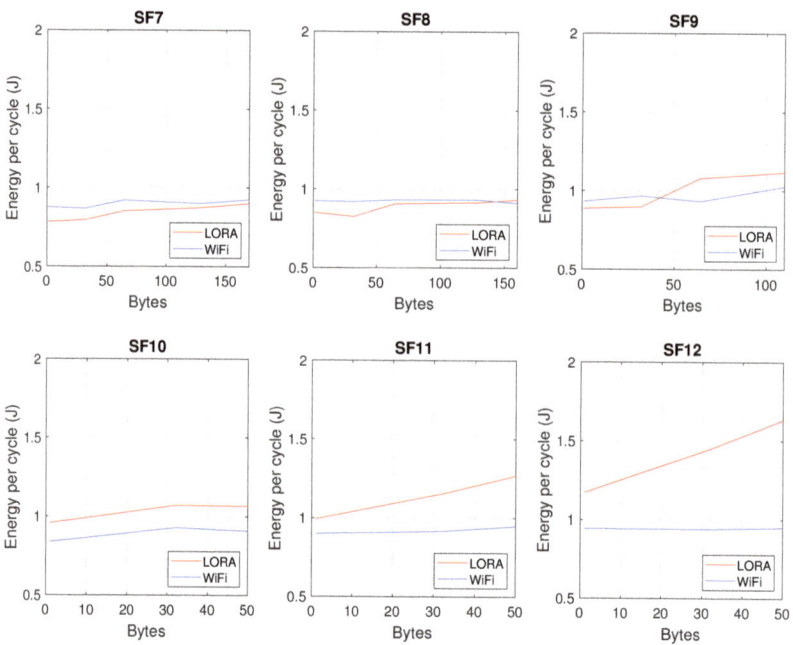

Figure 12. Energy consumption by the sensor node for different Spreading Factors (SFs).

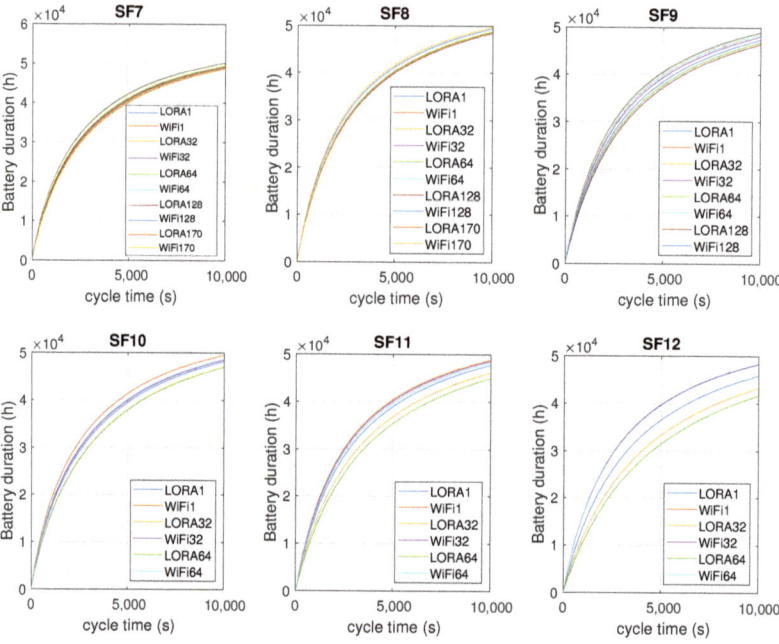

Figure 13. Battery duration for different cycle times and SFs.

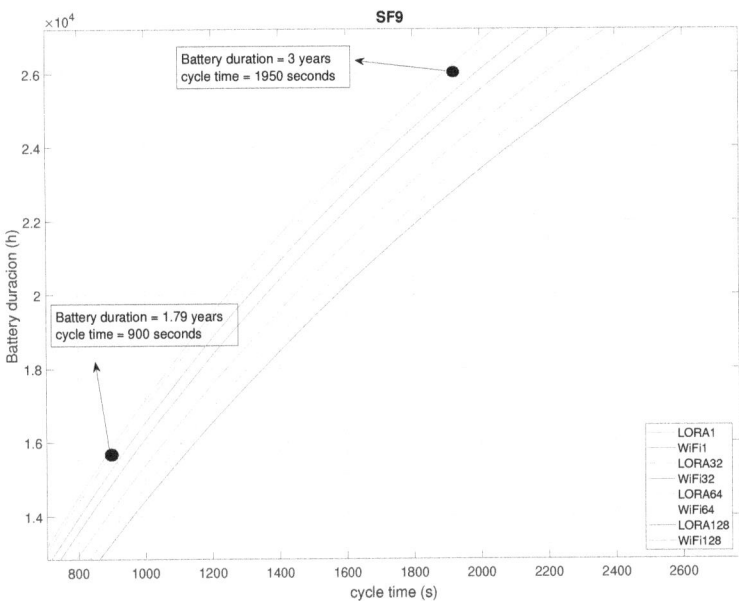

Figure 14. Battery duration with the parameters used in the STARPORTS case.

6. Conclusions

The new applications that have emerged from the IoT concept have generated a great growth of IoT devices connected to the Internet. This has resulted in a large amount of data flowing into the cloud, which can require a huge bandwidth and in consequence, an inefficient solution from the energy or storage point of view. In addition, certain applications require real-time processing or even make decisions without the need of an Internet connection. In this paper, a flexible Fog Computing architecture has been proposed. Thanks to that flexibility, this approach is capable of solving the previous issues related to the real-time processing and the communications bandwidth, as well as adding new advantages to the existing architectures, such as increasing security and privacy in the network and reducing the required resources at the node level, in order to increase autonomy without losing computational capacity.

In the proposed architecture, low-power strategies have been implemented in the sensor node in order to obtain autonomy for several years. These nodes are capable of selecting between two different communication links (LoRa and WiFi) on the fly, depending on the available coverage, the amount of data to be transmitted, or a trade-off between the energy consumption, coverage, and data to be transmitted. Furthermore, in the proposed architecture, a local server has been implemented within the IoT gateway, in which it is possible to process data at higher speed. This IoT gateway can work in real-time, with a very low latency in response to the data measured by the sensor nodes.

Different tests have been carried out by varying the parameters of the system, such as the duty cycle, the size of the data packet, and the Spreading Factor (SF), which only affects the LoRa communications. The objective of these tests has been to quantify the energy consumption of the sensor nodes focusing on the communication links. We have seen that, unlike WiFi, in the case of LoRa, the energy consumption increases as the number of bytes to be transmitted or the SF is increased. Additionally, there is a cut-off point between the

LoRa and WiFi curves, which, from an energy point of view and depending on the range we need to reach, can help us to determine which technology is more efficient.

The efficiency of the proposed architecture has been tested in a real scenario for a Smart Port application. It has demonstrated the capability of the sensor nodes to capture temperature, corrosion, acceleration, and pressure data and send them to the IoT gateway at a distance of 5.7 km, maintaining, even at that distance, a low energy consumption. Thus, the application has been running for more than one year in a hostile environment. Extrapolating the results obtained from the tests, we estimate that, with a 5800 mA/h battery capacity, these sensor nodes can monitor critical points of the port infrastructure and perform predictive maintenance of structural health for a duration of 1.7 years.

Author Contributions: Conceptualization, A.C. and A.I.; Formal analysis, A.I. and M.L.; Funding acquisition, A.I. and A.C.; Investigation, A.C., A.I., M.L., J.C., and A.P.; Methodology, A.I. and M.L.; Project administration, A.I.; Software, M.L., A.I., J.C., and A.P.; Supervision, A.I. and A.C.; Validation, M.L., A.I., and J.C.; Writing—Original draft, M.L.; Writing—Review & editing, A.I., M.L., and A.C. All authors have read and agreed to the published version of the manuscript.

Funding: This work was supported by STARPORTS-Sistema Inalámbrico Distribuido de monitorización, prevención y actuación para la Gestión Costera, a FEDER Innterconecta (Canary Island) funded project (ITC-20181029) in collaboration with FCC, Wellness Telecom, SensorLab and PLOCAN.

Institutional Review Board Statement: Not applicable.

Data Availability Statement: Not applicable.

Acknowledgments: This work has been possible thanks to the cooperation of CEIT with FCC, Wellness Telecom, SensorLab, and PLOCAN.

Conflicts of Interest: The authors declare no conflict of interest.

Abbreviations

The following abbreviations are used in this manuscript:

AGV	Autonomous Guided Vehicle
API	application programming interface
ABP	Activation by Personalization
CC	Cloudlet Computing
DHCP	Dynamic Host configuration Protocol
DSP	Digital Signal Processor
GPIO	General Purpose Input-Output
HW	Hardware
IoT	Internet of Things
IP	Internet Protocol
LoRa	Long Range Modulation
LoRaWAN	Long Range Wide Area Network
LPWAN	Low Power Wide Area Network
MCC	Mobile Cloud Computing
MEC	Mobile Edge Computing
NPU	Neural Processing Unit
OTAA	Over the Air Activation
PLOCAN	Plataforma Oceanica de Canarias
SSID	Service Set Identifier
SW	Software
TCP	Transmission Control Protocol
UART	Universal Asynchronous Receiver-Transmitter
RTC	Real Time Clock

SF	Spreading Factor
SOM	System on Module
UDP	User Datagram Protocol
USB	Universal Serial Bus
WiFi	Wireless Fidelity

References

1. Armbrust, M.; Fox, A.; Grifth, R.; Joseph, A.D.; Katz, R.; Konwinski, A.; Lee, G.; Patterson, D.; Rabkin, A.; Stoica, I. A view of cloud computing. *Commun. ACM* **2010**, *53*, 50–58. [CrossRef]
2. International Telecommunication Union. *Recommendation ITU-T Y.2060 Overview of the Internet of Things*; International Telecommunication Union: Geneva, Switzerland, 2012.
3. Raza, U.; Kulkarni, P.; Sooriyabandara, M. Low Power Wide Area Networks: An Overview. *IEEE Commun. Surv. Tutor.* **2017**, *19*, 855–873. [CrossRef]
4. Available online: https://www.statista.com/statistics/471264/iot-number-of-connected-devices-worldwide/ (accessed on 10 May 2020)
5. Dolui, K.; Datta, S.K. Comparison of edge computing implementations: Fog computing, cloudlet and mobile edge computing. *Proc. Glob. Internet Things Summit (GIoTS)* **2017**, *53*, 1–6
6. Jararweh, Y.; Otoum, S.; Ridhawi, I.A. Trustworthy and sustainable smart city services at the edge. *Sustain. Cities Soc.* **2020**, *62*, 102394 [CrossRef]
7. Balasubramanian, V.; Zaman, F.; Aloqaily, M.; Alrabaee, S.; Gorlatova, M.; Reisslein, M. Reinforcing the Edge: Autonomous Energy Management for Mobile Device Clouds. In Proceedings of the IEEE Conference on Computer Communications Workshops (IEEE INFOCOM 2019), Paris, France, 29 April–2 May 2019.
8. Roman, R.; Lopez, J.; Mambo, M. Mobile edge computing, fog et al.: A survey and analysis of security threats and challenges. *Proc. Glob. Int. Things Summit (GIoTS)* **2018**, *78*, 680–698. [CrossRef]
9. Gusev, M.; Dustdar, S. Going back to the roots: The evolution of edge computing, an IoT perspective. *IEEE Internet Comput.* **2018**, *22*, 5–15. [CrossRef]
10. Mach, P.; Becvar, Z. Mobile edge computing: A survey on architecture and computation of loading. *IEEE Commun. Surv. Tutor.* **2017**, *19*, 1628–1656 [CrossRef]
11. Donno, M.D.; Tange, K.; Dragoni, N. Foundations and Evolution of Modern Computing Paradigms: Cloud, IoT, Edge, and Fog. *IEEE Access* **2019**, *7*, 150936–150948. [CrossRef]
12. OpenFog Consortium Architecture Working Group. OpenFog Reference Architecture for Fog Computing. 2017. Available online: www.OpenFogConsortium.org (accessed on 17 December 2020).
13. Chang, C.; Srirama, S.N.; Buyya, R. Indie Fog: An Efficient Fog-Computing Infrastructure for the Internet of Things. **2017**, *50*, 92–98. [CrossRef]
14. Elkhatib, Y. On using micro-clouds to deliver the fog. *IEEE Int. Comput.* **2017**, *21*, 8–15. [CrossRef]
15. Sarker, V.K.; Queralta, J.P.; Gia, T.N.; Tenhunen, H.; Westerlund, T. A Survey on LoRa for IoT: Integrating Edge Computing. In Proceedings of the 2019 Fourth International Conference on Fog and Mobile Edge Computing (FMEC), Rome, Italy, 10–13 June 2019; pp. 295–300. [CrossRef]
16. Ferreira, C.M.S.; Oliveira, R.A.R.; Silva, J.S. Low-Energy Smart Cities Network with LoRa and Bluetooth. In Proceedings of the 2019 7th IEEE International Conference on Mobile Cloud Computing, Services, and Engineering (MobileCloud), Newark, CA, USA, 4–9 April 2019; pp. 24–29. [CrossRef]
17. Balasubramanian, V.; Otoum, S.; Aloqaily, M.; Ridhawi, I.A.; Jararweh, Y. Low-latency vehicular edge: A vehicular infrastructure model for 5G. *Simul. Model. Pract. Theory* **2020**, *98*, 101968 [CrossRef]
18. Sinha, R.S.; Wei, Y.; Hwang, S. A survey on LPWA technology: LoRa and NB-IoT. *ICT Express* **2017**, *3*, 14–21. ISSN 2405-9595. [CrossRef]
19. Yu, W. A Survey on the Edge Computing for the Internet of Things. *IEEE Access* **2018**, *6*, 6900–6919. [CrossRef]
20. Zhang, Q.; Sun, H.; Wu, X.; Zhong, H. Edge Video Analytics for Public Safety: A Review. *Proc. IEEE* **2019**, *107*, 1675–1696. [CrossRef]
21. Premsankar, G.; Francesco, M.D.; Taleb, T. Edge Computing for the Internet of Things: A Case Study. *IEEE Int. Things J.* **2018**, *5*, 1275–1284. [CrossRef]
22. Tomé, M.D.; Nardelli, P.H.J.; Alves, H. Long-Range Low-Power Wireless Networks and Sampling Strategies in Electricity Metering. *IEEE Trans. Ind. Electron.* **2019**, *66*, 1629–1637. [CrossRef]
23. Li, Y.; Yan, X.; Zeng, L.; Wu, H. Research on water meter reading system based on LoRa communication. In Proceedings of the 2017 IEEE International Conference on Smart Grid and Smart Cities (ICSGSC), Singapore, 23–26 July 2017; pp. 248–251.
24. Manoharan, A.M.; Rathinasabapathy, V. Smart Water Quality Monitoring and Metering Using LoRa for Smart Villages. In Proceedings of the 2018 2nd International Conference on Smart Grid and Smart Cities (ICSGSC), Kuala Lumpur, Malaysia, 12–14 August 2018; pp. 57–61.
25. Rajabi, A.; Saryazdi, A.K.; Belfkih, A.; Duvallet, C. Towards Smart Port: An Application of AIS Data. In Proceedings of the 2018 IEEE 20th International Conference on High Performance Computing and Communications, Exeter, UK, 28–30 June 2018. [CrossRef]

26. CC3220MODA Wireless Module Datasheet from Texas Instrument. Available online: https://www.ti.com/lit/ds/symlink/cc3220moda.pdf?&ts=1589201716200 (accessed on 10 May 2020).
27. RN2483 LoRa Transceiver Module Datasheet from Microchip. Available online: http://ww1.microchip.com/downloads/en/DeviceDoc/RN2483-Low-Power-Long-Range-LoRa-Technology-Transceiver-Module-Data-Sheet-DS50002346D.pdf (accessed on 10 May 2020).
28. ADXL355 Low Noise 3-Axis MEMS Accelerometer Datasheet from Analog Devices. Available online: https://www.analog.com/media/en/technical-documentation/data-sheets/adxl354_355.pdf (accessed on 10 May 2020).
29. BME280 Humidity and Pressure Sensor Datasheet from Bosch. Available online: https://www.bosch-sensortec.com/media/boschsensortec/downloads/datasheets/bst-bme280-ds002.pdf (accessed on 10 May 2020).
30. LDC1001 Inductance-to-Digital Converter Datasheet from Texas Instrument. Available online: https://www.ti.com/lit/ds/symlink/ldc1001.pdf?&ts=1589202383105 (accessed on 10 May 2020).
31. DS1374 32-Bit Binary Counter Watchdog RTC from Maxim Integrated. Available online: https://datasheets.maximintegrated.com/en/ds/DS1374-DS1374U.pdf (accessed on 10 May 2020).
32. DART-MX8M System-on-Module from Variscite. Available online: https://www.variscite.com/wp-content/uploads/2018/03/DART-MX8M-Datasheet.pdf (accessed on 10 May 2020).
33. i.MX 8M Processor Family-ARM Cortex-A53, Cortex-M4 Datasheet from NXP. Available online: https://www.nxp.com/products/processors-and-microcontrollers/arm-processors/i-mx-applications-processors/i-mx-8-family/i-mx-8m-family-armcortex-a53-cortex-m4-audio-voice-video:i.MX8M?&tab=Documentation_Tab&linkline=Data-Sheet (accessed on 10 May 2020).
34. DART-MX8M-PLUS System-on-Module from Variscite. Available online: https://www.variscite.com/wp-content/uploads/2020/10/DART-MX8M-PLUS_Datasheet.pdf (accessed on 10 May 2020).
35. i.MX 8M-Plus Processor Family-ARM Cortex-A53, Machine Learning, Vision, Multimedia and Industrial IoT Datasheet from NXP. Available online: https://www.nxp.com/products/processors-and-microcontrollers/arm-processors/i-mx-applications-processors/i-mx-8-processors/i-mx-8m-plus-arm-cortex-a53-machine-learning-vision-multimedia-and-industrial-iot:IMX8MPLUS (accessed on 10 May 2020).
36. RAK833 Gateway Concentrator Module Datasheet from Rak Wireless. Available online: https://doc.rakwireless.com/datasheet/rakproducts/rak833-LoRawan-gateway-concentrator-module-datasheet (accessed on 10 May 2020).
37. LoRa Network Packet Forwarder Software from Semtech. Available online: https://github.com/LoRa-net/packet_forwarder (accessed on 10 May 2020).
38. The Things Network: An Open LoRaWAN Network. Available online: https://www.thethingsnetwork.org (accessed on 10 May 2020).
39. MSP430FR2433 LaunchPad™ Development Kit. Available online: https://www.ti.com/tool/MSP-EXP430FR2433 (accessed on 16 November 2020).
40. ChirpStack, open-source LoRaWAN® Network Server stack. Available online: https://www.chirpstack.io/ (accessed on 10 May 2020).

Article

A Modular IoT Hardware Platform for Distributed and Secured Extreme Edge Computing

Pablo Merino, Gabriel Mujica *, Jaime Señor and Jorge Portilla

Centro de Electrónica Industrial, Universidad Politécnica de Madrid, José Gutiérrez Abascal 2, 28006 Madrid, Spain; p.merino@upm.es (P.M.); jaime.senors@alumnos.upm.es (J.S.); jorge.portilla@upm.es (J.P.)
* Correspondence: gabriel.mujica@upm.es; Tel.: +34-910-676-944

Received: 25 February 2020; Accepted: 18 March 2020; Published: 24 March 2020

Abstract: The hardware of networked embedded sensor nodes is in continuous evolution, from those 8-bit MCUs-based platforms such as Mica, up to powerful Edge nodes that even include custom hardware devices, such as FPGAs in the Cookies platform. This evolution process comes up with issues related to the deployment of the Internet of Things, particularly in terms of performance and communication bottlenecks. Moreover, the associated integration process from the Edge up to the Cloud layer opens new security concerns that are key to assure the end-to-end trustability and interoperability. This work tackles these questions by proposing a novel embedded Edge platform based on an EFR32 SoC from Silicon Labs with Contiki-NG OS that includes an ARM Cortex M4 MCU and an IEEE 802.15.4 transceiver, used for resource-constrained low-power communication capabilities. This IoT Edge node integrates security by hardware, adding support for confidentiality, integrity and availability, making this Edge node ultra-secure for most of the common attacks in wireless sensor networks. Part of this security relies on an energy-efficient hardware accelerator that handles identity authentication, session key creation and management. Furthermore, the modular hardware platform aims at providing reliability and robustness in low-power distributed sensing application contexts on what is called the Extreme Edge, and for that purpose a lightweight multi-hop routing strategy for supporting dynamic discovery and interaction among participant devices is fully presented. This embedded algorithm has served as the baseline end-to-end communication capability to validate the IoT hardware platform through intensive experimental tests in a real deployment scenario.

Keywords: extreme edge; embedded edge computing; internet of things deployment; hardware design; IoT security; Contiki-NG; trustability

---

1. Introduction

The Internet of Things paradigm has achieved an enormous integration level inside the technology distributed all around the world. It covers from consumer electronics, such as Wi-Fi controlled thermostats, to industrial or professional applications, such as a Wireless Sensor Network (WSN) registering data all along a whole forest. The future of communication protocols could also lead to bigger growths on new IoT system implementations, e.g., real-time systems collecting data from dozens of sensors around a fabric to optimize manufacturing operations dynamically. Therefore, the development of this kind of platforms looks promising.

The traditional hardware solutions that were used in Wireless Sensor Networks mostly relied on de-facto standard sensor motes, such as Micas and TelosB [1], or similar approaches where 8-bit or 16-bit-based microcontrollers were integrated as the core of the wireless devices, to perform simple yet energy-efficient tasks for the target application. During the last decade tens of hardware platforms for the Extreme Edge [2] of the IoT have appeared with different elements and focusing on aspects such as low power consumption, high processing capabilities or open HW philosophy, among others [3]. Although these hardware platforms have been valid for many WSN application contexts, the ongoing revolution of IoT is pushing the hardware implementation towards the integration of more complex capabilities that allow tackling the challenges of smart and highly dynamic scenarios [4], particularly concerning the arising end-to-end IoT security issues with such an amount of expected Edge devices in place. In this sense, the traditional behavior of a WSN, in which the devices remained in sleep modes for a very long period of time (thus the main consumption components to be considered were the deep power modes) and then wake up to transmit a sensing measurement to a root device, is changing to more active collaborations among participant sensors, in which the type of features they provide to the local or overall IoT Edge deployment becomes a key performance element of the system. In such scenarios, protecting the relationships among the nodes is crucial to assure data integrity and security on the Edge.

Nonetheless, it seems that practical implementation problems of IoT networks are always related to security and reliability issues. One of the many reasons is that those networks are usually built up from many nodes that have some restrictions on energy consumption and processing capabilities. Thus, they are often designed as tiny embedded systems with low-cost processors that do not have the enough computational power to implement security systems. However, if the problems associated with a lack of security capabilities are ignored, several disasters on the network and on the products related to it can indeed appeared. A common mistake on simple IoT products deployment is to think that data exchanged by the nodes on the Edge is not critical, as it does not contain private data about users, e.g., humidity sensors sensing moisture measurements to the central node that controls the overall climate of one house. However, since the security process is too simple or may not even exist on these nodes, an attacker could take control of one node and then scale privileges through upper layers of the network, reaching cloud server and the data located there.

The problem resides not only in the ability of the attacker to scale privileges in the network. Actions taken inside the nodes on the Edge might be also harmful for the system and for the users. Although many people might think that an attacker stealing data related to the temperature of their rooms is not a real threat, other systems may suffer from this uncontrolled access to the Edge. A good example of that is the research made by the authors in [5], where they analyzed the security problems within the Philips Hue lamps. In this case, the authors were able to infer the key that protects the firmware updates of the lamps, by measuring the patterns on the power consumption of the main chip while making cryptographic tasks. Then, they could upload new custom versions of the firmware to the lamps by just requesting it to the chip, once a minimum distance from the node is reached. Upon this update being accepted, the new firmware can be programmed to request the same update to other lamps on the network, propagating itself such as an infection. The ability to change the software that controls the nodes is the key to allow the attackers to cause several problems to the users. Looking at those lamps, the authors remark the possibility of causing epileptic attacks to users by generating stroboscopic lights. In this context, some solutions are being proposed by the community [6] in different ways, software-wise as well as hardware-wise. The security issue in IoT is certainly gaining more attention presently, and new approaches are being proposed to improve this aspect. For instance, some authors present testbeds to approach the difficult task of assessing security in IoT deployments [7].

In this work, these main concerns related to the security on the Edge of IoT are addressed, by creating a hardware platform that combines a main processing core with a Hardware Security Module in a modular and flexible architecture, so as to foster protection strategies for current and future sensor network deployments. Different techniques are used to guarantee privacy and integrity in the data collected by sensor nodes, as well as mechanisms to join the network in a trustable manner. The design and implementation of the hardware layer have been conceived to produce a trade-off solution between computational performance, power consumption awareness and high degree of protection with dedicated hardware resources, particularly considering the increasingly importance of the active operations of the nodes in IoT dynamic contexts. The runtime self-diagnosis management of the Edge node by providing power and functional islands, real-time current consumption monitoring and an extended range of operational modes for advanced power profiles are key features that this work takes into account to provide dynamic adaptation for the target application scenarios.

Secondly, in order to validate and provide a baseline hardware and software platform for supporting distributed IoT Extreme Edge applications, a lightweight and robust multi-hop communication strategy for the Extreme Edge of IoT is proposed in this work (called Extreme-LT Routing) that allows verifying the dynamic deployment, discovery, data processing and dissemination of IoT devices in a reliable yet low-power resource-constrained fashion. The presented routing algorithm is based on the self-composition of the network topology based on the deployment conditions of the wireless nodes to find the best possible routes for the given circumstances, so as to achieve an optimized data delivery from the sensing nodes to the Edge of the IoT layers. The design and implementation of this technique is included as an embedded software component of the proposed IoT platform, and it has been used as the support communication capability to analyze its behavior and performance in real IoT Extreme Edge deployments, through the realization of intensive experimental tests, as shown in the outcomes of the work.

The main contributions of this work can be summarized as follows:

- A modular hardware platform for the edge and extreme edge of the IoT, with HW enhancements for security, trustability and protection against hacking. It includes the implementation of enhanced low-power profiles to provide a trade-off solution between more demanding processing capabilities yet reduced energy consumption.
- An extreme lightweight transmission protocol for multi-hop packet routing in resource-constrained IoT edge sensor networks. Its main features are simplicity, robustness, efficiency and hardware Independence.
- A detailed and extensive set of real experimental tests to study the performance of the proposed solutions on the actual hardware implementation. The enhanced low-power profiles as well as the dynamics of the proposed transmission technique are deeply analyzed.

The rest of the article is organized as follows: Section 2 presents the Cookie modular platform, the particular design and implementation under study in this paper and its main features, as well as the porting and integration of the Contiki-NG operating system into the proposed hardware platform. Section 3 introduces the security aspects of the Internet of Things and their relevance on wireless sensor networks. The implementation of the security solution in the aforementioned platform is also proposed. Then, Section 4 is devoted to detail the lightweight multi-hop communication strategy for dynamic data processing and dissemination on the Extreme Edge, which is intensively tested and validated in Section 4.2, where the experimental results are presented and discussed. Finally, conclusions and future works are highlighted in Section 5.

2. Modular Hardware Platform for the Extreme Edge of IoT

The baseline architecture of the proposed solution for supporting security and distributed applications on the Edge and Extreme Edge relies on a modular hardware platform: The Cookie node [8,9]. This architecture follows a very flexible approach that promotes the implementation of IoT technologies with a very smooth integration effort, by considering the combination and reusability of hardware components in a seamless and modular fashion. The general structure of a Cookie node is composed of four main layers: The processing layer, which integrates the core elements to provide computational capabilities to the sensor node; the communication layer, which includes the wireless technology to provide connectivity to the surrounding network as well as the remote IoT infrastructure; the sensor layer that implements the physical interface to interact with the target environment; and the power supply layer, which is in charge of the voltage level provisioning and debugging capabilities to the rest of the modular platform. The vertical connectors of the Cookie architecture facilitate the plug-and-play philosophy of the platform, which means that new communication, sensing, processing and power supply technologies can easily be integrated without the need to replace or redesign the rest of the layers. Therefore, reusability and adaptability are the main pillars to facilitate fast prototyping upon the hardware architecture [8].

2.1. The Cookie Node

Targeting the provision of security and reliability capabilities on the Extreme Edge, a new IoT hardware platform has been developed in this work following the design style and the modularity of the Cookie architecture. This new self-contained version of the Cookie node aims at the next generation of IoT devices particularly considering key objectives such as trustability, scalability, flexibility and a security-based design, as well as adapting it to the hardware architecture and modularity of the Cookies. In this way, the new Cookie Edge Node is indeed an IoT oriented platform, which includes a Silicon Labs EFR32MG12 SoC as a core of the processing layer and several peripherals for sensing and security purposes. A general schematic view of the Cookie board architecture from a functional point of view is shown in Figure 1. The EFR32 MCU is a 32-bit Cortex-M4 SoC with a maximum operating frequency of 40 MHz, an IEEE 802.15.4 radio and enough memory to run applications with an increased demand on computational resources on the Edge and the Extreme Edge (256 kB RAM, 1 MB Flash). While being a 32-bit chip, it has been designed with the goal of energy efficiency, fast wake-up times and a scalable power amplifier [10]. These features are seized in the Cookie node, while bearing in mind the necessity of establishing a secure and trustable network.

It also includes a SI7021 temperature and relative humidity sensor [11], which can be interfaced via I^2C, and an ICM-20648 6-axis inertial sensor [12], which is accessed through SPI.

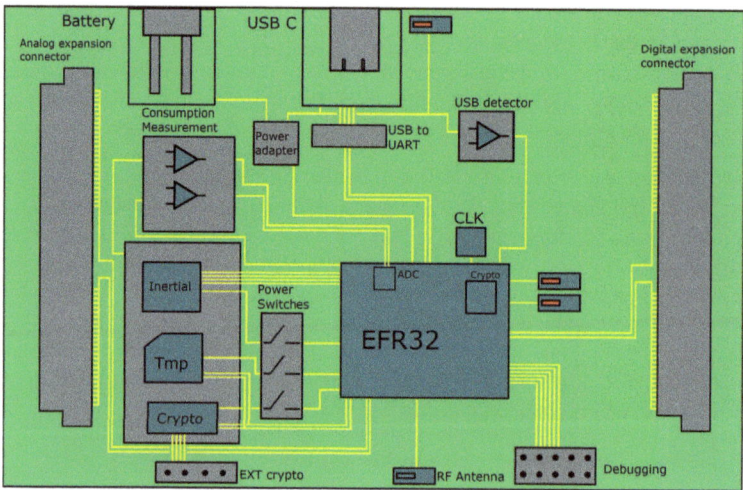

Figure 1. Block Diagram of the designed Cookie Node.

Besides the crypto accelerator integrated in the EFR32, the proposed Cookie node has another cryptographic co-processor. The Microchip ATECC608A encryption chip [13] is a core feature of the board, making it able to run several encryption algorithms and store the secure key on hardware, supporting the establishment of a chain of trust among the nodes in the sensor network. Also, its design makes the chip resistant to side-channel attacks.

With the aim of controlling its energy consumption, the new Cookie layer also includes two operational amplifier blocks at the input of the MCU and the consumption islands. These blocks enable the MCU to measure the consumption of the SoC and the sensors separately, and are directly connected to a 12-bits resolution ADC, therefore allowing the platform to perform self-adapting energy-aware strategies to switch to a better suited power profile, according to the application context needs. The implementation result of the new IoT Cookie node for the Extreme Edge is shown in Figure 2, where a top-layer view of hardware platform is presented.

Figure 2. Implementation of the Cookie node with Silicon Labs EFR32 MCU and Microchip ATECC608A Cryptographic Co-Processor.

2.2. Low-Power Strategies

2.2.1. EFR32 Low-Power Modes

According to Hyung-Sin Kim et al. [14], although the idle current of each hardware component is provided by its datasheet, the idle current of a sensor node may be impacted by many additional factors, making it significantly greater than the sum of the datasheet values [14]. The MCU of the Cookie, as part of the EFR32MG12 family, has a variety of low-power modes available. These modes allow the SoC to save energy by reducing the power consumption of the processor when it is not required to display its complete functionality. These modes are depicted as follows [15]:

- EM0 - Active/Run Mode: the normal running mode, everything is active.
- EM1 - Sleep Mode: the CPU clock is disabled. The memory can still be accessed through Direct Memory Access (DMA) and the peripherals can be handled using the Peripheral Reflex System (PRS).
- EM2 - Deep Sleep Mode: not only the CPU clock, but the high frequency oscillators are also disabled. The 32 kHz low frequency oscillator is still enabled.
- EM3 - Stop Mode: all high and low frequency oscillators are disabled except for the ultra-low frequency and, optionally, the auxiliary ones.
- EM4S - Shutoff Mode: all oscillators are disabled, there is no RAM retention and the MCU is shut down except for the recovery logic. The only way to wake up is through an external reset.
- EM4H - Hibernate Mode: similar to the EM4S mode, providing more options for the wake-up call. Mode EM4H can have RTCC running with the ultra-low frequency oscillator, while EM4S cannot. EM4H does also provide some RAM retention, which EM4S does not.

2.2.2. Enhanced Low-Power Profiles

Besides the low-power modes of the EFR32, the designed Cookie node for the Extreme Edge provides software access to enable or disable signals associated with the power supply of the external peripherals, such as the sensors and the cryptochip, then introducing the concept of power and functional islands. In this way, the power consumption of these islands can be arbitrarily controlled and adjusted to the combination that suits best each moment according to the target application and its dynamics. This feature can be combined with the aforementioned energy modes of the processor, therefore improving the consumption saving of the platform and enabling the creation of some more powerful and extended Low-Power Profiles.

All possible combinations of these options for the modes studied in Section 2.4 are highlighted in Table 1.

Table 1. Combined low-power modes of the Cookie Edge Node, allowing the creation of a more advanced range of power profiles.

	EM0	EM1	EM2
All islands disabled	EM0-000	EM1-000	EM2-000
Temp sensor enabled	EM0-100	EM1-100	EM2-100
Cryptochip enabled	EM0-010	EM1-010	EM2-010
Inertial sensor enabled	EM0-001	EM1-001	EM2-001
Temp + Crypto enabled	EM0-110	EM1-110	EM2-110
Temp + Inertial enabled	EM0-101	EM1-101	EM2-101
Crypto + Inertial enabled	EM0-011	EM1-011	EM2-011
All islands enabled	EM0-111	EM1-111	EM2-111

The naming code for each cell of the table (each combined mode) comes from the combination of the power mode of the processor (EMx) and three bits depending on the on/off state of the power switch of each consumption island, in the following order: the temperature sensor (x__), the encryption chip (_x_) and the inertial sensor (__x). For example, having the EFR32 in normal sleep mode while having the inertial sensor enabled and the other two power islands disabled would be coded as EM1-001.

2.3. Software Integration and Usability

To provide additional software support for the proposed Cookie node beyond the embedded libraries developed to use the platform (in case of needed), the Contiki-NG Operating System has been integrated in this hardware node. Contiki-NG started as a fork of Contiki OS [16], with the intent of focusing on the new 32-bits platforms, and the available partial porting of Contiki for EFR32 core [17] has been adapted to the Cookie Edge Node and completed using some of the libraries for the EFR32 from Silicon Labs. In addition to this, the porting has been conceived to provide fully support to the new hardware elements of the proposed solution, including the management of the power and functional islands, the self-diagnosis of the sensor node based on the power consumption monitoring cross-correlated with the advanced power profiles, and the enhanced security capabilities of the Cookie. Moreover, based on the modular architecture of the Cookie platform, and since the vertical connectors have been exploited to make full compatibility of the new hardware design with already existing or future Cookie layers, the different analog and digital signals and their relationship with the connected hardware elements are properly addressed in the implemented porting.

Most of the work to complement and enrich the initial porting and the adaptation to the proposed hardware node can be classified into the following categories:

- Adaptation of the pinout and other purely hardware-related issues, such as mapping ports to new locations.
- Completion of unfinished functions and missing parts of the Software Abstraction Layer (SAL). Since the porting is still a work in progress, some work needed to be done in this area.
- Particularization of generic functions calling to platform-specific ones for each target or board. Since each board provides the user with its own set of Hardware Abstraction Layer (HAL) functions and lower level functions belonging to each MCU, some parts of the higher level needed to be properly connected to the lower layers. This also includes adapting the drivers for the interaction with the peripherals.

2.4. Characterization

From a hardware perspective, this work is heavily focused on sensor nodes for the IoT, and not on the general wireless sensor networks domain. For this reason, it might not cover some of the most popular and traditional devices of the literature and include some others that better fit within the scope of next generation IoT Edge devices, as commented before. Also, it will not compare the proposed platform to smaller 8-bit or 16-bit-based platforms, since the performance and overall purpose of those differ from the aim of the proposed Extreme Edge platform.

To study the different low-power modes, every single combination of the state of the power islands has been tested on the Cookie Edge Node, going through all the energy modes of the processor for each one of them. The main approach was also to test the upper boundaries of the power profile sets in order to provide a trade-off relationship between power consumption and platform performance, seeking a good balance for those more demanding IoT scenarios, as described in the introduction section. The procedure started by initializing the board and forcefully staying in EM0 mode for a few seconds. After that, the MCU went into the next mode (EM1 - sleep) and waited for another 3 s, repeating this process successively from the highest to the lowest power mode. Before going into deep sleep mode (EM2), a low frequency clock was prepared to wake up the MCU and proceed into the next instruction.

During the tests, the peripherals in their enabled state were in idle mode waiting for the instruction to start a sensing cycle, and did not perform any operation or measure. In this way, the measurements obtained are closer to a real behavior since the sensing frequency in a real deployment is supposed to be low, i.e., the purpose of the low-power modes is to save energy when the board is idle, not during a measurement/transmission cycle.

The consumption of each one of the combined low-power modes can be seen in Table 2.

Table 2. Current consumption of the combined low-power modes for the upper active consumption states (mA).

	EM0	EM1	EM2
All islands disabled	11.93	10.43	6.80
Temp sensor enabled	11.94	10.44	6.81
Cryptochip enabled	11.99	10.45	6.82
Inertial sensor enabled	12.44	10.89	7.33
Temp + Crypto enabled	11.99	10.45	6.83
Temp + Inertial enabled	12.51	10.87	7.34
Crypto + Inertial enabled	12.45	10.95	7.35
All islands enabled	12.52	10.97	7.37

Table 3 shows the approximate current consumption of different platforms in their active state (MCU active, peripherals enabled) and their idle state (MCU sleeping, peripherals turned off). The platforms featured are OpenMoteB (CC2538 SoC based on ARM Cortex-M3, 32-bit), DotNOW emote (STM32F103ZG [18] ARM Cortex-M3, 32-bit) and Sparkfun freeSoC2 [19] (PSoC5LP ARM Cortex-M3, 32-bit). The consumption values shown for the platforms are taken from their respective datasheets, obtained by adding the manufacturer values for the processor consumption in similar circumstances than those of the Cookie for its testing: MCU active with the radio turned off and peripherals enabled but in a wait state. The values for the stm32 consumption (DotNOW emote) that correspond to sleep mode at 36 MHz with all peripherals enabled are shown. The consumption of OpenMoteB was obtained by adding 13 mA of core consumption at 32 MHz and the consumption of some common peripherals: GP timer, USB, SPI, I^2C, UART, but no ADC nor Flash being used. Consumption values for the freeSoC2 were obtained directly from the datasheet for a frequency of 24/48 MHz and 25 °C.

Table 3. Current consumption comparison for the different Edge nodes.

Board (MCU Clock Frequency)	Current
OpenMoteB [20] (32 MHz)	18 mA
DotNOW emote [21] (36 MHz)	17 mA
Sparkfun freeSoC2 [22] (24 MHz)	8.9 mA
Sparkfun freeSoC2 (48 MHz)	15.4 mA
Cookie Layer (38.4 MHz)	12.52 mA

2.5. Hardware Discussion

Figure 3 shows the differences in current consumption between the compared hardware platforms regarding the results shown in Table 3. Since the clock configurations are slightly different for each one of them, the plot has been normalized by considering the outcome of the current consumed per units of MHz. It can be seen that the Cookie layer outperforms the rest of the platforms even with one of the highest clock frequency operations, although in case of the freeSoC2 working at 48 MHz provides quite similar results but for a sleeper state, in contraposition to the Cookie Edge Node in normal mode. In the meantime, the results show that the Cookie layer obtains more than 40% of current consumption reduction in comparison with the OpenMoteB, whose results contribute to optimize the efficiency of the target approach regarding the balance between higher computational duty cycles (thus more presence of active operational modes in the functional profile of the sensor nodes) and power awareness on the Edge.

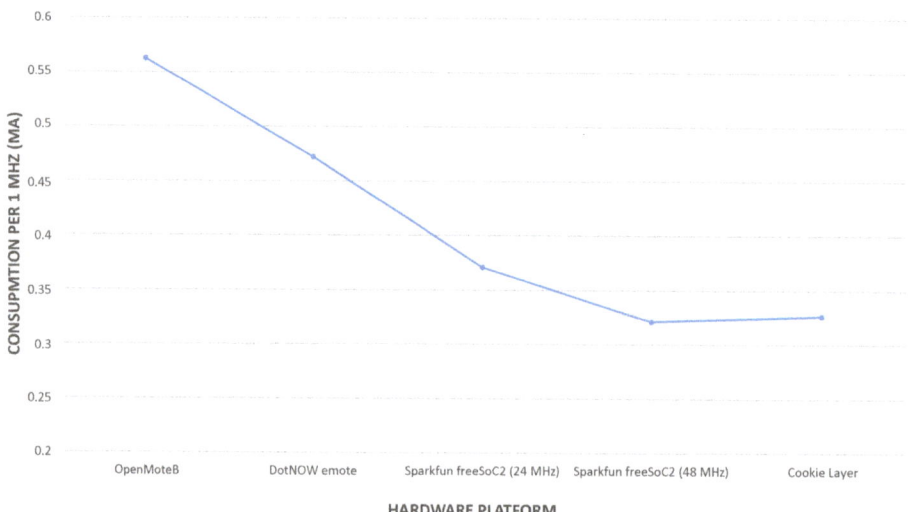

Figure 3. Results comparison of the Extreme Edge nodes considering the current consumption per MHz.

3. Security on the Extreme Edge

Protecting the Edge and particularly the Extreme Edge is one of the main pillars of the proposed modular platform, so as to provide trustability, robustness and reliability in the increasingly complex and diverse application scenarios of IoT. Traditionally, the security issue has been deeply studied in Internet, networking and computer science. However, the ubiquity of IoT devices introduces new elements to the equation, and more vulnerabilities should be considered to be protected from potential attackers. The security schemes are known to have a difficult implementation in real deployments of IoT networks. The operations that take place in common schemes may spend a large amount of time, in comparison with the usual time that a node should be active performing sensing, processing and communication tasks. This is an important issue when the approach for saving energy is to have the nodes in active mode the minimum required time, and move them to a sleep mode whenever possible. Thus, the addition of security capabilities to this type of networks must consider the extra power consumption that will appear.

Moreover, in the new IoT world, it is common to find networks composed of embedded devices that use communication protocols that do not necessarily have access to Internet, as in case of the wireless sensor networks (WSNs), which are oriented to low data rate and low-power consumption. Internet is a network that is continuously being monitored to find irregularities and attacks, but this is certainly not the case of the WSN domain.

The security on the Edge of the IoT is a very serious problem that is being addressed by the scientific community. In this regard, in [23] a security agent is introduced, which is a hardware element with enough resources to carry out advanced security algorithms. This element offloads the security tasks from the restricted sensor nodes, which are working on measuring and sending information to the network wirelessly, although they represent a source of vulnerability, as detailed before. This is the main reason tackling the security and trustability problem directly from the Extreme Edge perspective is gaining important attention.

In this way, one of the main aspects to be considered is that the security should rely on securing the criptographic key, and the ability to keep it hidden from potential attackers, so that a trustable communication between the different parties of the network can be guaranteed. Moreover, side-channel attacks should be foreseen, especially when an attacker may have physical access to deployed nodes. This work focuses on these principles by protecting the key inside the IoT nodes, using dedicated hardware with enhanced capabilities in this regard, with very few overheads in terms of cost and power consumption.

3.1. The Chain of Trust on the Edge

When two members do not know each other, they need to establish a root of trust. This technique is based on the fact that the manufacturer of the equipment or a Certificate Authority (CA) acts as a third member that provides confidence by giving legitimacy to the relationship between the public key and the member who claims to have it.

This process (known as Public Key Infrastructure, or PKI) is a combination of different elements and procedures that allow the execution of the encryption, signature and non-repudiation of transactions or electronic communications using asymmetric cryptography, with guarantees during the whole process. Using PKI, members that do not know each other can authenticate and trust among them before starting a communication. This is done by means of using signatures and certificates. The process consists of the creation of certificates, by the CA, for each device. Subsequently, each member has the public key of the CA with which it is possible to check the validity of the member's certificate with the one a communication (and thus an authentication process) has to be performed. The certificate is a data structure that contains relevant information about the device including its public key, and it is signed by the CA.

This concepts have been brought to the Extreme Edge by the design and implementation of the proposed new Cookie platform, combining the main processing core with a so-called Hardware Security Module (HSM). This dedicated accelerator allows providing the chain of trust with enhanced security capabilities in a transparent and efficient fashion, thus creating a protected modular and trustable hardware node for the Extreme Edge of IoT, as described in the following paragraphs.

3.2. Cookie Node with Enhanced Hardware Security

The Cookie node ensures security and trustability on the Extreme Edge by using the ATECC608A HSM designed by Microchip Inc., which is directly attached to the main I^2C bus, as stated previously in the description of the hardware modules. This chip accomplishes two main tasks. First, the power and time consumption of the cryptographic operations are moved from the software running at the microcontroller to a hardware accelerator, and second, it serves as a trustable module inside the node, meaning that it provides security to store sensitive data inside the platform that will not be discovered by side-channel attacks [24].

The most common strategy adopted when facing the security issue in IoT systems, is the use of symmetric and asymmetric schemes in a mixed fashion, where the authentication processes of the nodes relies on the asymmetric part, and the message exchange is done with symmetric algorithms. These are known to be more efficient if the communication channel is trustable [25]. For asymmetric authentication, usually Elliptic-Curve Cryptography (ECC) is the preferred choice, since the same security level can be achieved with smaller key sizes compared to other alternatives, such as RSA [26]. On the symmetric scheme, the most spread cypher is the Advanced Encryption Standard (AES) with a key length of 128 bits. With this scenario in mind, the ATECC608A was chosen because it provides hardware acceleration for both NIST standard P256 ECC and AES algorithms, and also, the corresponding procedure to switch from asymmetric to symmetric schemes, which is, in this case, the Elliptic-Curve Diffie–Hellman (ECDH) algorithm.

Regarding the capabilities of the HSM to work as an isolated trustable environment, many considerations about its configuration must be done before accessing it from the microcontroller. In order to provide authentication based on a chain of trust, two certificates must be generated prior to the final deployment of the network. The first one identifies the CA, and it is stored in all the HSMs. The second one identifies the HSM itself, and it is signed by the previous CA. Both certificates are stored in a compressed X.509 format in this isolated environment, and must be validated by all the parties involved in the authentication process, prior to verifying the private key associated with the public key included inside the device's certificate. Such a private key is also generated during the configuration stage inside the HSM, and it is never delivered outside the chip under any request. Shared keys for the AES-128 implementation are internally generated by this chip and thus they are never shown.

As already stated, the whole authentication process involves two stages, where the public keys are validated against the signed certificates, and the private key is later checked to be correct. In the first step, certificates are requested to the HSM by the microcontroller, and are exchanged over the network, to perform a validation of the signs and get the public ECC keys of each node. First, the CA's certificate is checked, followed by the device's certificate, where this public key actually resides. The second stage is to verify the private key that is supposed to be the corresponding one to the announced public key. This is done by generating a random number and request for the new node to sign it with its private key, and test the result against the already known public key. All of this is performed with the help of the hardware acceleration provided by the HSM, and the sequence of operations are described in Figure 4.

If the new node succeeds in the verification process, it is labelled as a trustable party. Thus, full communication availability should be allowed. Continuing with the previous ideas, a switch to a symmetric cyphering method is made. The sensor node benefits from the capabilities of the HSM to accelerate the ECDH key exchange that generates a shared secret between the two nodes from the asymmetric key pairs. Since the ECDH algorithm is computed on each node separately, an eventual "authentication confirmed" message should be sent to the new node to coordinate the operation. After both nodes get what is called the pre-master shared secret, a Key Derivation Function (KDF), also available in the HSM, hashes the result one more time. This extra step adds randomness to the previous ECDH operation, and makes the following digest more suitable to use as a symmetric key. A time diagram for this stage is shown in Figure 5.

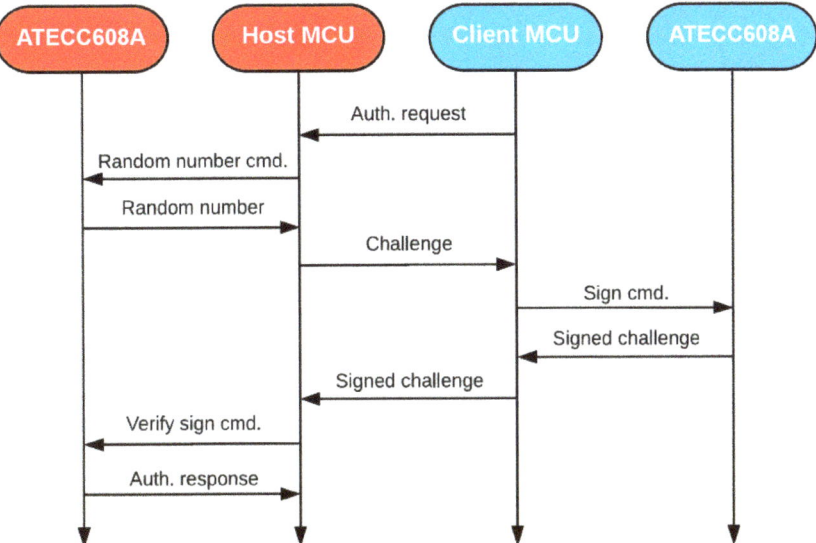

Figure 4. Time diagram of the steps followed in the authentication process between two nodes.

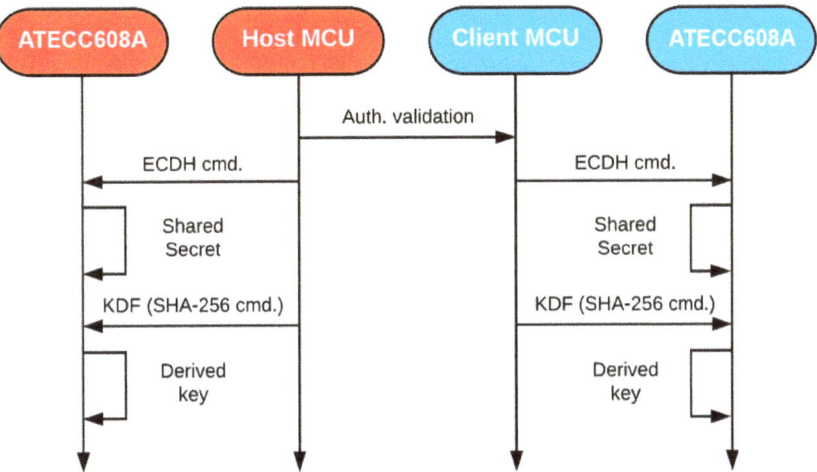

Figure 5. Time diagram of the steps followed to change from asymmetric cryptography to symmetric cryptography.

Once the secure channel for communications has been established, the rest of the messages can be cyphered with the AES-128 algorithm. Notice that the HSM does not support commonly used AES methods of operation, such as AES-CBC (Cypher-block chaining) or AES-CTR (Counter) [27]. Instead, it only provides acceleration of a basic AES engine that works with a single block of 16 bytes. Working only with the engine is not secure because it would not spread the information between different blocks of data, and the resulting cyphertext could not be random enough compared to the original plaintext source. Therefore, it is compulsory for a good performance of the symmetric scheme to coordinate the AES engine of the HSM with an extra help from the microcontroller, to get the behavior of the already mentioned modes of operation.

The main microcontroller of the platform running the software in the sensor nodes also provides its own inner hardware accelerator for AES. Table 4 compares the time spent between this accelerator and the HSM to perform the same encryption tasks, considering different AES modes. Notice that the external HSM provides a better time performance compared to the inner accelerator of the microcontroller, even with the need for additional support from the software part to coordinate the relationships between different blocks (128 bits each one) in the AES-CBC and AES-CTR modes. This reduction in the consumed time, in combination with the low-power characteristics of the HSM, makes this a suitable solution for securing real deployments of IoT edge networks. The added overheads and power consumption is minimum compared to the whole behavior of the network, even with the authentication processes that usually take more time to complete, since those are, in principle, only executed once, and the enhanced security justifies the approach of using a dedicated hardware.

Table 4. Experimental comparison of the two security modules included in the Cookie platform, considering the computational time for different AES modes

	AES-ECB (1 Block)	AES-CBC (16 Blocks)	AES-CTR (16 Blocks)
EFR32MG12	31 us	210 us	219 us
ATECC608A	7 us	165 us	183 us

Finally, each message exchange should be coupled with a Message Authentication Code (MAC), which allows the destination node to check if there was any error. This MAC can be generated by hashing the message with the SHA-256 function in the HSM. Another alternative would be to take advantage of the Galois field multiplication hardware accelerator of the HSM, which can be used to incorporate the AES-GCM (Galois/Counter Mode) operation [28] to the scheme. This mode calculates and adds the needed authentication code during the cyphering process, saving computational time.

4. The Extreme-LT Routing Protocol

As a means of validating and testing the performance of the Cookie platform in multi-hop distributed deployment contexts, the design and implementation of a dynamic and adaptive routing strategy is proposed in this work, seeking reliability yet lightweight operation for the Extreme Edge. The presented routing algorithm is based on the self-composition of the network topology based on the deployment conditions of the wireless nodes in the target scenario, to find and update the best possible routes for the given circumstances in a lightweight and dynamic fashion, so as to achieve an optimized data delivery from the sensing nodes to the Edge of the IoT layers.

There are some studies in the literature exploring the diverse options for the choice of IoT routing protocols. In [29], the authors focus on ad-hoc routing and study several protocols based on different mechanisms such as distance vector or link state. Another IoT routing protocol is RPL (Routing Protocol for Low-Power and Lossy Networks, [30]), which is widely used and supported by many IoT platforms and operating systems. This is reflected in the existence of many adaptations and variations for it, to enhance its performance in certain scenarios ([31–33]), as well as reviews of RPL-based protocols such as the one in [34].

The Extreme Edge Lightweight Transmission protocol (Extreme-LT) is a lightweight routing protocol developed at the Center of Industrial Electronics (CEI-UPM) for its use on the Cookie modular platform. It is a distance vector routing protocol for IoT networks, focused on simplicity, robustness and reduced processing load. It pursues the goals of reliability, robustness, efficiency and hardware independence set by CTP (Collection Tree Protocol, [35]), adapting and simplifying some mechanisms used by other protocols.

The protocol distinguishes between two node types: sending nodes and a root node. A network will always be composed of a root node, acting as a sink, and a variable number of sending nodes, establishing a tree topology. In this sense, Extreme-LT builds a Destination Oriented Directed Acyclic Graph (DODAG, [30]), similar to the ones used in other IoT routing protocols such as RPL.

The protocol is designed as a simple solution to route messages from the sending nodes to the sink, and since it is conceived to tackle the scenarios where the majority of traffic is directed to the sink node, and having in mind that the environment is lossy and routes are expected to change frequently, there is no necessity to store the whole upstream route in the node using routing tables, as seen in other protocols. Instead, each node only needs to know the route to its parent. Because of this, the choice of the best parent among the candidates is of utmost importance to the establishment of the tree and the optimization of the network topology. For the construction of the DODAG, the protocol uses the rank information and Received Signal Strength Indication (RSSI) as the metric to determine the best parent node from all the potential ones. The procedure to assign the rank of a node follows the following expression:

$$Rank(child) = Rank(parent) + HopIncrease \qquad (1)$$

With a rank increase per hop of 1 by default, the node rank is equal to the hop count from the root, resulting in the same metric that RPL implements for its Objective Function Zero (OF0, [36]). According to Yassien et al. [37], OF0 is not inferior to MRHOF (Minimum Rank with Hysteresis Objective Function, [38]) in terms of Packet Delivery Ratio (PDR) and power consumption, and even outperforms it in some scenarios. On top of that, Extreme-LT imposes a tie-break policy for equal rank candidates based on their RSSI.

Since a node has no routes stored other than the one pointing to its parent node, for downstream communications the protocol either uses unicast transmissions when it is a response to an upstream message, or uses broadcast messages for the nodes to filter in reception. The former is the usual solution, while the latter is restricted to specific situations to avoid flooding the medium.

For any given packet being transmitted, the network protocol header frame format includes data from the sender node, such as the node ID, its rank within the network topology or the DAG ID, as well as information related to the packet itself, such as the packet type or the packet number to keep track of the total number of packets sent from a sending node. Different DODAGs, with different DAG IDs, can coexist at the same time.

The protocol relies on the usage of several packet types, ranging from data packets to various kinds of control packets: Request, Discovery (network advertisement), Repair Unicast and Repair Broadcast. These packets have a common header, specific to the protocol, and an optional payload. In particular, data packets have a payload and control packets do not have it. The header frame format of the protocol is shown in Figure 6. To illustrate this frame format, different packet frames can be seen in the examples shown in Figure 7.

| 0 | 1-2 | 3-4 | 5-6 | 7-8 | 9-10 | 11-12 | 13-14 | 15+ |

Byte 0: packet type.
Bytes 1-2: rank of the sending node.
Bytes 3-4: node ID of the destination node.
Bytes 5-6: PAN ID of the network the sending node belongs to.
Bytes 7-8: node ID of the sending node.
Bytes 9-10: packet number.
Bytes 11-12: rank of the original sender of the message.
Bytes 13-14: sequence number of the original sending node.
Bytes 15+: rest of the message payload, if any.

Figure 6. Extreme-LT header frame format.

| 06 | FFFF | 0000 | 3412 | FFFF | 0100 | 0000 | 0100 |

Request message, short packet: 15B (no payload)

| 03 | 0100 | 0000 | 3412 | 3AC6 | 0A00 | 0100 | 0100 | 48E26300... |

Data message, long packet: 95B = 15B header + 80B payload

Figure 7. Extreme-LT header examples, with and without payload.

The general functionality of a sending node under the protocol can be seen as a state machine in Figure 8, and Figure 9 shows the corresponding one for the root node. The purpose of the sending nodes is to connect to the network in the best possible conditions, to then start measuring data from the sensors and sending it towards the sink node. For this, a sending node will broadcast a request message when booted. This is the first route creation mechanism provided by the protocol. Any node that receives this message will respond with a unicast discovery message directed to that node. The discovery message contains network advertisement information, including the rank of the node within the network topology. The new node will retrieve the network information from the message and store the node ID as its parent, assigning itself a rank one step higher than the rank of the parent. When other nodes in range also receive the request and send their discovery messages back to the new node, if their rank is better than the current parent or they have equal rank but a higher RSSI, the new node will accept them as its new parent node, replacing the former one. If the rank is lower, the discovery message will be ignored. This mechanism ensures that every node will connect to the reachable parent that offers the best connection to the sink, optimizing the route composition and reducing the number of relay hops as much as possible.

The same request-discovery mechanism triggers when a node loses connection to its parent. When a node encounters a fatal transmission problem at its data link layer, after retrying for a given amount of attempts, the node will delete its parent and broadcast a request, accepting a new parent with the best rank from the nodes within its range. After that, it will broadcast a repair command so that their child nodes can repair themselves, updating their routes and ranks. From the perspective of the rest of the network, this mechanism works as if the node had just been turned on as a new addition to the network, although internally the node will increase its sequence number, so it can track the number of times it has been forced to repair its route.

The second mechanism apart from the request-discovery method, is the network creation from the root. When the root node is booted, it will broadcast a discovery message to advertise the network. Every node in range will connect directly to it, since the sink has rank 0, and spread the network advertisement by broadcasting a discovery message with their own rank. Both mechanisms coexist so the creation of the network can be done in a flexible way, while also making it robust in case of new additions or changes in the topology. An example of a normal startup, depicting both mechanisms, is shown in Figure 10. The flow chart shows a situation where a node A is deployed on its own, with no other nodes nearby to connect to. It will request a rank and receive no answer. After that, the root node is plugged. It will create a network and broadcast a discovery message that node A will receive, accepting the root as its parent node. It will then spread the discovery to other nodes (none in this case). After a while, a node B is connected, and will broadcast a request as node A did. Assuming that the root node is out of range and node A is the only one able to respond to, it will send back a discovery message, being a unicast in this case. Node B will accept node A as its new parent and then it can begin the data transmission towards the network sink through it.

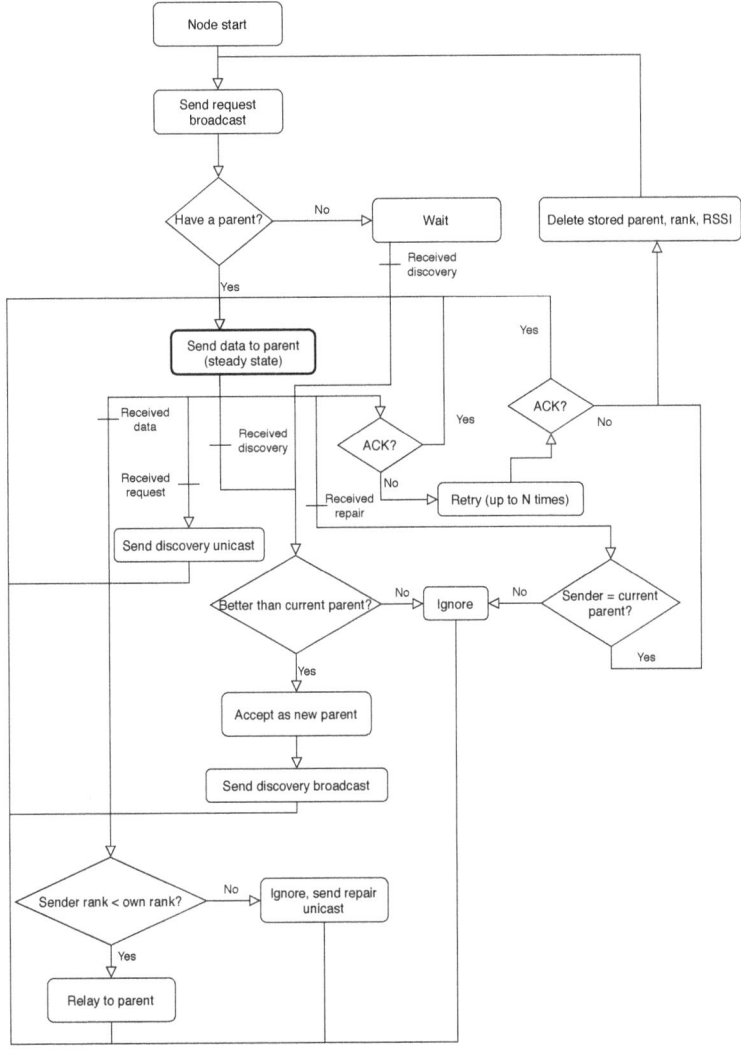

Figure 8. State machine of a sending node (non-root) under Extreme-LT.

After the network is established, the nodes will start sending their data to the sink node. For this, the data packets are always sent to the parent node. The node will first inspect the packet header, checking if the destination is their own node ID or another node ID upstream, i.e., the root ID. It will also check if the rank of the sending node is correct. If it is correct, it will relay the message upstream, or process the content of the payload if the destination was its own node ID. If not, there is an error in the network, since that node should not be sending data to this one. The node will ignore the data packet and send back a unicast repair message.

When a node receives a repair command, it will first filter it compared to its parent node ID. A node will only accept repair commands from its parent. If the sender node ID is the node ID stored as parent, the node will delete it and broadcast a request. After this, it will send broadcast a repair command so its child nodes, if any, will repair themselves and update their routes and ranks. The protocol can be condensed into these two rules:

- A node will only send data packets to its parent node. A data packet from a lower ranked node implies the network topology has changed and needs to be repaired.
- A node will only accept repair commands from its parent node. Repair commands received from any other node will be ignored.

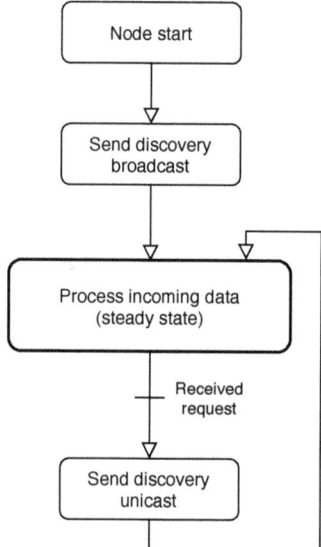

Figure 9. State machine of the sink node (root) under Extreme-LT.

The robustness of the protocol comes from its simplicity. Loops are avoided by ensuring a node will only accept a parent if its rank is the best among all reachable nodes, and will only accept repair commands from the node it has stored as its parent. Discovery messages from nodes with a rank that is not better than the current one will be ignored, and repair commands received from any node that is not its parent will be ignored as well.

As a summary, Extreme-LT is a distance vector protocol developed for the testing and validation of the Cookie platform, but not exclusive to it. It is based on the creation of DODAGs, relying on the robustness granted by the route creation mechanism to implement a reactive maintenance strategy. This way the control packet flow within the network is minimized, reducing the route overheads.

The following section presents the tests carried out on the hardware platform to validate its performance under the protocol, detailing the testing conditions and procedure, the parameters used and the results obtained, which are analyzed and discussed subsequently.

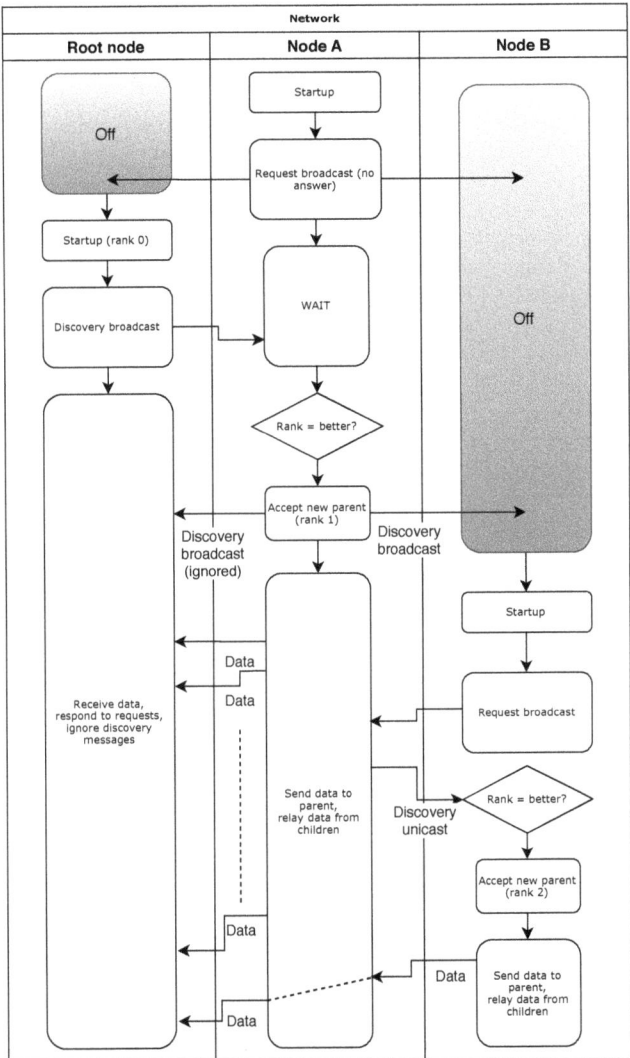

Figure 10. Message exchange in a normal operation under Extreme-LT.

4.1. Preliminary Tests

4.1.1. Range Tests

Before testing the performance of the nodes using the protocol, outdoor tests have been carried out to determine the transmission power of the Cookie platform and the maximum acceptable range of communication. The setup for the tests consisted on a sender node, deployed in a fixed position at ground level, sending packets periodically to a receiver node. The transmission power was set at 20 dBm, which is the maximum power gain of the antenna. The distance between the nodes was initially 1.5 m from which the receiver node was moved away, increasing the separation until the sink node was eventually unable to receive messages. This end condition was met at an approximate distance of over 130 m, beyond that distance the RSSI of the incoming messages was −85 dBm or lower and some of the packets were lost.

4.1.2. Traffic Tests

The next set of tests were designed to create heavy traffic conditions on the sink node and evaluate its capability to receive and process data from several nodes under such conditions. For this, the setup consisted on a receiver node connected to a terminal and 10 sending nodes deployed around it. Transmission power was set at −15 dBm. After being connected, all sender nodes started sending messages to the sink with the following parameters: sending interval = 0.1 s; packet size per transmission = 95 B; minimum number of iterations per node = 1000 (which means that the test lasted until every sending node had sent at least 1000 packets). This sets a worst-case scenario to analyze the performance of the protocol under such conditions. The results obtained are shown in Table 5, computing a total amount of 11041 packets, with PDR (number of packets received at the destination divided by the packets sent by the source, expressed as a percentage) mean equal to 98,4 %. From these outcomes, where the worst PDR was more than 96%, it can be concluded that the sink node is able to endure heavy traffic conditions, being able to receive and process most of the messages sent to it (certainly very close to 100%).

Table 5. Traffic test: saturation of the sink node.

	Node A	Node B	Node C	Node D	Node E
Received	1087	1079	1090	1094	1085
Total	1103	1099	1104	1103	1104
PDR (%)	98.606%	98.198%	98.808%	99.203%	98.308%
	Node F	Node G	Node H	Node I	Node J
Received	1095	1069	1090	1083	1089
Total	1103	1103	1112	1103	1107
PDR (%)	99.303%	96.1012%	98.24%	98.206%	98.414%

The results of these preliminary tests ensure the sink node will be able to support the incoming traffic and also determine the maximum transmission range of the nodes, and serve as the baseline for the following rounds of testing, in which the performance of the nodes under the routing protocol will be tested.

4.2. Extreme-LT Experimental Evaluation and Results

4.2.1. Setup, Test Procedure and End Conditions

Once the functionality of the platform was verified, a series of tests were performed to trial its behavior under the protocol dynamics, particularly pushing its operation to very extreme boundaries. For these tests, the nodes were deployed in an indoor environment, with the network distribution shown in Figure 11. In this schematic representation of the main lab room (approximately 238 m^2), the red dot represents the root node, acting as a sink, and the yellow dots represent the sensor nodes, able to both generate messages on their own and relay messages from other nodes. The rectangles represent the working disposition of the lab, just as a reference to show the distribution of the nodes and the different locations used during the deployment and testing process.

The setup parameters considered to perform the experimental tests are configured as follows: two packet sizes were used: small packets, with a length equal to 15 B, and large packets, with a length equal to 95 B. These two sizes correspond to those of control and data packets used by the protocol. The message interval for the sender nodes was established at 1 s, 0.5 s and 0.1 s respectively (so very aggressive traffic conditions, in which all the nodes are transmitting and routing packets intensively), with 3 different intervals tested over 2 different packet sizes, for a total of 6 test rounds, where each node generates a minimum of 1000 packets per iteration, as shown below. This setup parameters are summarized in Table 6.

Table 6. Parameters used for each round of testing.

Parameters	Round 1	Round 2	Round 3	Round 4	Round 5	Round 6
Packet size	15 B	15 B	15 B	95 B	95 B	95 B
Sending interval	1 s	0.5 s	0.1 s	1 s	0.5 s	0.1 s

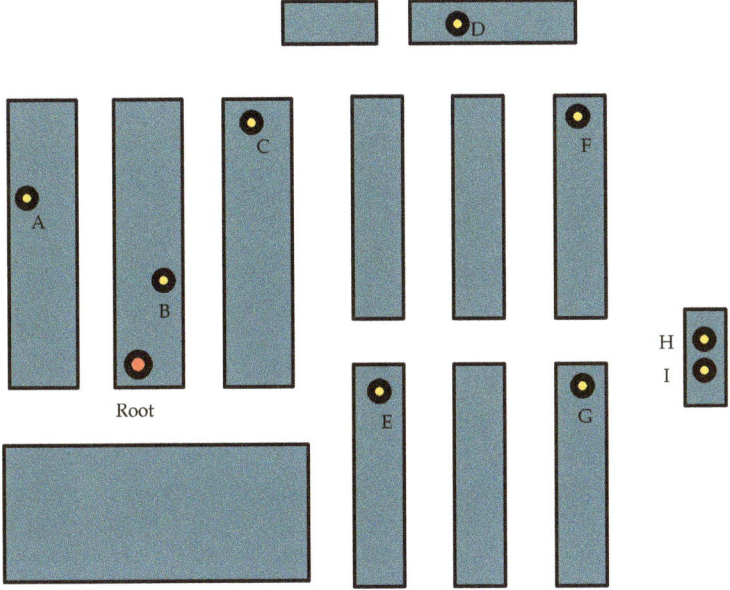

Figure 11. Distribution of the deployed sensor nodes for the routing protocol tests within the indoor scenario.

For each round of testing, the sensor nodes were deployed and turned on in the positions shown in Figure 11, then the root node was connected. By connecting the root node last, the route creation will start from the root node and propagate downstream to the rest of the nodes. This is the second network creation mechanism described in the protocol. An example of the network creation procedure for the setup used in the tests is shown in Figure 12. The topology is established by the network depending on the deployment conditions of the moment. After joining the network, each sensor node started sending packets towards the root node, be it directly or through multiple hops, bouncing in the intermediate sensor nodes. The distribution of the nodes in the lab was the same for all the tests, with their positions fixed, and the connections between them were established automatically according to the protocol, thereby creating some differences in the position of each individual node within the topology.

Because of these differences, the nodes will not be addressed individually but attending to their rank in the network: the sink node has rank 0, the nodes directly sending to it have rank 1, and so on.

Each round of testing was stopped after every node had sent a minimum of 1000 packets to the sink. With this, the PDR of the nodes can be measured and compared, to determine the impact of the packet size and sending interval.

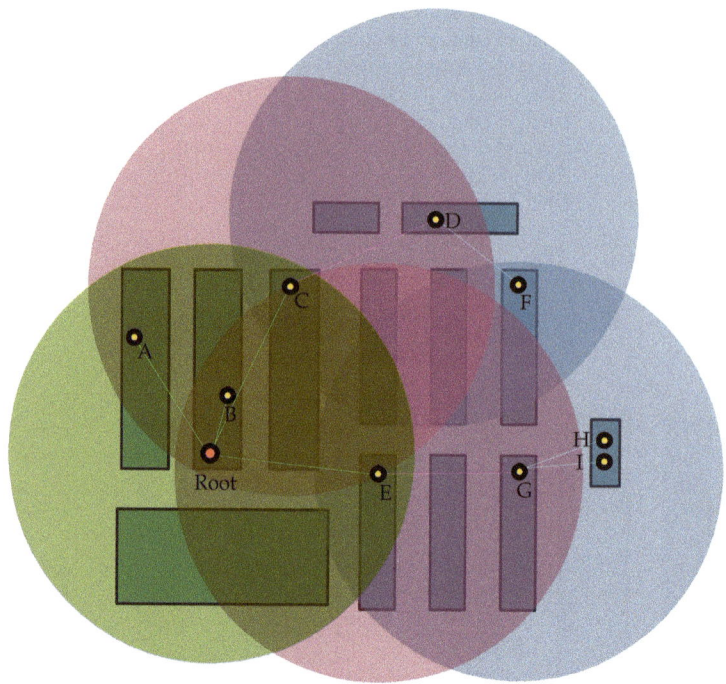

Route creation example:
1) Root connection (rank 0)
2) Root -> A, B, C, E (rank 1)
3) A -> root, B, C (ignored)
B -> root, A, C, E (ignored)
C -> D (rank 2), root, A, B, E (ignored)
E -> G (rank 2), root, B, C (ignored)
4) D -> C, F (rank 3)
G -> E, H, I (rank 3)
5) F -> D, H, I (ignored)
H -> G, F, I (ignored)
I -> G, F, H (ignored)

Figure 12. Example of network creation from the root.

4.2.2. Test results and discussion

The results obtained for each node, sorted by node rank, can be seen in Table 7. For each of the rounds of testing, the route creation mechanism established the network topology, resulting in the node distribution shown in Figure 13a–f.

From these results, it can be concluded that as expected, a lower sending interval increases the time the nodes are busy, making a node less capable of relaying messages. This condition makes the routing protocol produce more disperse routes with less child nodes per parent over a highly ramified tree, with many nodes connected to a single node in the same branch. This is, when the saturation of the nodes increases, the protocol tends to form N-ary subtrees with a lower N. In this way, the protocol avoids bottlenecks at route creation, even if it implies that the network will have a higher traffic overall (which ultimately compensates for the possibility of losing packets and/or the number of retransmissions produced by bottlenecks).

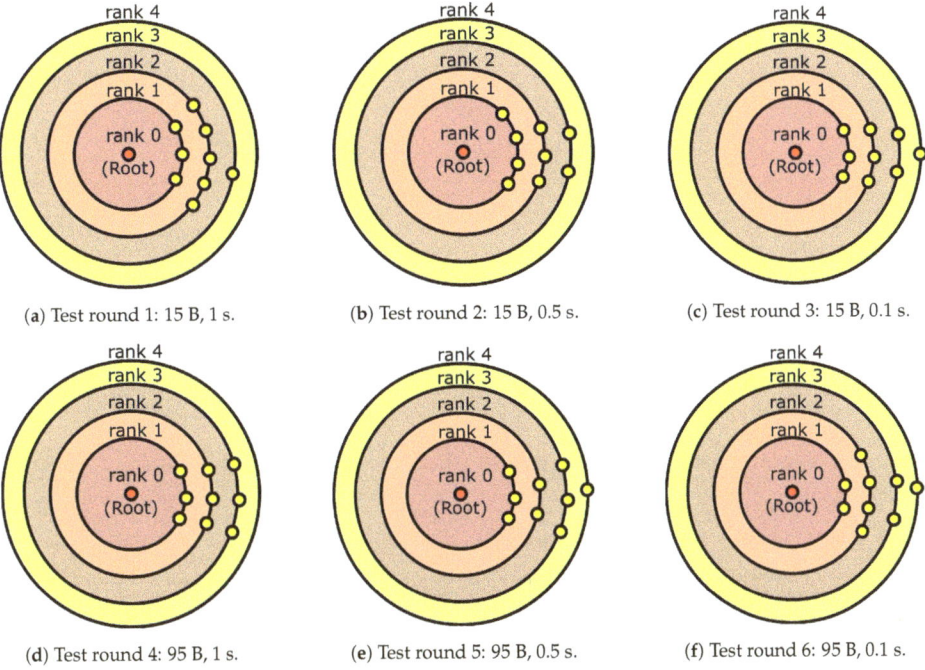

Figure 13. Node rank distribution generated for rounds 1 to 6.

In these circumstances, a node that could have rank 2 connecting directly to a rank-1 parent node has instead rank 3, because the rank 1 parent node is saturated and does not accept the request from a potential child node (which then connects to a higher rank node that is less saturated). On the other hand, this decision will effectively increase the traffic of the network, since the intermediate rank 1 node will have to route messages coming from all the nodes of its branch, regardless of whether they are sent directly to it or through a relay node.

Also, the congestion comes with a higher packet loss rate. By lowering the sending interval, the PDR from the higher rank nodes drops, reaching rates around 70% in the worst cases. This is due to the higher load put on the relay nodes, since those nodes must send their own messages and redirect messages coming from their child nodes.

For an easier interpretation, the results of each round of tests have been merged, grouping the received and total number of messages attending to the rank of the nodes and obtaining a combined PDR of the nodes with rank 1, rank 2 and so on. These combined results are depicted in Table 8.

A comparison of these results is presented in Figure 14. There is indeed a tendency to avoid bottleneck nodes and disseminate the routes. Such a tendency is accentuated as the sending interval decreases, as can be seen when comparing the results from round 3 to rounds 1 or 2, but there is no direct correlation between the increase in sending frequency and a lower PDR in some cases. As the figure shows for rounds 5 and 6, a faster sending interval (T = 0.1 s) for the same packet size forced the network to route packets in a different way, achieving better delivery rates for each rank than those obtained for a slower message frequency (T = 0.5 s). This is explained by the route creation mechanism. The protocol chooses the best available parent at route creation, selecting the node with the best rank and RSSI as a new parent. Once the route is created and all nodes have started sending, it may occur that the parent node is saturated most of the time due to the high message load from other nodes, being unable to route messages. Thus, the node will delete it and look for a new one, selecting a parent able to correctly receive and route its messages (event with a higher rank) due to having lower load.

In a less saturated scenario, the node might retain its initial parent and stay working under heavier traffic conditions, resulting in a lower PDR. In more saturated circumstances, this initial parent was rejected due to its high load and incapability to relay all the messages it received, resulting in a better PDR due to the reactive mechanism that establishes the routes.

Table 7. Individual node results for each test round.

Round 1	Node A	Node C	Node B	Node D	Node F	Node E	Node H	Node G	Node I
Received	1316	1366	1368	1365	1365	1367	1240	1362	1243
Total	1367	1369	1369	1369	1370	1368	1301	1370	1300
%	96.269%	99.781%	99.927%	99.708%	99.635%	99.927%	95.311%	99.416%	95.615%
Rank	1	1	1	2	2	2	2	2	3
Round 2	**Node A**	**Node C**	**Node E**	**Node B**	**Node F**	**Node G**	**Node D**	**Node I**	**Node H**
Received	1144	1137	1140	1132	1135	1132	1136	1136	1137
Total	1149	1179	1146	1135	1178	1149	1148	1179	1149
%	99.565%	96.438%	99.476%	99.736%	96.350%	98.520%	98.955%	96.353%	98.956%
Rank	1	1	1	1	2	2	2	3	3
Round 3	**Node A**	**Node B**	**Node G**	**Node D**	**Node C**	**Node E**	**Node I**	**Node F**	**Node H**
Received	1324	1339	1299	1172	1325	1280	1219	1189	915
Total	1342	1345	1341	1349	1345	1334	1333	1334	1088
%	98.659%	99.554%	96.868%	86.879%	98.513%	95.952%	91.448%	89.130%	84.099%
Rank	1	1	1	2	2	2	3	3	4
Round 4	**Node A**	**Node C**	**Node B**	**Node E**	**Node F**	**Node G**	**Node D**	**Node I**	**Node H**
Received	1184	1148	1169	1082	1120	1062	1105	1026	1035
Total	1203	1201	1201	1195	1190	1201	1189	1190	1191
%	98.421%	95.587%	97.336%	90.544%	94.118%	88.426%	92.935%	86.218%	86.902%
Rank	1	1	1	2	2	2	3	3	3
Round 5	**Node A**	**Node C**	**Node B**	**Node E**	**Node G**	**Node F**	**Node H**	**Node D**	**Node I**
Received	1322	1209	1369	1096	1044	994	918	930	823
Total	1382	1267	1380	1264	1266	1199	1267	1267	1197
%	95.658%	95.422%	99.203%	86.709%	82.464%	82.902%	72.455%	73.402%	68.755%
Rank	1	1	1	2	2	3	3	3	4
Round 6	**Node C**	**Node B**	**Node D**	**Node I**	**Node A**	**Node E**	**Node H**	**Node G**	**Node F**
Received	3653	4319	1486	764	2960	3326	834	1417	936
Total	3707	4345	1583	809	2983	3397	969	1473	1218
%	98.543%	99.402%	93.872%	94.438%	99.229%	97.910%	86.068%	96.198%	76.847%
Rank	1	1	2	2	2	2	3	3	4

Another aspect that stands out is the relationship between packet size and PDR. It is expected that bigger packet sizes will put a heavier load on the nodes and cause an increment in the time the nodes are busy processing the data, thus reducing the idle time they have left to relay messages from downstream nodes. A decrease in PDR is therefore expected, more noticeable as the number of hops increases. As it can be seen when comparing results obtained from rounds 1 and 4, or rounds 2 and 5, a bigger packet size for the same sending interval results in a worse PDR for nodes of the same rank. Also, it is important to highlight that the created traffic is a very extreme case of a normal application context, so it allowed to analyze experimentally the performance of the multi-hop communication strategy and the designed Cookie node under adverse traffic conditions.

Table 8. Combined PDR attending to node rank.

Test Round		Sum Rank 1	Sum Rank 2	Sum Rank 3	Sum Rank 4
Round 1					
	Received	4050	6699	1243	0
	Total	4105	6778	1300	0
	%	98.660%	98.834%	95.615%	0.000%
	Nodes	3	5	1	0
Round 2					
	Received	4553	3403	2273	0
	Total	4609	3475	2328	0
	%	98.785%	97.928%	97.637%	0.000%
	Nodes	4	3	2	0
Round 3					
	Received	3962	3777	2408	915
	Total	4028	4028	2667	1088
	%	98.361%	93.769%	90.289%	84.099%
	Nodes	3	3	2	1
Round 4					
	Received	3501	3264	3166	0
	Total	3605	3586	3570	0
	%	97.115%	91.021%	88.683%	0.000%
	Nodes	3	3	3	0
Round 5					
	Received	3900	2140	2842	823
	Total	4029	2530	3733	1197
	%	96.798%	84.585%	76.132%	68.755%
	Nodes	3	2	3	1
Round 6					
	Received	7972	8536	2251	936
	Total	8052	8772	2442	1218
	%	99.006%	97.310%	92.179%	76.847%
	Nodes	2	4	2	1

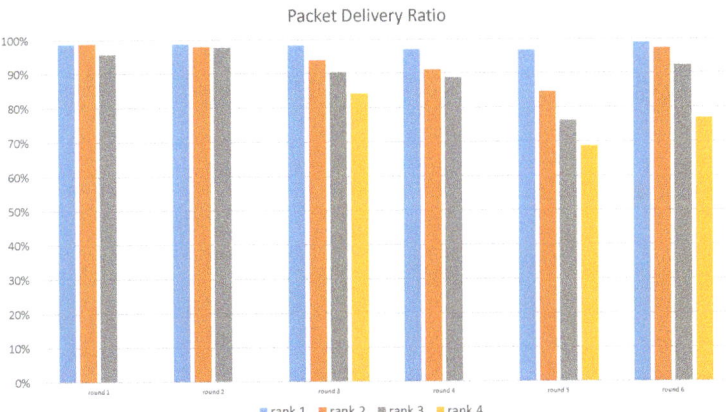

Figure 14. Results comparison of PDR for different packet sizes and sending intervals, grouped by node rank.

5. Conclusions and Future Work

In this work the new version of the Cookie node for the Extreme Edge of IoT is fully presented, a modular hardware platform conceived and designed to provide trustability and robustness necessary for the present and future of IoT applications, and based on the flexibility and scalability paradigm of the Cookie platform. The functionality of this Edge node has been showcased in real experimental performance tests to validate both the hardware and software integration of the proposed system. Additionally, a porting of the Contiki-NG operating system to the platform has been developed as an example of the flexibility and adaptability that is targeted with this new IoT sensor node, which opens the possibility of porting different operating systems into the platform in the future.

Moreover, a lightweight routing protocol designed for sink networks, one of the most commonly used topologies in IoT, is also presented. The protocol takes advantage of mechanisms used by other protocols and implements a simple, lightweight and robust multi-hop communication strategy for the Extreme Edge of IoT. Its performance has been tested on the Cookie platform, obtaining an extensive analysis of the routing mechanism within intensive communication scenarios with heavy traffic patterns, where the amount of data to be transmitted within the network has been overloaded to study the behavior of the sensor nodes within such extreme conditions.

On the other hand, security is a major concern in IoT, and the Edge is the most vulnerable part of the whole ecosystem. A hardware platform with a security-conscious conception during the design and implementation of the proposed Cookie Edge Node solution has been introduced. With very few costs and power consumption overheads, the security increases dramatically. Overall, the results show that a high balance between performance, security and power awareness, and self-diagnosis in dynamic scenarios (where the active operation, participation and collaboration among the nodes is an increasingly common feature in IoT), is certainly possible with the proposed design in this work. In this sense, the proposed Cookie platform is currently being used in practical use cases within the railway field, to provide trustability and chain of trust for on-board and on-track sensor network deployments. The presented platform is serving as the baseline IoT sensor node technology for such application contexts, and further in-field network deployments will be fully supported by this hardware platform.

Author Contributions: Conceptualization, P.M. and G.M.; Data curation, P.M. and G.M.; Formal analysis, P.M, G.M., J.S. and J.P.; Funding acquisition, J.P.; Investigation, P.M., G.M., J.S. and J.P.; Methodology, G.M. and J.P.; Project administration, G.M. and J.P.; Software, P.M. and J.S.; Validation, P.M. and G.M.; Writing—original draft, P.M, and J.S.; Writing—review & editing, G.M. and J.P. All authors have read and agreed to the published version of the manuscript.

Funding: This paper is a result of the SCOTT project (www.scottproject.eu) which has received funding from the Electronic Component Systems for European Leadership Joint Undertaking under grant agreement No 737422. This Joint undertaking receives support from the European Union's Horizon 2020 research and innovation program and several countries such as Austria, Spain, Finland, Ireland, Sweden, Germany, Poland, Portugal, Netherlands, Belgium and Norway..

Conflicts of Interest: The authors declare no conflict of interest.

References

1. Polastre, J.; Szewczyk, R.; Culler, D. Telos: Enabling ultra-low power wireless research. In *Proceedings of the 4th International Symposium on Information Processing in Sensor Networks*; IEEE Press: Piscataway, NJ, USA, 2005; p. 48.
2. Portilla, J.; Mujica, G.; Lee, J.; Riesgo, T. The Extreme Edge at the Bottom of the Internet of Things: A Review. *IEEE Sens. J.* **2019**, *19*, 3179–3190. doi:10.1109/JSEN.2019.2891911. [CrossRef]
3. Trilles Oliver, S.; González-Pérez, A.; Huerta, J. A Comprehensive IoT Node Proposal Using Open Hardware. A Smart Farming Use Case to Monitor Vineyards. *Electronics* **2018**, *7*, 419, doi:10.3390/electronics7120419. [CrossRef]
4. Mujica, G.; Portilla, J. Distributed Reprogramming on the Edge: A New Collaborative Code Dissemination Strategy for IoT. *Electronics* **2019**, *8*, 267, doi:10.3390/electronics8030267. [CrossRef]

5. Ronen, E.; Shamir, A.; Weingarten, A.; O'Flynn, C. IoT Goes Nuclear: Creating a Zigbee Chain Reaction. *IEEE Secur. Priv.* **2018**, *16*, 54–62, doi:10.1109/MSP.2018.1331033. [CrossRef]
6. Garg, H.; Dave, M. Securing IoT Devices and SecurelyConnecting the Dots Using REST API and Middleware. In Proceedings of the 2019 4th International Conference on Internet of Things: Smart Innovation and Usages (IoT-SIU), Ghaziabad, India, 18–19 April 2019; pp. 1–6, doi:10.1109/IoT-SIU.2019.8777334. [CrossRef]
7. Siboni, S.; Sachidananda, V.; Meidan, Y.; Bohadana, M.; Mathov, Y.; Bhairav, S.; Shabtai, A.; Elovici, Y. Security Testbed for Internet-of-Things Devices. *IEEE Trans. Reliab.* **2019**, *68*, 23–44, doi:10.1109/TR.2018.2864536. [CrossRef]
8. Mujica, G.; Rodriguez-Zurrunero, R.; Wilby, M.R.; Portilla, J.; Rodríguez González, A.B.; Araujo, A.; Riesgo, T.; Vinagre Díaz, J.J. Edge and Fog Computing Platform for Data Fusion of Complex Heterogeneous Sensors. *Sensors* **2018**, *18*, 3630, doi:10.3390/s18113630. [CrossRef] [PubMed]
9. Mujica, G.; Rosello, V.; Portilla, J.; Riesgo, T. Hardware-software integration platform for a WSN testbed based on cookies nodes. In Proceedings of the IECON 2012—38th Annual Conference on IEEE Industrial Electronics Society, Montreal, QC, Canada, 25–28 October 2012; pp. 6013–6018, doi:10.1109/IECON.2012.6389099. [CrossRef]
10. Silicon Labs. *efr32mg12 Datasheet*; Technical Report, 2018. Available online: https://www.silabs.com/documents/public/data-sheets/efr32mg12-datasheet.pdf (accessed on 18 March 2020)
11. Silicon Labs. *SI7021 Datasheet*; Technical Report, 2016. Available online: https://www.silabs.com/documents/public/data-sheets/Si7021-A20.pdf (accessed on 18 March 2020)
12. InvenSense. *ICM-20648 Datasheet*; Technical Report, 2017. Available online: http://www.invensense.com/wp-content/uploads/2017/07/DS-000179-ICM-20648-v1.2-TYP.pdf (accessed on 18 March 2020)
13. Microchip. *ATECC608A Datasheet*; Technical Report, 2017. Available online: http://ww1.microchip.com/downloads/en/DeviceDoc/ATECC608A-CryptoAuthentication-Device-Summary-Data-Sheet-DS40001977B.pdf (accessed on 18 March 2020)
14. Kim, H.S.; Andersen, M.P.; Chen, K.; Kumar, S.; Zhao, W.J.; Ma, K.; Culler, D.E. System Architecture Directions for Post-SoC/32-Bit Networked Sensors. In *Proceedings of the 16th ACM Conference on Embedded Networked Sensor Systems*; Association for Computing Machinery: New York, NY, USA, 2018; p. 264–277, doi:10.1145/3274783.3274839. [CrossRef]
15. Silicon Labs. *AN0007.1: MCU and Wireless SoC Series 1 Energy Modes*; Technical Report, 2017. Available online: https://www.silabs.com/documents/public/application-notes/an0007.1-efr32-efm32-series-1-energymodes.pdf (accessed on 18 March 2020)
16. Duquennoy, S. *More about Contiki-NG*; Technical report, 2017. Available online: https://github.com/contiki-ng/contiki-ng/wiki/More-about-Contiki%E2%80%90NG (accessed on 18 March 2020)
17. Eriksson, J. *Contiki-ng Porting to the EFR32 MCU*; Technical report, 2017. Available online: https://github.com/contiki-ng/contiki-ng/tree/046f283e241e7e73c454cfccc2783775076a3fe4 (accessed on 18 March 2020)
18. STMicroelectronics. *STM32F103ZG Datasheet*; Technical report, 2015. Available online: https://www.st.com/en/microcontrollers-microprocessors/stm32f103zg.html# (accessed on 18 March 2020)
19. Cypress Semiconductor Corporation. *PSoC5LP Datasheet*; Technical report, 2017. Available online: https://cdn.sparkfun.com/assets/e/6/1/8/4/PSoC_5LP_CY8C58LP_Family_DS.pdf (accessed on 18 March 2020)
20. Texas Instruments. *cc2538 Datasheet*; Technical report, 2015. Available online: http://www.ti.com/lit/ds/symlink/cc2538.pdf (accessed on 18 March 2020)
21. Samraksh. *DotNOW Emote Specification Sheet*; Technical report, 2012. Available online: https://samraksh.com/files/products/DotNOW/emote-spec-sheet.pdf (accessed on 18 March 2020)
22. Sparkfun Electronics. *Sparkfun freeSoC2 Retail Page*; Technical report, 2017. Available online: https://www.sparkfun.com/products/13714 (accessed on 18 March 2020)
23. Hsu, R.H.; Lee, J.; Quek, T.Q.S.; Chen, J.C. Reconfigurable Security: Edge-Computing-Based Framework for IoT. *IEEE Netw.* **2018**, *32*, 92–99, doi:10.1109/MNET.2018.1700284. [CrossRef]
24. Maletsky, K. Attack Methods to Steal Digital Secrets. White Paper, Atmel Corporation. 2015. Available online: http://ww1.microchip.com/downloads/en/DeviceDoc/Atmel-8949-CryptoAuth-Attack-Methods-Steal-Digital-Secrets-WhitePaper.pdf (accessed on 18 March 2020)

25. Henriques, M.S.; Vernekar, N.K. Using symmetric and asymmetric cryptography to secure communication between devices in IoT. In Proceedings of the 2017 International Conference on IoT and Application (ICIOT), Nagapattinam, India, 19–20 May 2017; pp. 1–4, doi:10.1109/ICIOTA.2017.8073643. [CrossRef]
26. Maletsky, K. RSA vs ECC Comparison for Embedded Systems. White Paper, Atmel Corporation. 2015. Available online: http://ww1.microchip.com/downloads/en/DeviceDoc/Atmel-8951-CryptoAuth-RSA-ECC-Comparison-Embedded-Systems-WhitePaper.pdf (accessed on 18 March 2020)
27. Dworkin, M. *Recommendation for Block Cipher Modes of Operation*; National Institute of Standards and Technology Special Publication 800-38A 2001 ED; National Institute of Standards and Technology: Gaithersburg, MD, USA, 2005; pp. 1–23, doi:10.6028/NIST.SP.800-38d. [CrossRef]
28. Dworkin, M. *SP 800-38D: Recommendation for Block Cipher Modes of Operation: Galois/Counter Mode (GCM) and GMAC*; NIST Special Publication; National Institute of Standards and Technology: Gaithersburg, MD, USA, 2007; volumn 800, pp. 1–39.
29. Xin, H.; Yang, K. Routing Protocols Analysis for Internet of Things. In Proceedings of the 2015 2nd International Conference on Information Science and Control Engineering, Shanghai, China, 24–26 April 2015; pp. 447–450, doi:10.1109/ICISCE.2015.104. [CrossRef]
30. Winter, T.; Thubert, P.; Brandt, A.; Hui, J.W.; Kelsey, R.; Levis, P.; Pister, K.; Struik, R.; Vasseur, J.P.; Alexander, R.K. RPL: IPv6 Routing Protocol for Low-Power and Lossy Networks. RFC 6550, 2012. Available online: https://tools.ietf.org/html/rfc6550 (accessed on 18 March 2020)
31. Jenschke, T.L.; Papadopoulos, G.Z.; Koutsiamanis, R.A.; Montavont, N. Alternative Parent Selection for Multi-Path RPL Networks. In Proceedings of the 2019 IEEE 5th World Forum on Internet of Things (WF-IoT), Limerick, Ireland, 15–18 April 2019; pp. 533–538, doi:10.1109/WF-IoT.2019.8767236. [CrossRef]
32. Bhandari, K.S.; Hosen, A.S.; Cho, G.H. CoAR: Congestion-Aware Routing Protocol for Low Power and Lossy Networks for IoT Applications *Sensors* **2018**, *18*, 3838, doi:10.3390/s18113838. [CrossRef] [PubMed]
33. Sheu, J.P.; Hsu, C.X.; Ma, C. A Game Theory Based Congestion Control Protocol for Wireless Personal Area Networks. In Proceedings of the 2015 IEEE 39th Annual Computer Software and Applications Conference, Taichung, Taiwan, 1–5 July 2015; pp. 659–664, doi:10.1109/COMPSAC.2015.21. [CrossRef]
34. Kharrufa, H.; A.A., A.K.H.; Kemp, A.H. RPL-Based Routing Protocols in IoT Applications: A Review. *IEEE Sens. J.* **2019**, *19*, 5962–5967, doi:10.1109/JSEN.2019.2910881. [CrossRef]
35. Gnawali, O.; Fonseca, R.; Jamieson, K.; Moss, D.; Levis, P. Collection Tree Protocol. In *SenSys '09: Proceedings of the 7th ACM Conference on Embedded Networked Sensor Systems*; ACM: Berkeley, CA, USA, 2009; pp. 1–14, doi:10.1145/1644038.1644040. [CrossRef]
36. Thubert, P. Objective Function Zero for the Routing Protocol for Low-Power and Lossy Networks (RPL). RFC 6552, 2012. Available online: https://tools.ietf.org/html/rfc6552 (accessed on 18 March 2020)
37. Pradeska, N.; Widyaman.; Najib, W.; Kusumawardani, S.S. Performance analysis of objective function MRHOF and OF0 in routing protocol RPL IPV6 over low power wireless personal area networks (6LoWPAN). In Proceedings of the 2016 8th International Conference on Information Technology and Electrical Engineering (ICITEE), Yogyakarta, Indonesia, 5–6 Octorber 2016. doi:10.1109/ICITEED.2016.7863270. [CrossRef]
38. Gnawali, O.; Lewis, P. The Minimum Rank with Hysteresis Objective Function. RFC 6719, 2012. Available online: https://tools.ietf.org/html/rfc6719 (accessed on 18 March 2020)

© 2020 by the authors. Licensee MDPI, Basel, Switzerland. This article is an open access article distributed under the terms and conditions of the Creative Commons Attribution (CC BY) license (http://creativecommons.org/licenses/by/4.0/).

Article

Energy Efficiency of Machine Learning in Embedded Systems Using Neuromorphic Hardware

Minseon Kang, Yongseok Lee and Moonju Park *

Department of Computer Science & Engineering, Incheon National University, Incheon 22012, Korea; kangpenguin@naver.com (M.K.); dyd9422@gmail.com (Y.L.)
* Correspondence: mpark@inu.ac.kr

Received: 25 May 2020; Accepted: 29 June 2020; Published: 30 June 2020

Abstract: Recently, the application of machine learning on embedded systems has drawn interest in both the research community and industry because embedded systems located at the edge can produce a faster response and reduce network load. However, software implementation of neural networks on Central Processing Units (CPUs) is considered infeasible in embedded systems due to limited power supply. To accelerate AI processing, the many-core Graphics Processing Unit (GPU) has been a preferred device to the CPU. However, its energy efficiency is not still considered to be good enough for embedded systems. Among other approaches for machine learning on embedded systems, neuromorphic processing chips are expected to be less power-consuming and overcome the memory bottleneck. In this work, we implemented a pedestrian image detection system on an embedded device using a commercially available neuromorphic chip, NM500, which is based on NeuroMem technology. The NM500 processing time and the power consumption were measured as the number of chips was increased from one to seven, and they were compared to those of a multicore CPU system and a GPU-accelerated embedded system. The results show that NM500 is more efficient in terms of energy required to process data for both learning and classification than the GPU-accelerated system or the multicore CPU system. Additionally, limits and possible improvement of the current NM500 are identified based on the experimental results.

Keywords: embedded system; artificial intelligence; hardware acceleration; neuromorphic processor; power consumption

1. Introduction

An Artificial Neural Network (ANN) consists of a large group of nodes, each of which is assigned a value or synaptic weight to act as an artificial neuron. Calculation of the weight for each neuron for learning and the weighted function value of the input vectors for classification requires large computing power; thus, massively parallel processing can be beneficial. Many-core CPUs and GPUs can be employed in a server for the acceleration of neural network computation to exploit the inherent parallelism of the ANN. Currently, GPUs are the most widely used hardware accelerator of artificial intelligence because GPUs are specialized in performing the same operations on many data instances simultaneously, which is inherently required in the ANN. However, CPUs and GPUs are power-hungry devices, and the energy-intensive computation of the ANN is one of the critical problems that make it difficult for the ANN to be used for power-limited embedded systems.

To make the neural network less power-hungry, the use of specially designed hardware dedicated to neural network performance has been studied. The use of Field-Programmable Gate Arrays (FPGAs) is one such effort; FPGAs consume less energy and can be configured as a custom neural-network-specific hardware [1,2]. A study comparing energy efficiency between an FPGA and GPU in [3] found that simple and parallel computations were performed well on the GPU, but the FPGA outperformed the

GPU in terms of energy efficiency as the complexity of the computational pipeline grew. FPGAs and GPUs offer suitability depending on the application specifications [4]. Thus, the hybrid use of both FPGAs and GPUs [5] has been researched as an efficient implementation of neural networks, especially on embedded systems that require both performance and energy efficiency [6].

Another approach to accelerate the neural network is the ASIC (Application-Specific Integrated Circuit) implementation of neural network models. In particular, neuromorphic chips have been developed to implement brain-like computation to overcome the memory bottleneck problem in parallel processing with von Neumann architecture processors. There are commercial neuromorphic chips available on the market, such as Intel's Loihi and General Vision's NeuroMem. ZISC (Zero Instruction Set Computer) is a hardware implementation of the ANN (Artificial Neural Network) commercialized by IBM, allowing massively parallel processing of digital data [7]. Its feed-forward network provides a nonlinear classifier, which can be used for unknown and uncertainty detection. Based on ZISC technology, General Vision developed the CM1K chip, which consists of 1,024 neurons that can store and process 256-byte length vectors [8,9]. The CM1K chip has been applied to face recognition [9], a fish inspection system [10], and an authentication system by face and speech recognition [8]. The NM500 chip is a successor of CM1K and consists of 576 neurons [11]. Neurons of NM500 have exactly the same behavior as those of CM1K, but it is operated at a higher clock rate and consumes less power. The possibility of adopting the NM500 chip for an ADAS (Advanced Driver Assistance System) has been discussed in [12].

While much research has been done to compare the performance and the energy efficiency of FPGAs and GPUs, little work can be found on neuromorphic chips. IBM's TrueNorth chip is reported as highly energy efficient in [13], and NM500's power consumption is available in the hardware manual. In [14], the authors studied the energy efficiency of a neuromorphic computing system using ReRAM (Resistive RAM). Others compared the performance of neuromorphic computing systems by simulation [15]. However, most research has focused on the neuromorphic chip's performance and power consumption. When it is used as an accelerator in a system, other factors such as data transfer from the host system and control subsystem for interconnection should be considered because the energy cost of data movement is much higher than that of computation [16]. Examining the benefits and the problems of the neuromorphic hardware accelerator for a real-world application needs to include an evaluation of the performance with a real target system.

In this paper, we study the performance and the energy efficiency of a neuromorphic chip employed in an embedded system using a currently available commercial neuromorphic chip, NM500, by comparing its performance and power consumption with those of CPU and GPU cores. To this end, a pedestrian image detection system was implemented and tested on a real target equipped with NM500 chips. The number of neurons in the tested neural network ranges from 576 to 4032 due to the hardware restriction of the evaluation board containing the neuromorphic chips. For these three different configurations (neuromorphic chips, GPUs, and CPUs) of embedded systems, the processing time and power consumption for learning and classification are measured, and the energy efficiency for processing a data instance is calculated and compared.

This paper is organized as follows. Section 2 provides a brief description of the neuromorphic hardware tested in this work. Section 3 explains the datasets and how they are preprocessed for evaluation. In Section 4, experimental results on the power consumption and performance in detecting pedestrian images using NM500 hardware are presented and compared with those on a CPU-only system and a GPU system. Finally, Section 5 discusses applications and possible improvements of the neuromorphic hardware.

2. Neuromorphic Hardware

The neuromorphic chip used in our work to accelerate AI processing in an embedded system is NM500 by Nepes, which is based on the NeuroMem technology of General Vision. An NM500 chip has 576 hardware neurons; a hardware neuron is an identical element that can store and process information simultaneously. They are all interconnected and working in parallel. NM500 makes these hardware components (neurons) collectively behave as a KNN (K-Nearest Network) or RBF (Radial Basis Function) classifier [11].

Figure 1 shows the interconnection architecture of the NM500. Logically, the network is three-layered: one input layer, one hidden layer, and an output layer. All the neurons in the chip can be considered as nodes in the hidden layer. Each hardware neuron has 256-byte storage, which limits the input size to less than or equal to 256 bytes. The output size is 2 bytes, so the number of candidate class labels for training data is limited to 65,536. Input data and commands are fed to each cell in parallel, and neurons are daisy-chained to signal to the next neuron to accept the input data in training neurons sequentially. Though the layers cannot be made deeper, the hidden layer is extendable by stacking up multiple NM500 chips. The "Neuron interconnect" module shown in Figure 1 enables the use of multiple chips in parallel to expand the size of the neural network by an increment of 576 neurons.

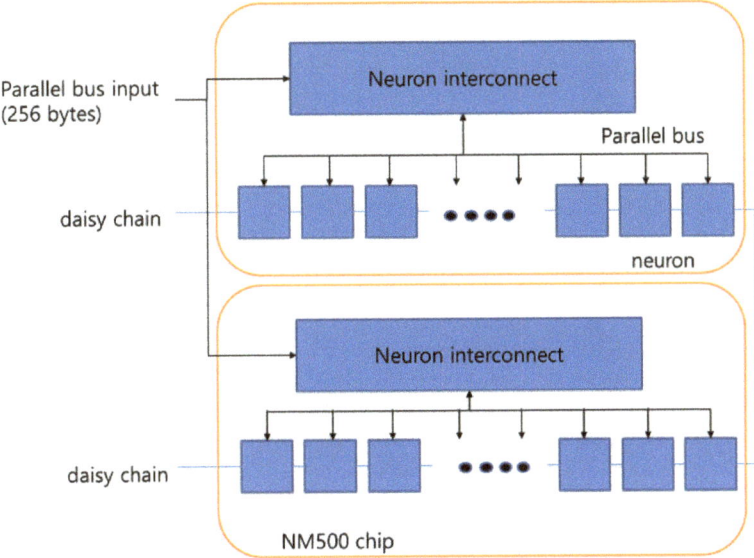

Figure 1. The interconnection architecture of the NM500.

A neuron has a model and IF (Influence Field) value after its learning process, stored in its volatile memory. When data are provided for classification, each neuron calculates the distance of a data point from its model and fires if the distance is less than the IF value. Each neuron examines the response of others on the parallel bus, and if another neuron reports a smaller distance value, then it withdraws itself [11].

The NM500's architecture is not meant to be configured to have a deeper neural network, which may affect accuracy for specific applications. However, because the neural network has only one hidden layer, the classification time of the neuromorphic hardware becomes almost constant. Considering the simplicity of the hardware configuration, it could be suitable for embedded systems whose requirements can be fulfilled by a relatively simple neural network.

3. Benchmark Problem and Data Preprocessing

Because embedded systems have scarce computing resources and power constraints, machine learning problems with a complex model are often infeasible to execute on the system. For example, AlexNet requires about 727 MFLOPS to process a 227 × 227-pixel image, while BCM2835 MCU in Raspberry Pi B development board delivers about 213 MFLOPS at peak operating frequency, which requires 3.4 s to process an image. Thus, we need to select a machine learning problem that can be feasibly executed on embedded systems.

Pedestrian detection is an important problem in computer vision and has broad application prospects, such as video surveillance, robotics, and automotive safety [17,18]. As autonomous driving systems emerge, detecting small-size pedestrians in images becomes more important [19]. Furthermore, pedestrian detection on an embedded system using GPUs has been studied by researchers, including a recent example in [20]. Thus, because of its practical importance and implementation feasibility, pedestrian detection using the RBF classifier was selected to benchmark the hardware accelerators for embedded systems in our experiments.

For test datasets, the INRIA Person Dataset [21,22], which is very popular in pedestrian detection research [23], was used for our experiments. From the dataset, HOG (Histogram of Oriented Gradient) features with the SVM classifier were extracted to detect a human in [21]. Normalized images in 128-by-64-pixel format were used in our experiments. A pedestrian data point consists of an image pair in which one is a mirror image of another. Non-pedestrian images were generated by randomly selecting 128-by-64-pixel areas from the original image. Table 1 summarizes the images used in our experiments.

Table 1. Dataset for experiments.

Use	Category	No. of Images
Training	Pedestrian	2416
	Non-Pedestrian	2416
Classification	Pedestrian	1132
	Non-Pedestrian	4531

First, the HOG is used as a feature descriptor for human detection to identify a pedestrian. The HOG descriptor methods have shown high performance in human detection and have been widely used for pedestrian detection [24,25]. The image is divided into local regions, where the gradient, direction, and size are computed using the differences in brightness between adjacent pixels. Histograms are generated using the calculated values to make feature vectors.

Because the NM500 chip has a memory of only 256-byte input, the HOG descriptors that are first generated with a high dimension (3780 in our implementation) are not suitable to be used. To reduce the dimension of the features, the PCA (Principal Component Analysis) method was adopted. PCA is a linear transformation feature extraction method that uses less data than the input data while maintaining the most important information of the input data [25,26]. Using the PCA method, the HOG features are transformed into 40-dimensional data. Finally, 32-bit floating-point features are quantized to 8-bit data using the vector quantization method in [27], which results in 160-byte input vectors.

4. Experimental Results

The neuromorphic chips are packaged into a hardware module named NeuroShield. The NeuroShield module is an evaluation board with one NM500 chip containing 576 neurons, on top of which three more extension modules can be stacked at most. The extension module has two NM500 chips and is called NeuroBrick. Thus, a NeuroShield module supports at most 4032 neurons. Because the NeuroShield module has one NM500, and each NeuroBrick module has two NM500 chips, the neuromorphic processing can be done with four different numbers of neurons: 576 with only the NeuroShield module, 1728 with one NeuroBrick on it, 2880 with two NeuroBricks, and 4032 at maximum.

To compare the neuromorphic chip-based system with other systems, the same pedestrian detection neural network was implemented on a CPU-only system and a GPU system. The CPU-only system is an embedded board with the Exynos5422 processor. The Exynos5422 CPU of the embedded board used in our experiments has an 8-core CPU, which consists of 4 fast (big) cores and 4 slow (little) cores. Because little cores are too slow to be used for neural network processing, only big cores were used in the experiments.

As a GPU system for comparison, Nvidia's Jetson Nano board with 128 GPU cores was used. The neural network on the GPU system was implemented using the Tensorflow-GPU library. The NeuroShield module was connected to the Jetson Nano board using an SPI (Serial Peripheral Interface) connection at 2 MHz. The power consumption of the NeuroShield module was measured separately from the Jetson Nano board. Table 2 summarizes the hardware configurations of each system test in the experiments. The neuromorphic system (NeuroShield) does not have a CPU or external memory because NM500 is not a Von Neumann architecture.

Table 2. Hardware specifications.

System Type	Accelerator	CPU	Memory
CPU system	None	Octa-core ARM @2 GHz (A15 × 4 & A7 × 4)	2 GB LPDDR4
GPU system	GPU (128 cores)	Quad-core ARM @1.43 GHz A57 × 4	4 GB LPDDR4
Neuromorphic system	NM500 (up to 7 chips)	-	256 B per each neuron

Figure 2 shows the power consumption of three implementations with different underlying hardware: NM500, GPU, and CPU-only. For the CPU-only system, we measured the power consumption in two cases: using only one core and using all four big cores. The GPU system consumes about 4.85–4.89 Watts on average. The power consumption of the GPU system includes the power consumed by the CPU in the system. For a fair comparison with the neuromorphic hardware, the power consumed only by the GPU cores needs to be measured, which could not be done because the GPU cores are integrated with CPU cores in the Jetson Nano SoC. Therefore, to estimate the power consumption of the GPU cores, the power consumption of the board with GPU cores off at idle state was measured, which is about 1.41 Watts on average. The GPU line in Figure 2 shows the power consumption of the entire system, while the GPU–idle line shows the power consumption estimated by subtracting the average power consumption of the Jetson Nano board at idle state with the GPU cores off.

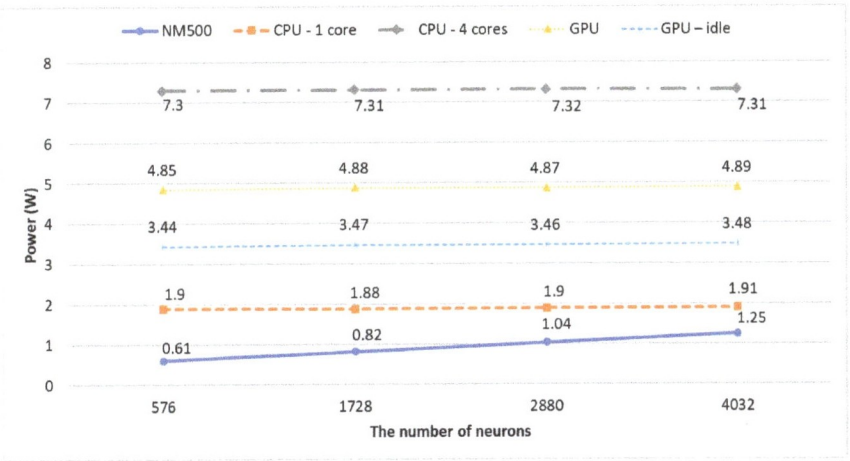

Figure 2. Average power consumption for varying numbers of neurons.

The GPU cores cannot be turned off partially; thus, the power consumption remains the same regardless of the number of neurons. The power consumptions of both the CPU-only and GPU systems are barely changed, while that of the NM500 system linearly increases as the number of chips (hardware neurons) employed increases. An additional NM500 chip containing 576 hardware neurons consumes approximately 100mW, so the total power consumption increases by 0.2 W for every additional 1172 neurons. The power consumption of the NeuroShield is a little higher than that of the NeuroBrick because the NeuroShield has an FPGA for interfacing with SPI, I2C, and USB.

Figure 3 shows the amount of time needed to train a neural network for the three systems. The time in the graph is in a base-10 log scale. Training on the CPU-only system takes much longer than other systems, about 15–185 times longer than the GPU system even though four cores are used. The learning time of the neuromorphic chip-based system is even shorter than that of the GPU system, by about 1300–1500%.

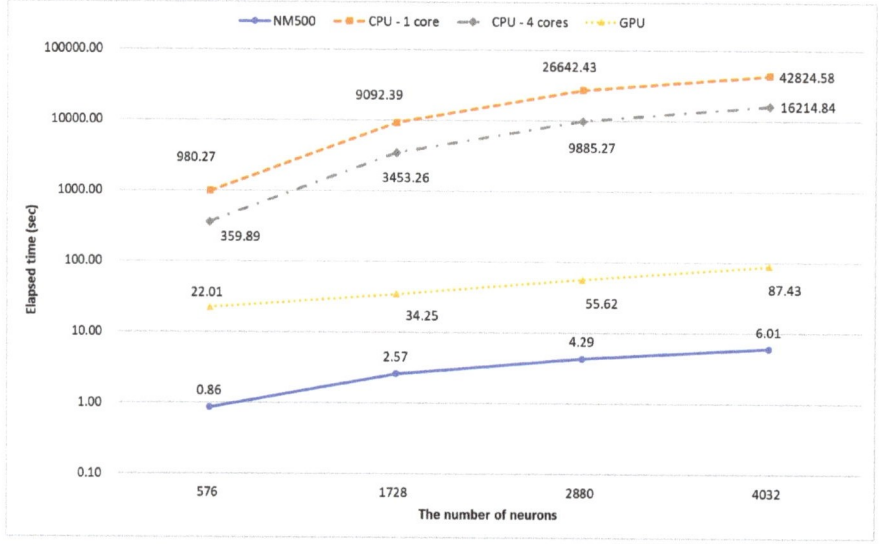

Figure 3. Time to train the model.

To determine the classification performance, 1132 pedestrian images and 453 non-pedestrian images were tested. The processing time of the neuromorphic-based system is unchanged even though the number of neurons used in the system is increased, as shown in Figure 4, because all hardware neurons are in the same layer and execute in parallel. On the other hand, the processing times of the CPU-only system and the GPU system increase as the number of neurons increase. Nevertheless, the GPU system is the fastest among the systems to process all the test images. We could not test with more neurons because the current NeuroShield does not support more than three NeuroBricks on it.

To determine the energy efficiency of the neuromorphic hardware, we calculated the amount of energy needed to process an image when each system is learning or classifying. The consumed energy for learning is shown in Figure 5, while the energy for image detection is shown in Figure 6.

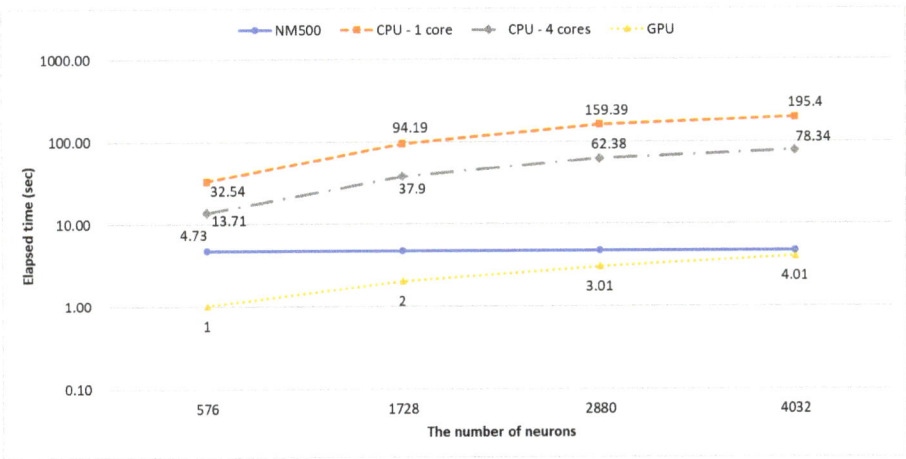

Figure 4. Time for processing all test data.

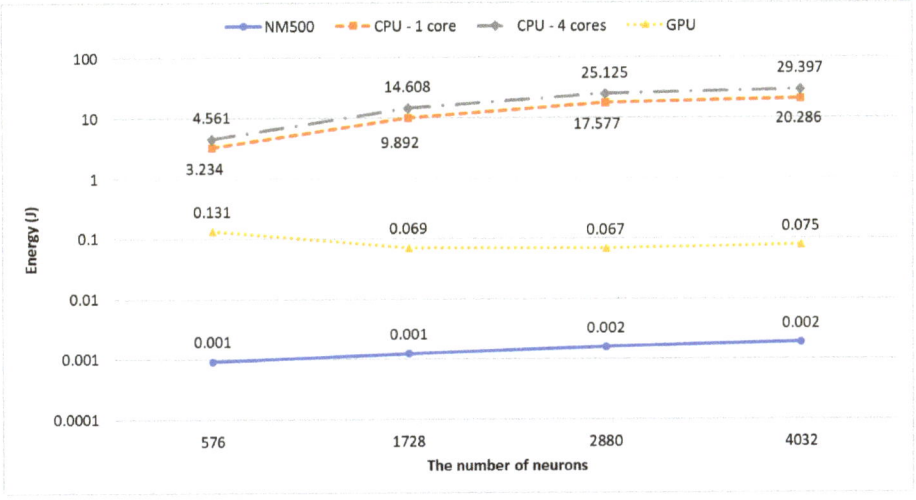

Figure 5. Energy per training data.

When training the neural network, the system with NM500 requires the least amount of energy to process an image data instance. The GPU system's energy efficiency is much better than that of the CPU-only system, but the efficiency of the neuromorphic chip-based system is over an order of magnitude higher than that of the GPU system in terms of per-data energy consumption. This is because both the power consumption and the processing time of the NM500 are much lower than those of the GPU system.

For classification, the required amount of energy consumed for a data instance by the GPU system is more than that of the neuromorphic system but is not very high (<2.5 times). Though the power consumption of the GPU system is higher than that of the NM500 system, the processing time of the GPU system is shorter than that of the NM500 system. The energy consumption of the GPU system in classification is much lower than that in training because less computation is needed in classification. However, the NM500 system consumes about 80% more energy for classification than learning.

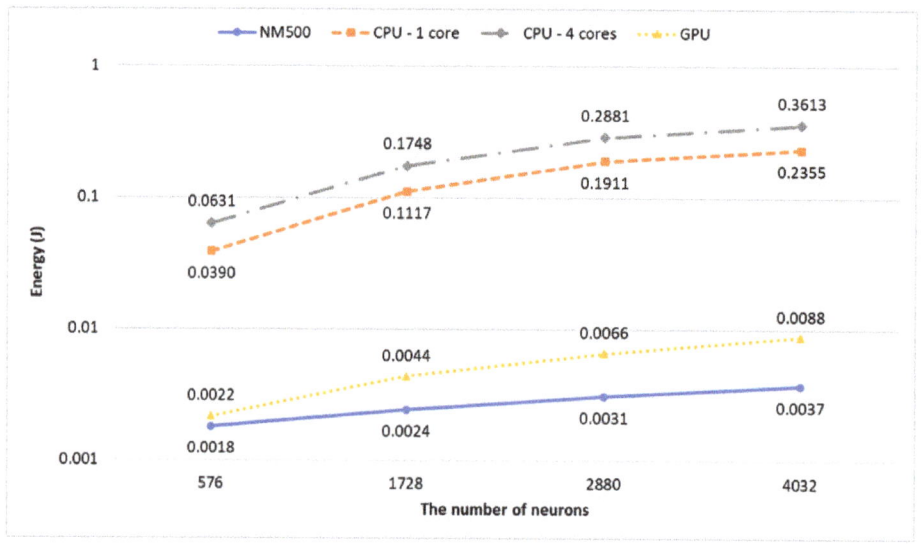

Figure 6. Energy per test data.

5. Conclusions

In this work, we compared the performance and the energy efficiency of a commercially available neuromorphic chip with those of GPU and CPU cores on embedded devices. The processing time and power consumption were measured while increasing the number of neurons in the neural network. The experimental results show that the time required for the neuromorphic chips to learn the same amount of data is about 13–15 times shorter than that required for the embedded system with 128 GPU cores. On the other hand, the time required to classify a dataset remains almost constant for the neuromorphic processor due to its neural network architecture with only one hidden layer. In classification, the GPU processes data faster than the neuromorphic chip, but the processing time tends to increase as the number of neurons increases. Thus, it is expected that the neuromorphic chips can outperform the GPU system with a larger number of neurons, but this could not be tested due to the restriction in the expandability of the evaluation board for the neuromorphic chips.

As most embedded systems depend on limited power supply such as batteries, energy efficiency is a critical factor in designing a system. In our experiments, the energy required for NM500 chips to process an input data instance is less than 1/35 of that required by the GPU accelerated embedded system in training the neural network, while the energy consumption of the GPU system in classification is only 1.22–2.37 times higher than that of NM500 chips. Because the neural network of NM500 has only one hidden layer, the processing time for classifying the given dataset remains almost the same even though the number of neurons increases, while the power consumption increases linearly. On the contrary, the classification time of the GPU system is almost linearly proportional to the number of neurons, while the power consumption remains unchanged. Therefore, the energy for the neuromorphic chips to classify data is expected to be close to 50% of that for the GPU system as the number of chips increases. It is interesting to note that the neuromorphic chips are especially energy efficient in training the neural network in comparison with the GPU system.

However, despite the high energy efficiency of the neuromorphic chip, it still needs to be improved. First of all, NM500's architecture can support only one hidden layer, which may restrict the possible benefit of deeper neural networks. Second, the lack of the ability to dynamically switch on and off a partial group of chips makes it difficult to manage power consumption. Finally, if high-speed interconnection such as AMBA or other high-speed bus protocols is supported, the processing time can be reduced further. The current SPI connection of the NM500 requires about 10 us to write a byte, a total 1660 us for learning a 160-byte data instance, which is done in about 2045 us. Therefore, communication via SPI interconnection accounts for about 82% of the total processing time. Integration of the neuromorphic chips into an SoC could be considered to improve the performance and the energy efficiency of machine learning on embedded systems using the neuromorphic hardware.

Author Contributions: M.K. performed most of the experiments in this paper, Y.L. performed preprocessing and analysis, M.P. performed analysis and wrote the original draft preparation. All authors have read and agreed to the published version of the manuscript.

Funding: This research received no external funding.

Acknowledgments: This work was supported by Incheon National University Research Fund in 2019.

Conflicts of Interest: The authors declare no conflicts of interest.

References

1. Guo, K.; Zeng, S.; Yu, J.; Wang, Y.; Yang, H. A survey of FPGA-based neural network interface accelerator. *ACM Trans. Reconfig. Technol. Syst.* **2018**, *12*, 2.
2. Shawahna, A.; Sait, S.M.; El-Maleh, A. FPGA-based accelerators of deep learning networks for learning and classification: A review. *IEEE Access* **2019**, *7*, 7823–7859. [CrossRef]
3. Qasaimeh, M.; Denolf, K.; Lo, J.; Vissers, K.; Zambreno, J.; Jones, P.H. Comparing energy efficiency of CPU, GPU and FPGA implementations for vision kernels. In Proceedings of the IEEE International Conference on Embedded Software and Systems, Las Vegas, NV, USA, 2–3 June 2019; pp. 1–8.
4. Jahnke, M.D.; Cosco, F.; Novickis, R.; Rastelli, J.P.; Gomez-Garay, V. Efficient neural network implementations on parallel embedded platforms applied to real-Time torque-vectoring optimization using predictions for multi-motor electric vehicles. *Electronics* **2019**, *8*, 250. [CrossRef]
5. Liu, X.; Ounifi, H.A.; Gherbi, A.; Lemieux, Y.; Li, W. A hybrid GPU-FPGA-based computing platform for machine learning. *Procedia Comput. Sci.* **2018**, *141*, 104–111. [CrossRef]
6. Tu, Y.; Sadiq, S.; Tao, Y.; Shyu, M.; Chen, S. A power efficient neural network implementation on heterogeneous FPGA and GPU devices. In Proceedings of the IEEE 20th International Conference on Information Reuse and Integration for Data Science, Los Angeles, CA, USA, 30 July–1 August 2019; pp. 193–199.
7. Zhang, D.; Ghobakhlou, A.; Kasabov, N. An adaptive model of person identification combining speech and image information. In Proceedings of the 8th Control, Automation, Robotics and Vision Conference, Kunming, China, 6–9 December 2004; pp. 413–418.
8. Suri, M.; Parmar, V.; Singla, A.; Malviya, R.; Nair, S. Neuromorphic hardware accelerated adaptive authentication system. In Proceedings of the IEEE Symposium Series on Computational Intelligence, Cape Town, South Africa, 7–10 December 2015; pp. 1206–1213.
9. Sardar, S.; Tewari, G.; Babu, K.A. A hardware/software co-design model for face recognition using Cognimem Neural Network chip. In Proceedings of the International Conference on Image Information Processing, Himachal Pradesh, India, 3–5 November 2011.
10. Menendez, A.; Paillet, G. Fish inspection system using a parallel neural network chip and the image knowledge builder application. *AI Mag.* **2008**, *1*, 21–28.
11. General Vision. NeuroMem Technology Reference Guide, Version 5.4. Available online: https://www.general-vision.com/documentation/TM_NeuroMem_Technology_Reference_Guide.pdf (accessed on 30 June 2020).
12. Kim, J. New neuromorphic AI NM500 and its ADAS application. In Proceedings of the International Conference on Advanced Engineering Theory and Applications, Ostrava City, Czech Republic, 11–13 September 2018; pp. 3–12.
13. Esser, S.K.; Merolla, P.A.; Arthur, J.V.; Cassidy, A.S.; Appuswamy, R.; Andreopoulos, A.; Berg, D.J.; McKinstry, J.L.; Melano, T.; Barch, D.R.; et al. Convolutional networks for fast, energy-efficient neuromorphic computing. *Proc. Natl. Acad. Sci. USA* **2016**, *113*, 11441–11446. [CrossRef] [PubMed]
14. Li, P.; Yang, C.; Chen, W.; Huang, J.; Wei, W.; Liu, J. A neuromorphic computing system for bitwise neural networks based on ReRAM synaptic array. In Proceedings of the IEEE Biomedical Circuits and Systems Conference, Cleveland, OH, USA, 17–19 October 2018; pp. 1–4.

15. Zhao, Z.; Wang, Y.; Zhang, X.; Cui, X.; Huang, R. An energy-efficient Computing-In-Memory neuromorphic system with on-chip Training. In Proceedings of the IEEE Biomedical Circuits and Systems Conference, Nara, Japan, 17–19 October 2019; pp. 1–4.
16. Sze, V.; Chen, Y.-H.; Yang, T.-J.; Emer, J.S. Efficient processing of deep neural networks: A tutorial and survey. *Proc. IEEE* **2017**, *105*, 2295–2329. [CrossRef]
17. Dollar, P.; Wojek, C.; Schiele, B.; Perona, P. Pedestrian detection: A benchmark. In Proceedings of the IEEE Conference on Computer Vision and Pattern Recognition, Miami, FL, USA, 20–25 June 2009; pp. 304–311.
18. Dollar, P.; Wojek, C.; Schiele, B.; Perona, P. Pedestrian detection: An evaluation of the state of the art. *IEEE Trans. Pattern Anal. Mach. Intell.* **2012**, *34*, 743–761. [CrossRef]
19. Zhang, X.; Cao, S.; Chen, C. Scale-aware hierarchical detection network for pedestrian detection. *IEEE Access* **2020**, *8*, 94429–94435. [CrossRef]
20. Barba-Guaman, L.; Naranjo, J.E.; Ortiz, A. Deep learning framework for vehicle and pedestrian detection in rural roads on an embedded GPU. *Electronics* **2020**, *9*, 589. [CrossRef]
21. Dalal, N.; Triggs, B. Histograms of oriented gradients for human detection. In Proceedings of the IEEE Conference on Computer Vision and Pattern Recognition, San Diego, CA, USA, 20–26 June 2005; pp. 886–893.
22. INRIA Person Dataset. Available online: https://dbcollection.readthedocs.io/en/latest/datasets/inria_ped.html (accessed on 24 February 2020).
23. Taiana, M.; Nascimento, J.C.; Bernardino, A. An improved labelling for the INRIA person data set for pedestrian detection. *Lect. Notes Comput. Sci.* **2013**, *7887*, 286–295.
24. Zhu, Q.; Avidan, S.; Yeh, M.; Cheng, K. Fast human detection using a cascade of histograms of oriented gradients. In Proceedings of the IEEE Conference on Computer Vision and Pattern Recognition, New York, NY, USA, 17–25 June 2006; pp. 1491–1498.
25. Kim, J.-Y.; Park, C.-J.; Oh, S.-K. Design & Implementation of Pedestrian Detection System Using HOG-PCA Based pRBFNNs Pattern Classifier. *Trans. Korean Inst. Electr. Eng.* **2015**, *64*, 1064–1073.
26. Jiang, J.; Xiong, H. Fast pedestrian detection based on HOG-PCA and gentle AdaBoost. In Proceedings of the 2012 International Conference on Computer Science and Service System, Nanjing, China, 11–13 August 2012; pp. 1819–1822.
27. Benoit, J.; Skirmanta, K.; Bo, C.; Zhu, M.; Tang, M.; Howard, A.; Adam, H.; Kalendichenko, D. Quantization and training of neural networks for efficient integer-arithmetic-only inference. In Proceedings of the IEEE Conference on Computer Vision and Pattern Recognition, Salt Lake City, UT, USA, 18–22 June 2018; pp. 2704–2713.

© 2020 by the authors. Licensee MDPI, Basel, Switzerland. This article is an open access article distributed under the terms and conditions of the Creative Commons Attribution (CC BY) license (http://creativecommons.org/licenses/by/4.0/).

Article

A Dynamically Reconfigurable BbNN Architecture for Scalable Neuroevolution in Hardware

Alberto García *, Rafael Zamacola, Andrés Otero and Eduardo de la Torre

Center for Industrial Electronics (CEI), Tecchnical University of Madrid (UPM), José Gutiérrez Abascal 2, 28006 Madrid, Spain; rafael.zamacola@upm.es (R.Z.); joseandres.otero@upm.es (A.O.); eduardo.delatorre@upm.es (E.d.l.T.)
* Correspondence: alberto.garcia.martinez@alumnos.upm.es

Received: 9 April 2020; Accepted: 9 May 2020; Published: 13 May 2020

Abstract: In this paper, a novel hardware architecture for neuroevolution is presented, aiming to enable the continuous adaptation of systems working in dynamic environments, by including the training stage intrinsically in the computing edge. It is based on the block-based neural network model, integrated with an evolutionary algorithm that optimizes the weights and the topology of the network simultaneously. Differently to the state-of-the-art, the proposed implementation makes use of advanced dynamic and partial reconfiguration features to reconfigure the network during evolution and, if required, to adapt its size dynamically. This way, the number of logic resources occupied by the network can be adapted by the evolutionary algorithm to the complexity of the problem, the expected quality of the results, or other performance indicators. The proposed architecture, implemented in a Xilinx Zynq-7020 System-on-a-Chip (SoC) FPGA device, reduces the usage of DSPs and BRAMS while introducing a novel synchronization scheme that controls the latency of the circuit. The proposed neuroevolvable architecture has been integrated with the OpenAI toolkit to show how it can efficiently be applied to control problems, with a variable complexity and dynamic behavior. The versatility of the solution is assessed by also targeting classification problems.

Keywords: neuroevolution; block-based neural network; dynamic and partial reconfiguration; scalability; reinforcement learning

1. Introduction

Artificial Neural Networks (ANN) are computational models inspired by the structure and physiology of the human brain, aiming to mimic their natural learning capabilities. ANNs excel in complex tasks, such as computer vision, natural language processing or intelligent autonomous systems, which are difficult to handle by using conventional rule-based programming languages. In addition, biological evolution has inspired the development of evolutionary engineering methods that exploit the benefits of Evolutionary Algorithms (EA) [1] as optimization and solution searching tools. Evolutionary engineering techniques have been applied in areas such as robotics [2], bioengineering [3], electrical engineering [4] or electromagnetism [5]. EAs have also been used to design and adjust digital circuits, which is known as Evolvable Hardware (EH) [6].

Natural learning and biological evolution are not independent processes. Natural brains are themselves products of natural selection. Similarly, EAs can be combined with ANNs to discover computing structures featured with learning capacities. The combination of both bio-inspired fields is known as neuroevolution [7]. It includes techniques to create neural network topologies, weights, building blocks, hyperparameters and even learning algorithms. One of the pioneering algorithms in neuroevolution is NeuroEvolution of Augmenting Topologies (NEAT). NEAT and their variants have been applied to evolve topologies along with weights of small recurrent neural networks, showing outstanding performance in complex reinforcement learning tasks [8,9]. Other researchers have focused on the evolution of deep neural network topologies and the optimizer hyperparameters, substituting handcrafted design and re-design steps with automated methodologies [10]. Deep neuroevolution requires intensive gradient-based training and evolution cycles, only appropriate to cloud facilities.

Differently to the state-of-the-art, a hardware-accelerated integrated solution for neuroevolution is proposed in this paper. In addition to the design automation benefits inherent to neuroevolution and the expected acceleration produced by hardware, implementing a neuroevolvable hardware architecture allows training (and re-training) the neural network, in an edge computing device, during its whole lifetime. This approach enables the continuous adaptation of systems working in dynamic environments. Continuous adaptation is not possible in conventional ANNs that use gradient-based backpropagation algorithms for training since the high computational demands associated with these algorithms require cloud or GPU-based computing resources, not available in the edge. However, the different nature of evolutionary algorithms makes possible the design of custom hardware accelerators for learning weights and topologies to be used directly in the edge.

The proposed neuroevolvable hardware architecture is based on the Block-based Neural Network (BbNN) template, initially conceived in [11]. A BbNN is a particular type of ANN, in which neurons are arranged as a two-dimensional grid of Processing Elements (PEs). Each PE is connected to its four nearest neighbors through four ports (north, south, east and west), which are configurable as inputs or outputs. Internally, each PE features one, two or three artificial neurons, depending on its configuration. The parallelism, regularity and high modularity of the BbNN model make it appropriate to be implemented in hardware. In this paper, we propose using a System-on-a-Chip (SoC) FPGA, in which a dual-core ARM processor and reconfigurable logic are combined in the same chip. The EA is executed in the processor, while candidate BbNN solutions are evaluated in the programmable logic, increasing the evaluation (and inference) throughput.

The size of the BbNN structure determines the complexity of the problems it can solve. It also has a significant impact on training time. The more complex a problem is, the bigger the BbNN has to be. However, bigger networks increase the design space to be explored during evolution, which may even prevent its convergence. Since the optimal size for a given problem is unknown in advance, it may be necessary to discover it by trial and error. In addition, when a network is applied to different problems during different system operation stages, it is expected that its size could be changed. For these reasons, the BbNN implementation we propose in this paper is dynamically scalable. Thus, the BbNN can be scaled up and down in size at run-time during the training process, adapting the number of neurons to the complexity of the task.

Dynamic scalability is achieved by using the Dynamic Partial Reconfiguration (DPR) technique, which allows modifying part of the logic while the rest of the device continues working. The proposal of this paper consists in composing the network at run-time by replicating the primary PE of the network, taking benefit of its regularity. This strategy reduces the memory footprint and the time required for scaling the network. It is enabled by the advanced reconfiguration capabilities provided by the IMPRESS [12,13] reconfiguration tool. Moreover, advanced fine-grain reconfiguration features are used in the proposed architecture to modify the parameters of the network during evolution, without requiring a global configuration infrastructure reaching each PE. Differently, the device reconfiguration port is used to modify the configuration parameters by writing the appropriate positions in the device configuration memory. This approach also reduces configuration time and resource occupancy.

The run-time adaptation features provided by the proposed architecture are applied in this work for controlling Cyber-Physical Systems (CPSs) working under dynamic conditions. Different environments included in the OpenAI toolkit [14] are used to benchmark the performance of the proposed architecture for control applications. The OpenAI toolkit defines control problems with different complexities. In particular, we have selected the inverted pendulum and the mountain car problems, as the test bench. When applied to control problems, the feedback provided by the environment after applying the actions generated by the BbNN is used as a reward, guiding the evolutionary algorithm. This means that evolvable BbNNs can be considered a form of reinforcement learning. We also prove how the proposed network can be applied in classification problems, such as the XOR.

The original contributions of this paper can be summarized as follows:

- A scalable BbNN hardware architecture with reduced usage of DSPs and BRAMs. The proposed architecture supports feedback loops, includes a novel synchronization mechanism and a simplified implementation of the activation function.
- A novel approach for the network adaptation that exploits the advanced dynamic and partial reconfiguration features offered by the IMPRESS tool to obtain dynamic scalability and an efficient parameter and topology configuration during evolution.
- The integration of the proposed architecture, implemented on an SoC FPGA, with the OpenAI toolkit, conforming a hardware-in-the-loop simulation platform. This platform shows the applicability of the proposed neuroevolvable hardware architecture as a reinforcement learning solution for control problems.

The rest of the paper is organized as follows: first, in Section 2, the basic operation principles and previous works on BbNNs are presented. In Section 3, the different approaches existing in the literature to implement dynamically scalable architectures are discussed. Then, Section 4 describes the proposed implementation for the BbNN architecture, while Section 5 provides the evolutionary algorithm used in this work. A description of how dynamic scalability and fine-grain reconfiguration are implemented in the architecture is included in Section 6. Section 7 provides use cases and implementation results, while conclusions and future work are tackled in Section 8.

2. Block-Based Neural Networks

In this section, the main background concepts related to Block-based Neural Networks and the existing implementations in the literature are described.

2.1. Basic Principles

BbNNs are a type of ANN in which neurons are arranged as a two-dimensional array of $n \times m$ PEs, as shown in Figure 1. The number of inputs of the architecture corresponds to the number of columns (m) in the matrix. Outputs are obtained from the PEs in the last row, leaving unconnected those that are not needed. Each PE is linked with its four closest neighbors, at the north, south, east and west directions. PEs placed at the last column are connected to those in the first column, forming a cylinder. Each PE has, therefore, four ports, which are configurable as inputs or outputs. Vertical links can be configured upwards or downwards, and horizontal links can be configured to the right or the left. Depending on the configuration of the ports, different types of processing elements are defined. Thus, PEs with 1-, 2- or 3-inputs (i.e., 3-, 2- or 1-outputs) are possible, up to a total amount of fourteen PE types, as shown in Figure 2. These types result from combining all the PE inputs with the outputs, with the only limitation that every input must be connected to, at least, one output. PEs with all inputs or all outputs are discarded to avoid inconsistencies within the network. Each processing element applies a neuron operator in each port configured as an output. Neuron operators in BbNNs do not differ from traditional units used in ANNs [11]. They perform a weighted addition of all the inputs and transmit the result to the output node, after invoking an activation function [15]. The activation function is non-linear, being the sigmoid or the hyperbolic tangent the most widely used. These functions are applied to introduce non-linear relations in the network, needed to approximate functions that involve non-linear relations between variables. Performing non-linear operations on hardware platforms, such as FPGAs, entails a high logic resource utilization, especially in terms of DSPs or LUTs.

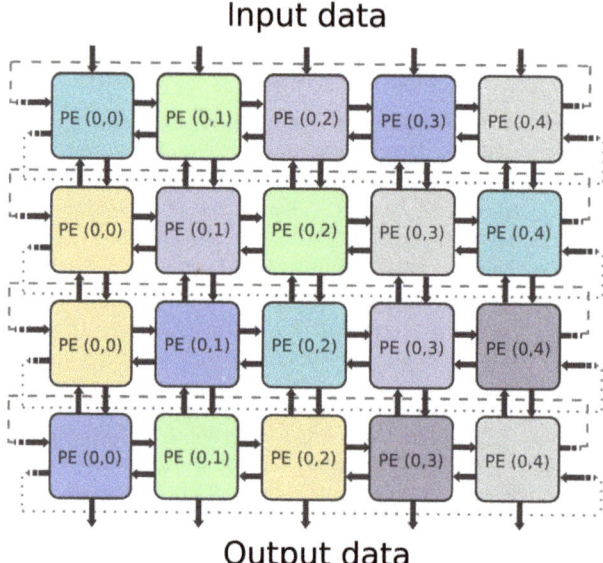

Figure 1. Block-based Neural Network layout.

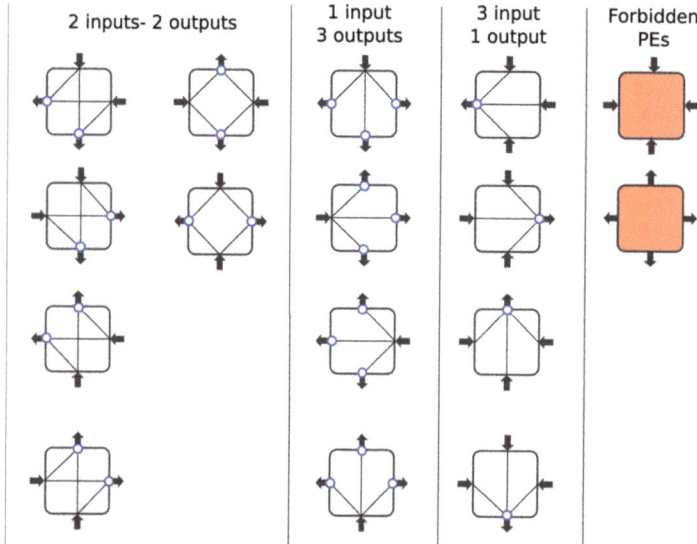

Figure 2. Processing Element (PE) schemes considered for the Block-based Neural Network.

Since the evolutionary algorithm can decide the direction of every link during the training stage, internal loops may appear. Internal loops feature the network with memory capabilities, so data from a previous state are combined with new data flowing through the network in subsequent time instants. Some examples of feedback loops are shown in Figure 3. Feedbacks are essential when solving time-dependent problems such as control or time series prediction. However, inner loops create data-paths with different lengths, and so they complicate discovering when input data have been completely processed. Knowing when the output data is valid requires synchronizing neuron activities. As it is exposed in Section 4, a synchronization mechanism based on tokens has been implemented in this work.

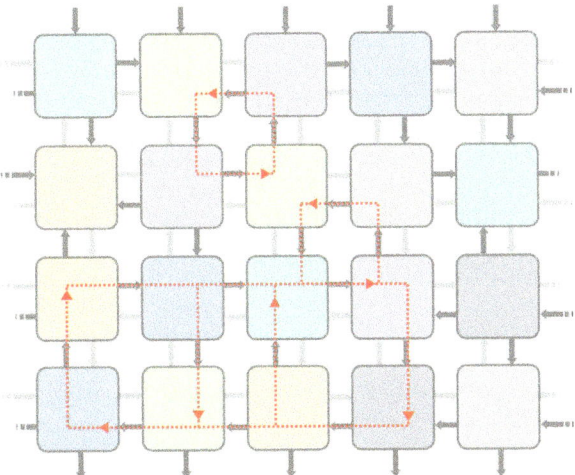

Figure 3. Inner feedback loops of a Block-based Neural Network (BbNN) configuration.

Authors in [11] demonstrate mathematically that for structures with a maximum of five inputs, the number of interconnections in a BbNN is higher than the corresponding value in a fully connected network. Therefore, BbNNs can replace traditional neural networks with a similar number of inputs while providing parallelism and scalability. Parallelism given by hardware acceleration enhances the throughput of the system, while the high regularity of the BbNN layout facilitates its scalability.

2.2. Related Works

Moon and Kong conceived the BbNN model in 2001 [11], as an alternative to general neural network models, specially designed to be implemented in reconfigurable hardware devices. Beyond the architecture, they also proposed the use of genetic algorithms for optimizing the structure and weights of the network. Following this initial work, various researchers have improved the architecture, the optimization method and the applications of the BbNNs, as described next.

The works by Merchant et al. present significant contributions in terms of the BbNN architectures [16,17]. They implemented a BbNN on an SoC FPGA device, that can be evolved online. In particular, the authors selected a Xilinx Virtex-IIPro FPGA featured with two on-chip PowerPC 405 processors. The EA, which is in charge of adapting the system when the operational environment changes, is executed in the on-chip processor, while the configurable BbNN model runs in the programmable logic. This approach is known as intrinsic evolution, since the EA directly changes the final hardware, instead of evolving it offline, using a software model. In this implementation, the Smart Block-based Neuron (SBbN) is proposed as the basic element of the BbNN. The SBbN is a software-configurable neuron, in which the on-chip processor controls the operation of the neuron. The authors present this approach as an alternative to include all the possible configurations of the neuron simultaneously and then selecting the appropriate one with a multiplexer. Differently, in this work, we propose a dynamically reconfigurable processing element, in which the modification of its functionality is carried out by writing in the device configuration memory. A mechanism for latency control using tokens, inspired by Petri networks, is also proposed in the works by Merchant. The token synchronization of this work is slightly different since our proposal also implements accept signals to avoid overwriting unconsumed data. In contrast to the solution proposed by Merchant, our architecture is fully pipelined, and it allows inner loops. These loops require a proper initialization of the tokens to avoid deadlocks in the network, which is shown in Section 4.4.

A new variant of the BbNN model, known as the Extended Block-based Neuron Network (EBbN), is presented in [18]. In contrast with classic BbNN implementations, the EBbN presents six input/output ports instead of four. However, possible configurations are limited since the north and south ports are always configured downwards. The two east and the two west ports can be configured to provide both side horizontal data flow, right or left data flow, or they may not provide either side data flow. The EBbN has a lower hardware overhead when compared with the SBbN. Authors achieve this by using the internal resources more efficiently since resource redundancy within the PE is eliminated. Pipeline registers are introduced to separate every row in the network. However, the EBbN model cannot be applied on large networks since the critical path still becomes longer as the number of stages increases. Differently, our approach is fully pipelined at all the outputs of each neuron (i.e., at horizontal and vertical directions). This pipeline scheme achieves higher operating frequencies than previous works, and hence the throughput of the proposed architecture is incremented.

Focusing on the implementation of the activation function, some works [16,19,20] present a LUT-based approximation of its non-linear section, where discrete values of the function are stored. This method achieves high accuracy but increases memory utilization unless all the PEs share a single LUT-based function, which in turn, constitutes a bottleneck. An alternative to the LUT-based activation function was presented in [21]. In that work, a sigmoid-like activation function is implemented as a piecewise-quadratic (PWQ) function (i.e., as a function defined by multiple sub-functions).

There have also been contributions in terms of the training algorithms. Although most of the BbNN-based systems are trained by using EAs, some works rely on alternative optimization methods. In [22], the problem is posed as a set of linear equations solved with the linear least-squares method. This approach provides good training accuracy for time-series prediction and nonlinear system identification problems. Authors in [23] propose the use of a multi-population parallel genetic algorithm (GA) targeting implementations on multi-threading CPUs.

Most of the implementations reported for the BbNN do not allow the inner feedback loops defined in the original model. Only in works by Nambiar [21,23] and Kong [11,24], topologies with feedback loops are addressed, showing how these feedback loops can lead to non deterministic results if all the PE outputs are not registered. The authors tackled this issue by introducing latency as a parameter to be controlled by the EA, encoded in the chromosome. In the present work, the uncertainties induced by feedback loops are controlled with the token synchronization.

In previous works, the BbNN model has succeeded in solving tasks of different domains such as classification, time series forecasting and control. In [25], it has been applied to ECG signal analysis and classification, such as arrhythmia detection [26] or driver drowsiness detection [27]. Hypoglycemia detection has been another use case of the BbNN related to the healthcare domain [28]. Time series prediction [22,24] and dynamic parameter forecasting [23] show the BbNN capabilities to solve tasks with temporal dependencies. This ability to solve problems where time is an intrinsic factor makes BbNN a good option to deal with control problems, like mobile control problems [11] or dynamic fuzzy control [29]. Real-time intrusion detection systems have also been developed in [30].

Apart from the works related to BbNNs, there are almost no hardware implementations of neuroevolvable systems providing continuous learning in the state-of-the-art. One of the most relevant works in this regard is the GenSys [31], an SoC prototype that includes an accelerator for the NEAT algorithm and an inference engine that accelerates in hardware the neural networks described by the evolutionary algorithm. At this regard, the work by A.Upegui on the evolution of spiking neural networks using DPR on commercial FPGAs is also notable [32].

In a more general sense, different circuit topologies have been proposed in the state-of-the-art to be used as part of evolvable hardware systems. Relevant examples are the Cartesian Genetic Programming (CGP) [33] or Systolic Arrays (SA) [34]. Both of them are based on meshes of interconnected processing elements that perform different functions from their inputs. In its standard form, the CGP corresponds to a computing graph that is directed and feed-forward. Therefore, a PE may only receive inputs from either input data or the output of a PE in a previous column [33,35]. Connectivity is CGP is achieved by adding large multiplexers at the input of each PE, which has a resource overhead that limits the size of the structure. In turn, SAs do not have such a high connectivity overhead since their dataflow is fixed and restricted to the closest neighbors of each PE.

3. Existing Approaches to Scalability

Scalable architectures offer significant advantages compared to fixed architectures. Their size can be adapted to change the quality of the results, to operate with inputs of different width or to modify its computation performance (e.g., adding more modules to exploit data parallelism). An architecture can be scaled at design-time (e.g., using generics in HDL descriptions [36]), or it can be scaled dynamically to deal with changing external conditions. Dynamic scalability requires using SRAM-based FPGAs, with dynamic partial reconfiguration (DPR) capabilities. DPR makes it possible to adapt part of the device fabric at run-time, while the rest of the system (i.e., the static part) remains uninterrupted. There are two concepts that are important to understand in dynamically reconfigurable systems, which are reconfigurable regions (RRs) and reconfigurable modules (RMs). The RMs are accelerators that can be exchanged in the system at run-time. On the other hand, the RRs are regions of the FPGA that have been reserved for allocating the RMs. This section introduces different approaches found in the literature to implement dynamically scalable architectures.

The most direct way to implement scalable architectures is to synthesize offline different variants of the same accelerator, with different sizes, and then to swap them in one Reconfigurable Region (RR) of the FPGA. This approach has been used in [37] to generate a scalable family of two-dimensional DCT (discrete cosine transform) hardware modules aiming at meeting time-varying constraints for motion JPEG. A similar approach is used in [38] to vary the deblocking filter size to adapt it to different constraints in H.264/AVC coding. In [39], the authors implement a CORDIC accelerator that can be scaled at run-time to work with different data types when the required dynamic range and accuracy change. A sharp drawback of this approach is that the whole RR remains occupied when the size of the architecture decreases, so it can not be reused for other modules.

A more efficient alternative to achieve real footprint scalability is to create several RRs, as shown in Figure 4a, and changing the size of the architecture by replicating modules in parallel. With this approach, free RRs can be reused for other RMs. This approach has been used in [40] with four RRs to allocate a scalable H.264/AVC deblocking filter. When the architecture can not be divided into different RMs, it is possible to arrange contiguous RRs in slot or grid styles [41]. In these configurations, one RM can be allocated in several RRs, as shown in Figure 4b. In this way, when the size of the architecture increases, the RM can use more RRs. This approach has been used in [42] to generate an architecture for DCT computation with three size levels that can be allocated in up to three contiguous slots.

The previous approaches can be used when the modules are connected directly to the static system. However, they are not valid in two-dimensional mesh-type architectures (e.g., BbNNs or systolic arrays) that have direct interconnections among neighboring processing elements. The most natural solution to interconnect RMs is to use static resources crossing the boundaries of their RRs. This approach is followed in [43], where the authors generate a triangular systolic array architecture for computing the DCT. The systolic array can be scaled using different RRs that can allocate a whole diagonal of PEs. The main drawback of this approach is that the communication among RRs is fixed, and therefore, it is not very easy to reuse the RRs for other accelerators. The authors in [44] solve this problem by using switching boxes that can be configured to adapt the interconnection among the PEs.

Using static but configurable interconnections among PEs offers excellent flexibility at the cost of having a considerable resource overhead. It is possible to reduce this overhead by using reconfigurable interfaces instead of a fixed infrastructure. A reconfigurable interface is composed of specific device routing nodes located at the border of the PE; if a neighbor module uses a compatible set of nodes in its interface, the communication between neighboring modules is enabled without requiring fixed interconnections. The authors in [34,45] used this approach to build a scalable systolic array for evolvable hardware and a scalable wavefront array to implement a deblocking filter. In both cases, the static system contains one RR that interfaces with the static system through specific nodes located at the border of the RR. The RR does not have static resources, and therefore it can be deemed as a grid-based RR that can allocate multiple PEs. In this way, the same RR can allocate several architectures with different communication schemes. Authors relied on the academic tool Dreams [46] to build these applications since commercial tools did not, and still do not provide these advanced reconfiguration features.

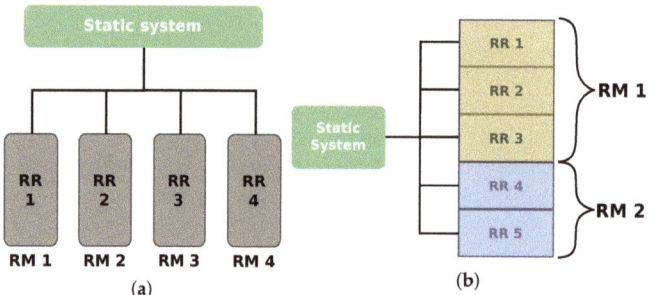

Figure 4. (a) Scalable architecture using multiple isolated reconfigurable regions connected to the static system. (b) Scalable architecture using multiple reconfigurable regions arranged in a slot style, where one reconfigurable module (RM) can span multiple reconfigurable regions (RRs).

It must be noticed that every module of the architecture does not have a fixed position in the device when its size changes. This fact limits the connection of the scalable architecture with the static system. The solution provided by the authors is to use only one input/output module located in one corner of the RR and to surround the architecture with communication and control modules that communicate the outer blocks of the architecture with the input/output instance. When using this approach, the RR can allocate several modules. One example could be connecting the static system to the 4 corners of the RR and allocating two-dimensional architectures or monolithic reconfigurable modules, as shown in Figure 5. In this case, the architectures can only grow at the expense of reducing the size of the other modules.

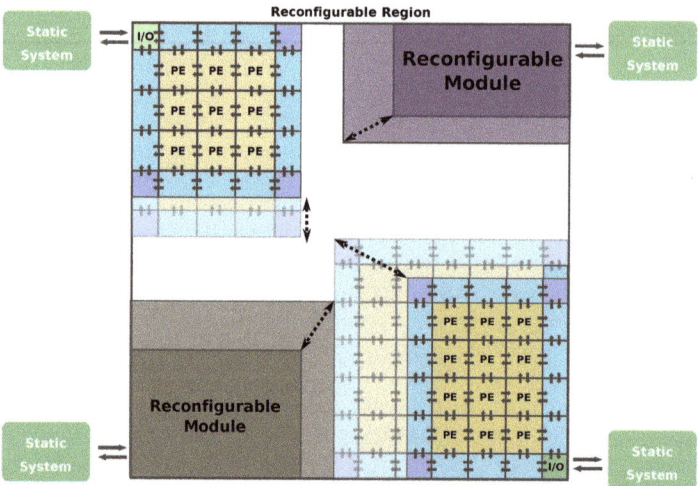

Figure 5. Scalable architectures using reconfigurable interconnections.

4. Proposed Bbnn Architecture

This section describes the reconfigurable and scalable architecture proposed to implement BbNNs in hardware. It aims to reduce the utilization of resources while keeping modularity and scalability. First, we focus the discussion on the implementation of the processing elements used as the basic building block for the BbNN. Then, the modules used for connecting the neurons and handling data within the network are described.

Each PE in the BbNN computes a variable number of outputs (K) with a given number of inputs (J) using the following expression:

$$y_k = g\left(b_k + \sum_{j=1}^{J} w_{jk} x_j\right), k = 1, 2, \ldots K \qquad (1)$$

where:

- g: is the activation function of the neuron.
- x_j: is the j_{th} input of the neuron.
- w_{jk}: is the is the connection weight between the j_{th} input and the k_{th} output.
- b_k: is the bias applied to the k_{th} output.
- y_k: is the k_{th} output of the neuron.

These arithmetic operations are proposed in the original model to be computed as floating-point numbers, including the non-linear activation function. A set of numerical optimizations are proposed first to provide an optimized hardware implementation.

4.1. Numerical Optimizations

We have studied first the most convenient fixed-point data representation and the approximation of the activation function to be used in the proposed hardware implementation.

4.1.1. Numerical Range for Inputs and Parameters

The numerical range has a straightforward impact on the hardware resource utilization and the size of the chromosomes used during training since the algorithm directly evolves these values. Therefore, it also affects the size of the design space to be explored.

In this work, we have decided to use a range of $(-4, 4)$. Experimentally, we have validated that this range is appropriate to activate or deactivate the network nodes during training. This choice is also coherent with the proposals existing in the literature. For instance, in [21], authors use the range of $[-3, +3]$. Notice that in both cases, the number of bits required for the representation of the integer part is the same. The complete fixed-point representation scheme is explained in the next section.

4.1.2. Fixed-Point Representation Scheme

A fixed-point representation has been chosen for the input data and all the intermediate computations, aiming at reducing the logic resources required when compared to the floating-point counterpart. We now describe the details of the selected representation, which is graphically shown in Figure 6.

All the registers and data ports are implemented using 16 bits. Since the integer part requires three bits to allocate the integer range of $(-4, 4)$, 13 bits remain for the fractional part. This scheme is used for inputs, weights and bias, but it is modified for the internal neuronal computations within a PE. The maximum number of concurrent connections to a single PE output is 3, as shown in Figure 2. It corresponds to a PE with a single output and three inputs, represented by Equation (2). Considering that weights have been limited to the range $(-4, 4)$, the range of values passed to the activation function is (−16, 16) as Equation (3) illustrates. The integer part of these values can be represented with 4 bits, plus an extra bit for the sign.

$$output = g\left(x_1 w_1 + x_2 w_2 + x_3 w_3 + b\right) \tag{2}$$

$$max.output = g\left(1 \times 4 + 1 \times 4 + 1 \times 4 + 4\right) = g(16) \tag{3}$$

Instead of enlarging the accumulation registers inside the PE, we opt for redistributing the 16 bits as follows. We dedicate now the 5 bits required for the integer part and the remaining 11 bits for the fractional part. This decision reduces the flip-flops required for the implementation of each PE.Output data from the activation function and input data to the PE are coded with the same fixed-point representation. Figure 6 shows the data representation at each computation stage.

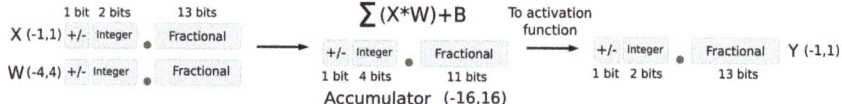

Figure 6. Fixed-point representation used in this work.

4.1.3. Approximation of the Activation Function

We use the sigmoid function as the activation function since it has proven in the literature to provide good results when used in BbNNs [21,25]. Other well-known activation functions reported in the neural network literature, such as the Rectified Linear Unit (ReLU), could also be appropriate from the algorithmic point of view. However, we have discarded the functions that are not constrained to a value range, which creates overflows and inconsistencies when dealing with fixed-point data types in hardware implementations.

As mentioned in Section 2, some authors used an LUT-based approximation for the approximation of the non-linear function, where discrete values of the sigmoid function are stored in pre-computed look-up tables. Thus, computing the activation function is reduced to finding in the table the value corresponding to the required point. However, this look-up table constitutes a bottleneck if multiple PEs require simultaneous access to this table. In an architecture with massive parallelism like BbNNs, sharing the activation function has a considerable impact on the processing throughput. As an alternative, piecewise quadratic (PWQ) functions can approximate the sigmoid without the necessity of LUTs. PWQ function technique implies performing multiplications, which require the usage of DSP units.

Differently, the proposal of this work consists in splitting the function domain into sub-functions whose operands can be represented as the addition of powers of 2, as shown in Equation (4). The selection of the appropriate sub-function (i.e., the corresponding tranche of the function) is carried out by evaluating the integer part (x_{int}) of the function argument. In turn, the fractional part (x_{frac}) is used to compute the output within each sub-function, by applying bit-shifting transformations.

$$g(x) = \begin{cases} 0, & \text{if } x_{int} < -4 \\ \dfrac{x_{frac}}{32}, & \text{if } -4 < x_{int} < -3 \\ \dfrac{x_{frac}}{32} + \dfrac{1}{16}, & \text{if } -3 < x_{int} < -2 \\ \dfrac{x_{frac}}{16} + \dfrac{1}{8}, & \text{if } -2 < x_{int} < -1 \\ \dfrac{x_{frac}}{8} + \dfrac{1}{4}, & \text{if } -1 < x_{int} < 0 \\ \dfrac{x_{frac}}{4} + \dfrac{1}{2}, & \text{if } 0 < x_{int} < 1 \\ \dfrac{x_{frac}}{4} + \dfrac{3}{4}, & \text{if } 1 < x_{int} < 2 \\ \dfrac{x_{frac}}{8} + \dfrac{7}{8}, & \text{if } 2 < x_{int} < 3 \\ \dfrac{x_{frac}}{16} + \dfrac{15}{16}, & \text{if } 3 < x_{int} < 4 \\ \dfrac{x_{frac}}{32} + \dfrac{63}{64}, & \text{if } 4 < x_{int} < 5 \\ 1, & \text{if } x_{int} > 5 \end{cases} \quad (4)$$

In Figure 7, the comparison of the approximate sigmoid function and the real function is exposed. Mean squared error between both functions in the non-linear section is 1.254×10^{-4}. This error is only calculated for the $(-6, 6)$ range since out of this range the sigmoid function is practically linear.

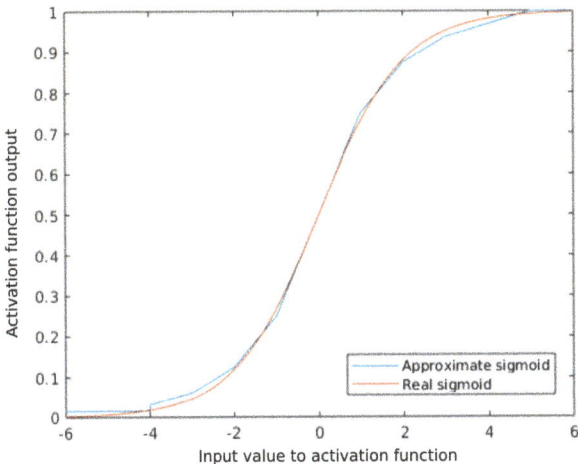

Figure 7. Comparison of the approximate sigmoid function and the real function.

4.2. Proposed Processing Element Architecture

As shown in Figure 8a, the interface of the processing element includes the following signals:

- Input data: one input signal per PE side (x_n, x_e, x_s, x_w)
- Output data: one output signal per PE side (y_n, y_e, y_s, y_w).

- Token signals: one token signal per input/output port. They are part of the synchronization mechanism. They indicate that intermediate results are ready to be consumed. They are set to one by the producer PE and set to zero by the consumer PE.
- Accept signals: one accept signal per input/output port. These signals avoid overwriting unconsumed data. They are also part of the token-based synchronization scheme. Accept signals are set to zero when the consumer has not consumed inputs or while it is triggered, and they are set to one when the link has no data, and the consumer PE is idle.

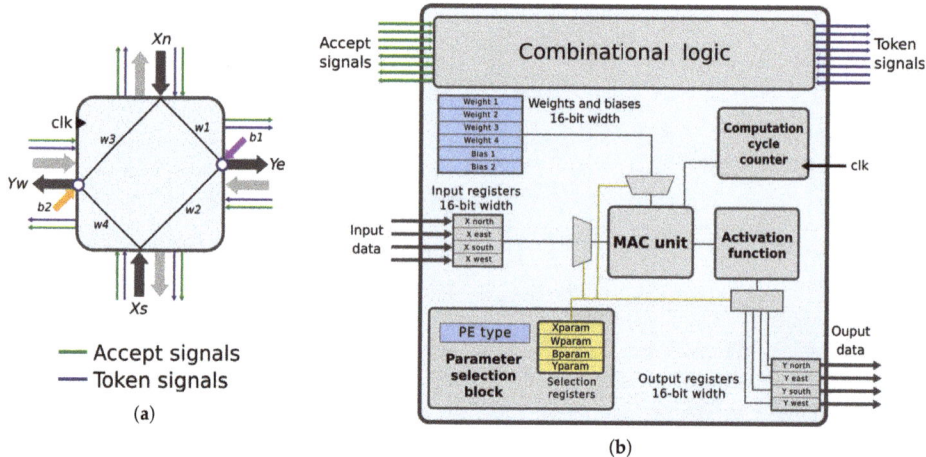

Figure 8. Proposed structure for the BbNN processing element. (**a**) Shows the interface and internal connections of one possible type of processing element (PE). (**b**) Exposes internal blocks of a generic PE.

Each PE is characterized by a set of parameters, represented as blue boxes in Figure 8b. These parameters fully define the behavior of the PE, including the PE type, the weights and the biases. They are implemented with LUTs that can be configured using the fine-grain reconfiguration technique detailed in Section 6. This way, each PE of the BbNN is configured without the need for a global configuration infrastructure. Thus, enhancing the scalability of the BbNN.

Apart from the PE parameters, each PE is composed of the following modules:

- Parameter selection block: it generates the signals that select the proper operands at the right clock cycles depending on the values stored in the parameter selection registers (*Xparam*, *Wparam*, *Bparam* and *Yparam*). These values are chosen from the PE type.
- MAC Unit: it performs all the calculations to generate the weighted sum during the computation cycle.
- Computation cycle counter: this counter controls the computation cycle stage.
- Activation function: this block computes the approximation of the sigmoid function, as it was described in the previous section.
- Synchronization logic: this logic checks the values of the token signals to trigger the computation cycle. When the operations are executed, it generates the output ports tokens. This logic also manages the accept signals.

Only one DSP per PE is needed, which is included in the MAC Unit. All the calculations of the neuron block are performed throughout seven clock cycles. The DSP is used sequentially during these clock cycles performing *multiply and accumulate (MAC)* operations with the appropriate operands. During the computation cycle, the Parameter Selection Block generates selection signals to indicate which input, weight, bias value and output is required at each cycle. This selection depends on the coded sequence stored in the fine-grain reconfigurable LUTs of the Parameter Selection Block. These values constitute the internal configuration of the PE. Once the weighted sum of a neuron's output is ready, its value is passed to the activation function block to generate the final output value. Table 1 illustrates how each parameter of the neuron is encoded.

Table 1. Signal coding for parameter selection.

SelX	Input	SelW	Weight	SelB	Bias	SelY	Output
00	X_n	00	W_1	0	B_0	0001	Y_n
01	X_e	01	W_2	1	B_1	0010	Y_e
10	X_s	10	W_3	-	-	0100	Y_s
11	X_w	11	W_4	-	-	1000	Y_w
-	-	-	-	-	-	0000	Reset acc.

The operations carried out in the seven clock-cycles are shown with an example in Figure 9. In the first clock cycle, the triggering condition of the PE is checked, and the values stored in the accumulator from previous clock cycles are reset. If the triggering condition is fulfilled, the PE parameters are read sequentially and decoded on the subsequent clock cycles. This decoding uses the values in Table 1 to generate the selection signals for each operand and the proper output at each clock cycle. Each neuron type has an unique codification for each selection signal (*SelX*, *SelY*, *SelB* and *SelY*).

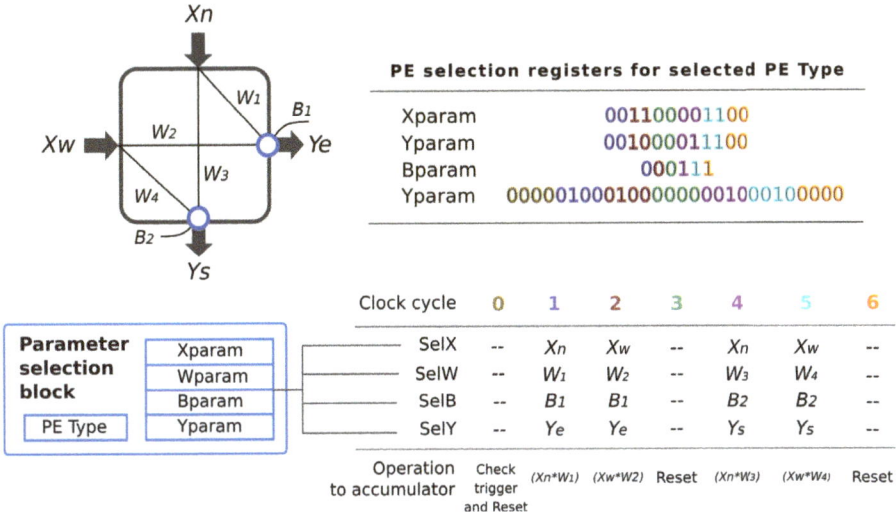

Figure 9. Values of the selection parameter register for the subscribed neuron type and read sequence.

Not all PE types require the seven clock cycles to compute the output. This value is defined by the worst case, which corresponds to a PE with the maximum number of outputs (i.e., 1-input/3-outputs). As the DSP is used sequentially, the accumulated results must be reset before computing a different PE output. With three outputs, two clock cycles are needed per output: one clock cycle to multiply the input and the corresponding weight, and an extra clock cycle to reset the accumulator. Therefore, six clock cycles are used as computation cycles, besides the additional clock cycle needed to check the triggering condition. In any case, the clock cycles not required by a given PE are lost, since all the PEs are synchronized every seven clock cycles.

4.3. From the Basic PE to the Block-Based Neural Network IP

The proposed BbNN has been integrated into an Intellectual Property (IP) core, as shown in Figure 10. The main component of the IP is the BbNN itself. At design-time, the BbNN is a dummy block reserved in a reconfigurable region. This reconfigurable region is then used to allocate PEs at run-time to compose a BbNN of a given size. The composition of the BbNN is carried out by reconfiguring individual PEs into the reconfigurable region. Each PE has compatible interfaces to neighboring PEs so that they connect directly without predefined static interconnections. Composing the BbNN in this modular way allows scaling its size efficiently by adding or removing PEs.

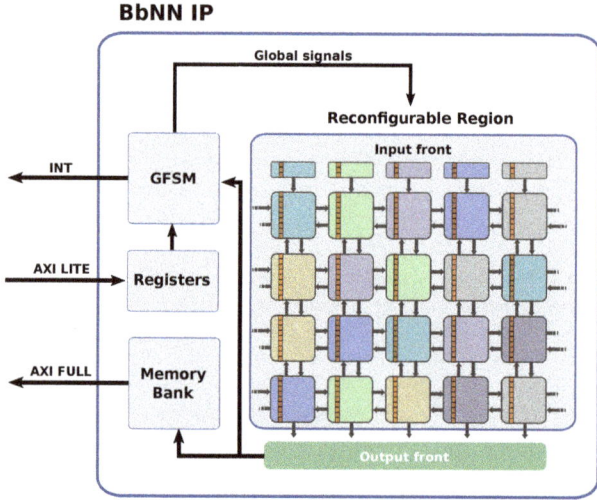

Figure 10. Block-based Neural Network Intellectual Property (IP) with fine-grain reconfigurable elements in each PE.

Once the BbNN has been composed, it can be configured using a technique called fine-grain reconfiguration that has been used in state of the art to reconfigure specific elements of an FPGA (e.g., LUTs) [47,48]. In the proposed BbNN each PE parameter (e.g., weights, biases) is implemented using LUTs whose output values can be modified by adapting the LUTs truth table using fine-grain reconfiguration. The IP also contains specific logic to provide the inputs to the BbNN via fine-grain reconfiguration. This way, a direct connection between the BbNN and the static system is not required, which enhances the scalability of the network. However, output signals are connected through the southern border of the reconfigurable region, independently of the size of the network. A memory bank accessible by the processor using an AXI interface has been included to store the outputs temporarily.

In summary, the proposed BbNN implementation relies on dynamic partial reconfiguration to (1) compose the BbNN on the fly by stitching together individual neuron blocks, (2) change the configuration of each neuron in the training phase and (3) providing the input values to the network. Details regarding the scalability and the configuration of the BbNN are described in Section 6.

The processor is also connected to the BbNN IP through an AXI lite interface that can be used to modify the BbNN configuration registers. These registers can be used to enable or disable the BbNN, asserting that a new input has been provided to the network or to select which network outputs are used. The General Finite State Machine (GSFM) controller is the component that reads the registers written by the user and writes the necessary control signals to the BbNN. These signals are connected to every PE of the network. To allow scalability, these signals use specific routing resources of the FPGA reserved to clocks and other global signals. Once the BbNN generates a set of valid outputs, the GSFM asserts an interrupt signal to indicate that the processor can read the output values and generate a new input signal.

4.4. Management of Latency and Datapath Imbalance

All the PE outputs include a pipeline register to keep the critical path of the circuit constant regardless of the BbNN configuration. Therefore, the latency of the network depends on the length of the paths between the inputs and outputs. By latency, we mean the number of cycles needed to process all the BbNN inputs until a valid output is generated. Since the dataflow is fully configurable, this latency is variable. This circumstance is shown in Figure 11, where two BbNN configurations with the same size and selected output, but different dataflows, are represented. Configuration in Figure 11a has a latency of 10 cycles, and configuration Figure 11b has a latency value of 18 cycles.

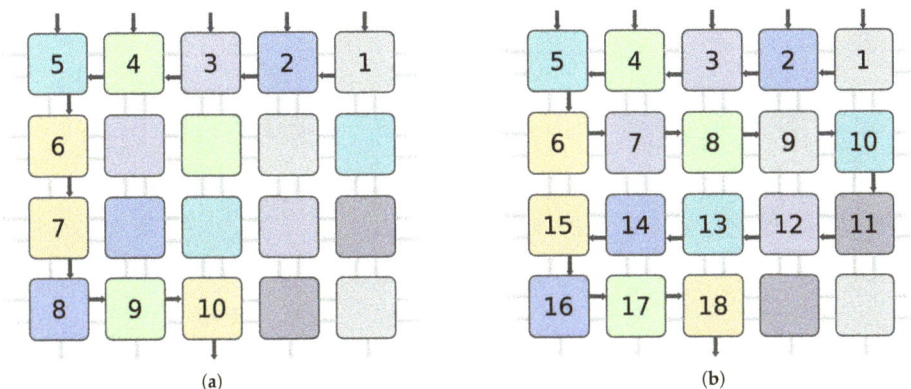

Figure 11. Configurations with the same dimensions and selected output but different latency. (**a**) shows a configuration with a 10 latency cycles; meanwhile (**b**) exposes a configuration with 18 latency cycles.

The dependency of the datapath length with the network configuration might also cause the computing imbalance at the PE level. If two paths arriving the same PE have different lengths, valid data will arrive at the PE at different control steps. In this work, the network latency and the datapath imbalance are controlled with a synchronization scheme based on tokens and accept signals. When an output from a neuron is ready to be used, a token is set at the pertinent link. PEs are only triggered if all the tokens at their input nodes are activated. Accept signals avoid overwriting a link with unconsumed data. This approach may cause deadlocks during the first calculation cycle if the BbNN configuration under test has feedback loops. Neurons influenced by feedback loop wait for other neurons in the loop to produce an output, leading to a deadlock. This scenario is avoided by setting to one the tokens in the upward vertical links by default at the first calculation cycle.

5. Proposed Evolutionary Algorithm

This section presents the EA used as the optimization mechanism in the proposed BbNN. EAs have been selected for driving the training of the network since they require fewer memory resources and a lower numerical precision when compared with other alternatives, including gradient-based methods. This makes them suitable for their intrinsic implementation in the SoC. The EA runs on the processor of the system, and its goal is to optimize data structures called chromosomes. These chromosomes encode complete configurations of the network, including weights, biases and port directions for every PE. BbNN codification within the chromosome structure is exposed in Figure 12. The size of the chromosome depends on the BbNN size. Larger networks require larger chromosomes since the EA uses a direct encoding. Weights and biases of each PE are represented with 16-bits per parameter (see Figure 12a). Dataflow configuration of the whole network is encoded with two bitstrings: E_param for East ports and N_param for North ports. Two bits per PE are needed to configure the dataflow. Figure 12b shows an example of the dataflow configuration generated by this combination of parameters. Therefore, each PE adds 98 bits to the chromosome size. A problem-dependent fitness score is assigned to every chromosome during the evaluation stage. This value is stored in each chromosome with a float variable. Each chromosome also has an associated age, whose functionality is explained next in this section, stored as an integer variable.

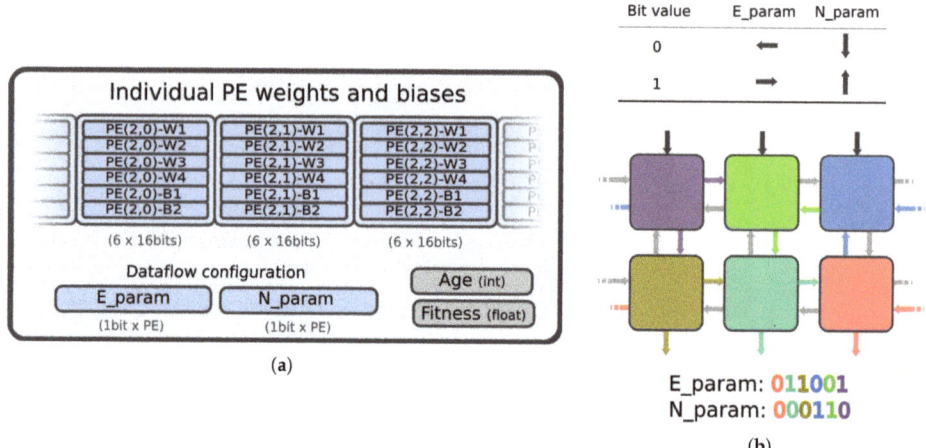

Figure 12. BbNN configuration encoded in the chromosome structure. (**a**) presents the representation of the chromosome structure. (**b**) exposes and example of dataflow configuration from bits in E_param and N_param.

The proposed algorithm is detailed in Algorithm 1. The algorithm takes as many iterations (generations) as needed to achieve a fitness score that exceeds the value defined as the target. The initial population of chromosomes is created randomly (line 1). At every generation, a mutation operator is applied over the whole population of chromosomes with different mutation rates (line 6). Thus, producing copies of the chromosomes with altered data. These copies are the offspring. The portion of altered data injected by the mutation operator is given by the mutation rate, which in the proposed algorithm decays in chromosomes with high fitness values. Therefore, good chromosomes suffer lighter mutations. Decaying the mutation rate enhances the performance of the algorithm since aggressive mutations on the dataflow may worsen the behavior of chromosomes with a high fitness value. In turn, chromosomes with undesired performance are removed from the population with two mechanisms: extinction and age threshold.

Each chromosome has an associated age. This value is incremented if any offspring chromosome improves the performance of the original one (line 12). A chromosome is removed if its age is over the maximum age, defined as an algorithm parameter (lines 13–15). This mechanism prevents the stalling of the evolutionary algorithm. After some generations, the extinction operator is applied over chromosomes with the lowest fitness values (lines 19–22). This strategy constitutes a kind of elitism: only the best chromosome is protected from extinction. Extinction is the second mechanism to prevent the algorithm from stalling while it increases the diversity of the population, thus avoiding to fall into local minimum points. All operators of the proposed EA are configurable with the parameters represented in Table 2. The values of these parameters have been set empirically to enhance the convergence of the EA. Another mechanism to prevent the stalling of the EA is the dynamic scalability of the network. If fitness value remains constant for several generations, the EA scales up the architecture by adding a row to the network.

The design of the fitness function is crucial for accomplishing a successful evolution process. This function must be adapted to the problem by the designer. In classification problems, the goal of the function is to assign a high score to chromosomes that result in higher classification accuracy. Meanwhile, in control problems, the fitness function is designed to assign high scores to those chromosomes which behavior achieves the requirements for the physical problem to be considered as solved. The design of each fitness function for each of the use cases described in this work is detailed in Section 7.

Algorithm 1: Evolutionary algorithm

```
1  Initialization(population);
2  bestFitness = evaluate(population);
3  generations = 0;
4  while bestFitness < targetFitness do
5      for chromosome in population do
6          offspring = mutation(chromosome);
7          bestFitnessMut = evaluate(offspring);
8          if bestFitnessMut > (chromosome.fitness) then
9              replaceChromosome(chromosome, offspring);
10             chromosome.age = 0;
11         else
12             chromosome.age++;
13             if chromosome.age > maxAge then
14                 remove(chromosome);
15             end
16         end
17     end
18     selectBest(population);
19     if subgenerations > ExtinctionFreq then
20         extinction(population);
21         subgenerations = 0;
22     else
23         subgenerations++;
24     end
25     generations++;
26 end
```

Table 2. Parameters of the Evolutionary Algorithm.

Parameter	Type	Value	Functionality
TargetFitness	Float (0, 1.0)	Application dependant	Desired fitness
Pop-size	Int	15	Number of chromosomes in the population
N-offspring	Int	10	Number of mutated copies from one chromosome
MaxAge	Int	7	Maximum number of stalled generations
ExtinctionFreq	Int	5	Generations between extinctions
MutationRate	Float (0, 1.0)	0.3	Percentage of data altered in the mutation

6. A New Approach to Build a Scalable Bbnn

Enhancing the BbNN model with dynamic scalability allows handling the size of the network as a parameter to be optimized at run-time, instead of being fixed at design-time. This way, the optimization algorithm can find the appropriate size, as a trade-off between the size of the design space under exploration and the capability of the architecture to undertake complex problems. Dynamic scalability is also useful in applications in which changing the network size leads to different quality levels. In these applications, it is possible to adapt the size of the BbNN according to different run-time constraints, such as energy consumption, quality of results or available logic resources in the FPGA.

Its modular design and the distributed nature of its control make the BbNN an excellent candidate to be implemented in a grid-based RR, using specific reconfigurable interfaces. The proposed implementation is possible thanks to the use of the advanced reconfiguration features provided by the IMPRESS reconfiguration tool [12,13]. IMPRESS is an open-source (https://des-cei.github.io/tools/impress) design tool developed by the authors targeting the implementation of reconfigurable systems. IMPRESS has been designed with a particular focus on implementing scalable two-dimensional mesh architectures (i.e., overlays). Some features of IMPRESS that are of significant importance to build scalable overlays are the following: direct reconfigurable-to-reconfigurable interfaces, module (i.e., bitstream) relocation, the implementation of multiple RMs in the same clock region and decoupling the implementation of the static system and the reconfigurable modules. All these features allow the reconfiguration of multiple individual PEs in a single RR to compose at run-time a BbNN of any given size. Another feature of IMPRESS that is of great importance to implement scalable BbNNs is the possibility to instantiate LUT-based constants inside reconfigurable modules. This feature, known as fine-grain reconfiguration, allows changing these logic constants by reconfiguring a single device frame that spans one clock region column. A frame is the minimum reconfigurable unit of an FPGA. Fine-grain reconfiguration accelerates the reconfiguration of logic constants distributed throughout the device fabric. LUT-based reconfigurable components can be used to access the inside of a RR without needing a direct link to the static system. In the case of BbNNs, the purpose of fine-grain reconfiguration is twofold. First, it allows changing the configuration of the PEs without using any global bus interface. It also enhances scalability as it is possible to provide inputs to the network without using external communication modules that add overhead to the system.

The following is a description of the process of building a scalable BbNN with the aid of IMPRESS. First, it is necessary to generate the static system with a single RR that contains the interface of the output BbNN blocks. The interface of the RR can be easily defined by selecting which border (e.g., south) is used, and then IMPRESS automatically selects which routing nodes are used as interface points. Figure 13a shows an example of an empty RR with a south interface. The next step is implementing the reconfigurable PE. IMPRESS allows relocating reconfigurable modules in different RRs, whenever they have the same resource footprint (i.e., regions with the same resource distribution). Once all the modules have been implemented, it is possible to compose a BbNN of arbitrary size at run-time by reconfiguring individual blocks, as shown in Figure 13b. Notice that contrary to the Xilinx reconfiguration flow where each RM has to be allocated in a unique RR, IMPRESS can allocate inside a single RR multiple RMs that are interconnected to each other through reconfigurable interfaces.

During the run-time training of the BbNN, it is necessary to configure each PE of the BbNN to modify the weights, biases and the neuron type configuration. Fine-grain reconfiguration needs to be fast enough to be usable in the training phase of the BbNN, where a large number of potential candidate configurations have to be evaluated. To reduce the reconfiguration time, IMPRESS automatically groups all the LUT-based constants in the same column of device resources so that all the constants can be reconfigured by modifying a minimum amount of frames. This feature makes fine-grain reconfiguration fast enough to be used in the training phase of the BbNN. Fine-grain reconfiguration can also be used to enhance scalability. As explained before, the works presented in [34,45] surrounded the scalable architectures with communication and control modules that passed the input/output signals to the corresponding modules. This strategy can lead to considerable resource overhead for small overlays. This overhead is avoided in this work by providing the inputs to the BbNN with fine-grain reconfiguration. Figure 13c shows an example of a scalable BbNN with fine-grain constants grouped in columns to modify the BbNN configuration and the input modules.

As we have seen, the BbNN relies on two different reconfigurations techniques. The first one is used to allocate RMs inside the RR to change the size of the BbNN. The BbNN size is usually selected before launching the application. However, the EA can change it at run-time if the fitness value is stalled after a given number of generations, as shown in the experimental results. The second technique is the fine-grain reconfiguration, which is used to provide the inputs of the BbNN and also to configure the BbNN parameters during the training phase.

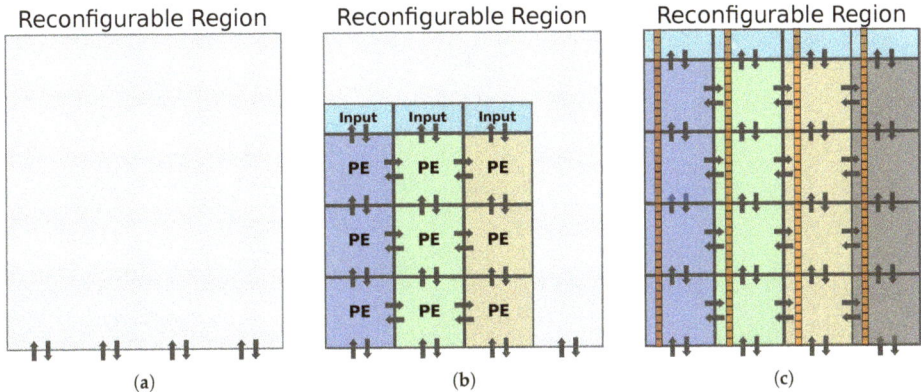

Figure 13. (a) Empty reconfigurable region. (b) reconfigurable region with 3 × 3 BbNN. (c) reconfigurable region with 4 × 4 BbNN showing LUT-based constants grouped in columns.

One difficulty that arises when building scalable BbNNs with reconfigurable interfaces and fine-grain reconfiguration is how to connect the edges of the network. This means, to close the structure as a cylinder, which is a convenient feature to increase the connectivity between input variables. The proposed implementation connects the edges by routing the signals through the interior of the BbNN, as shown in Figure 14. This approach increases the heterogeneity of the PEs. Instead of using the same RM, this solution requires three different RMs depending on the location (i.e., center or edge of the BbNN), which hinders PE relocation. Moreover, bypass signals crossing the BbNN form a combinatorial path which size increases with the size of the BbNN. When building larger BbNNs, these routes can become the critical path, thus limiting the maximum system frequency. In the cases where the maximum frequency limit is achieved, it is possible to connect dummy blocks (i.e., blocks that output a constant value) at the edges of the BbNN. While this solution does not connect the edges of the BbNN, it has the advantage that it keeps the frequency of the system independent of the BbNN size.

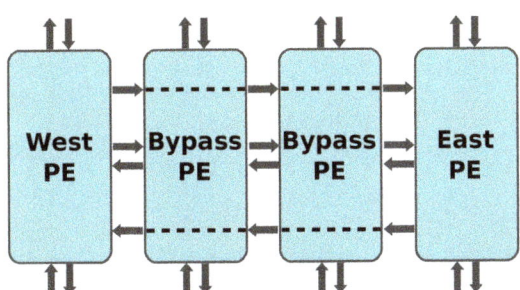

Figure 14. Connecting the external edges of the BbNN using reconfigurable interconnections.

Figure 15a shows the implementation of the BbNN static system in a Xilinx Zynq xc7z020clg400-1 SoC, including the area reserved for the RR. The RR can be populated at run-time with PEs to compose a BbNN with up to 3 × 5 neurons. Figure 15b shows the implementation of the different neurons and input modules and how they can be arranged at run-time to compose a 1 × 5 BbNN. It is important to remark that the BbNN is rotated compared to the one shown in Figure 15c. In this case, the data flow goes from the west to the east. This modification allows placing all the input modules in the same column, aligning all the fine-grain reconfigurable inputs in the same frame. Thus, speeding-up the reconfiguration process. The main drawback of rotating the BbNN is that it hinders the relocation of the neurons in the column. PEs in the bottom and top columns have a different interface to those in the middle of the column, and therefore their partial bitstreams are not compatible with relocation.

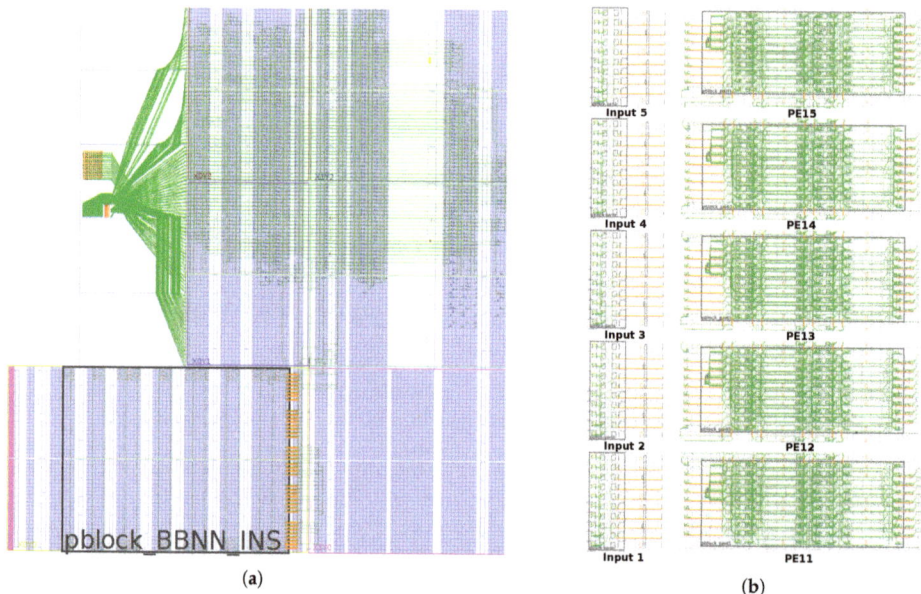

Figure 15. (a) Shows a BbNN static system implementation that can allocate up to 3 × 5 PEs. (b) Shows how neuron blocks can be arranged inside the reconfigurable region at run-time to form a 1 × 5 BbNN.

IMPRESS incorporates a library to manage the reconfiguration of mesh-type architectures. This library includes a bidimensional variable that represents the current configuration of the architecture. Each element in this variable has two parameters. The first one is a pointer to a reconfigurable module in the library. The second one is the location where the reconfigurable module is allocated in the device. When any of these parameters are changed, IMPRESS automatically initiates the reconfiguration process to allocate the specified reconfigurable module in the desired FPGA location.

Moreover, IMPRESS includes a run-time hardware reconfiguration engine specialized for fine-grain reconfiguration. The reconfiguration engine receives the configuration of the constants, and it automatically reconfigures the FPGA with the required configuration.

7. Results

This section illustrates the performance of the system in terms of logic resource utilization, the reconfiguration time and the capability to resolve different problems in two different domains, which are classification and control tasks.

7.1. Logic Resource Utilization and Reconfiguration Times

Table 3 contains the resource utilization of the static system and each PE in the BbNN implementation shown in Figure 15. The static system includes the BbNN controller, the fine-grain reconfiguration engine and an empty RR where the BbNN PE blocks can be allocated at run-time. Table 3 also shows the resources used by each individual processing element. Each PE uses 473 LUTS, 163 flip-flops and 1 DSP. As the PE can be implemented in different reconfigurable regions, there are small variations in the percentage of used resources among RRs. The size of the partial bitstreams also depends on the region where the PE is implemented. The PE bitstream size varies from 21.8 kB to 26.9 kB, depending on the reconfigurable region where the PE is implemented, while the input module bitstream size is 5.8 kB.

As shown in Figure 14, the PE can adopt three different configurations, which have to be implemented as three different RMs. To implement each possible BbNN size, we have to analyze all the possible locations where the RMs can be allocated. The bypass RMs can only be allocated in the inner regions of the RR. However, the edge RMs (e.g., west and east PEs) can be placed in every region except the opposite edge regions (i.e., a west RM cannot be allocated on the east side of the RR). When using the Xilinx reconfiguration flow, it is necessary to generate one partial bitstream for each RM location, which would result in 33 (12 × 2 for edge RMs and 9 for the bypass RM) different partial bitstreams to generate all possible combinations. However, generating all the possible combinations is avoided by the flexibility benefits provided by IMPRESS, which allows relocating one partial bitstream to compatible regions (i.e., regions that have the same resource distribution). In the BbNN implementation shown in Figure 15, the total number of partial bitstreams needed to generate all the possible combinations is reduced to 9.

Table 3. Resource utilization of the BbNN implemented on a Zynq XC7Z020.

Resource Type	Static System	Individual PE
LUTs	7966	473 (95.84%) *
FFs	7939	163 (16.98%) *
DSPs	0	1 (25%) *
BRAMs	2	0

* Percentage of the resources available in the RR used by the PE.

Table 4 shows a comparison of the proposed PE implementation and existing proposals in the state-of-the-art in terms of logic resources. The proposed architecture presents the lowest footprint in memory elements and DSPs. This is achieved by the proposed implementation for the sigmoid function and the strategy proposed to reuse the single DSP over different clock cycles. The downside of the dynamic scalability and flexibility of the proposed architecture is reflected in the high utilization of logic elements. This logic overhead is a consequence of the online training feature. One downside of dynamic partial reconfiguration is that other circuits cannot use the unused resources of the reconfigurable region where the PE is implemented. Table 3 shows that in our PE proposal, the LUTs are the bottleneck and leave several FFs, DSP and BRAMs unused.

Table 4. Resource utilization per individual PE in comparison with other works in the state-of-the-art.

Work	Platform	Logic Elements *	Memory Elements	DSP Elements	Activation Function
Proposed architecture	Zynq XC7Z020	473	163 FFs	1	Sigmoid-no DSP
Nambiar [21]	Stratix III	231	276 FFs	2	Tanh-piecewise
Jewajinda [49]	Virtex V	263	341 FFs	1	Sigmoid-LUT based
Merchant [19]	Virtex-II Pro	338	4BRAM	1	Sigmoid-LUT based
Lee and Hamagami [18] **	Stratix IV	186	40 FFs	8	Linear

* Logic element implementation depends on the selected platform: 4-inputs LUTs (Virtex-II Pro), 6-inputs (Zynq XC7Z020, Stratix III, Virtex V) LUTs or 8-inputs (Stratix IV). ** Only resource consumption for 8 × 16 BbNN size provided. Approximate metrics per PE.

Table 5 shows the breakdown of the time spent in each operation stage, both during the training and the inference phases. The time the BbNN needs to process a set of inputs depends on the latency. In a 3 × 3 BbNN, the maximum latency is 9. As each PE needs 7 clock cycles to compute its outputs, the BbNN takes a maximum of 63 clock cycles to make the computation, which results in 0.63 µs at 100 MHz. The transference of inputs to the BbNN is carried out using the fine-grain reconfiguration engine, and it takes 6.1 µs. In turn, the outputs are read with the AXI interface in 4.3 µs. Therefore, the maximum throughput in the inference phase is 90.66 Kilo Operations per second (KOPS). By operation, we mean to process a new set of inputs completely to obtain the desired output from the BbNN. In the training phase, it is also necessary to configure the BbNN. The configuration of each parameter of the BbNN also relies on the fine-grain reconfiguration, and it takes 41.7 µs. In the training phase, it is also necessary to take into account the time required by the software to calculate the fitness and to generate the chromosomes, which is application dependant. The computing times for fitness computation are reported next for each use case. All the design operates at 100 MHz, except the fine-grain reconfiguration engine that works at 175 MHz. While the ICAP configuration port has a nominal value of 100 MHz, it has been demonstrated in [50] that it is possible to overclock it at higher frequencies without behavior malfunction. This overclocking aims at reducing the total time needed to reconfigure the BbNN during evolution.

Table 5. Time breakdown for a 3 × 3 BbNN.

Task	Inference	Training
BbNN computation	<0.63 µs	<0.63 µs
Input data transference	6.1 µs	6.1 µs
Output data transference	4.3 µs	4.3 µs
BbNN configuration	-	41.7 µs
Fitness computation	-	Application dependant
Throughput	90.66 KOPS	Application dependant

Table 6 shows how the BbNN size impacts the time spent in each stage. Reconfiguration times shown in the table are a consequence of how IMPRESS carries out the fine-grain reconfiguration process, which is described next. First, when the evolutionary algorithm commands to change one parameter in an RM, IMPRESS has to search the device column where the parameter is placed and then modify the column configuration accordingly. Once the user has changed all the parameters, the new configuration values are sent to the reconfiguration engine, a hardware component in charge of reconfiguring the selected columns with the new configuration data. The time spent on this first stage depends on the number of parameters that have to be changed. In contrast, the second phase only depends on the number of columns that have to be reconfigured. In the implementation shown in Figure 15a, the number of frames that have to be reconfigured increases with the BbNN depth. Therefore, the BbNN configuration time of a 3 × 3 BbNN increases significantly compared to a 1 × 3 BbNN. However, when increasing the width of the BbNN, the number of frames that have to be reconfigured is kept constant, thus resulting in a more efficient reconfiguration process. Table 6 shows that increasing the size from a 3 × 3 to a 3 × 5 BbNN results in a more efficient reconfiguration time, especially in the case of the input data that only increases 0.5 µs. The increment in the BbNN configuration time is higher because more parameters have to be changed in the first phase of the reconfiguration process.

Table 6 also shows the comparison between using fine-grain reconfiguration (working at 175 MHz) and using an AXI lite interface in a non-reconfigurable BbNN operating at 100 MHz. Using fine-grain reconfiguration to configure the BbNN parameters is more efficient than using an AXI lite interface for all the three different sizes. In contrast, the best option to transfer the input data to the BbNN depends on the number of inputs. Fine-grain reconfiguration is convenient when there are five inputs, while the AXI lite interface is the preferred option when the BbNN only contains three inputs.

Table 6. Performance comparison for different BbNN sizes.

BbNN Size	BbNN Computation (µs)	Input Data (µs)		Output Data (µs)		BbNN Configuration (µs)	
		Fine-Grain	AXI	Fine-Grain	AXI	Fine-Grain	AXI
1 × 3 BbNN	<0.21 µs	6.1	4.5	-	4.3	15.8	19.7
3 × 3 BbNN	<0.63 µs	6.1	4.5	-	4.3	41.7	58.9
3 × 5 BbNN	<1.05 µs	6.6	7.7	-	7	56	94.1

7.2. Case Studies

This section provides three different case studies showing how the neuroevolvable hardware system can be adapted to different problems. All the results provided are the average of 100 training processes. The EA finishes if a candidate configuration achieves the goal fitness or 1000 generations are exceeded. At each generation, 150 candidate configurations (i.e., chromosomes) are evaluated.

We expose here one classification problem and two control problems. In the classification problem, each chromosome is evaluated with all samples in the dictionary. In control problems, a new set of initial states is evaluated at each generation to avoid inconsistent solutions.

7.2.1. Classification Domain: the Xor Problem

The XOR problem involves two inputs and one output, all 1-bit width. The goal is to evolve the BbNN, so it behaves like a logic XOR gate. If two inputs have the same value, the output is zero. Otherwise, the output must be one.

This problem is solved by using the truth table of the XOR gate as the reference. The selected output of the BbNN is compared with the reference result for each input data pair. The fitness function used to evaluate each configuration is based on the mean squared error of the BbNN output and the reference (see Equation (5)). Both values are float data type. The fitness function expresses the accuracy of the chromosome to approximate the output values to the binary values of the XOR truth table. A fitness over 0.9 corresponds to a mean squared error below 10% for the four cases in the XOR truth table. This problem is considered solved if the achieved fitness is over 0.9.

$$XOR fitness = 1 - \left(\frac{1}{4} \sum_{i=1}^{4} (y_i - y_{real})^2 \right) \quad (5)$$

Fitness computation for this problem takes 21 µs, and it is executed once per sample in the batch. The batch contains four samples, so the fitness is computed four times per chromosome. Figure 16 shows the fitness progression along the evolution process and Figure 17 the selected configuration for a 2 × 2 network that solves the problem. It should be noted that the links connecting the edges of the network are used by the solution (i.e., the structure is closed as a cylinder). Figure 18 and Table 7 show the influence of the BbNN size in training. Experimental results showed that the minimum BbNN that can solve this task is a 2 × 2 BbNN. BbNNs with more than 2 × 2 elements facilitate the evolution towards a solution evaluating fewer configurations.

The four graphs in Figure 18 show the influence of the BbNN size on the convergence of the XOR problem. For each size, the generations needed by the EA to solve the problem are registered. Each graph covers up to 1000 generations. Beyond this value, the execution of the EA is considered as non-convergent. From these measurements, it can be concluded that the more convenient BbNN size for XOR proves to be 4 × 2 BbNN since it has the lowest rate of non-convergent executions and the highest rates of executions below 100 generations. This BbNN size has the lowest number of evaluated chromosomes and generations on average, as exposed in Table 7.

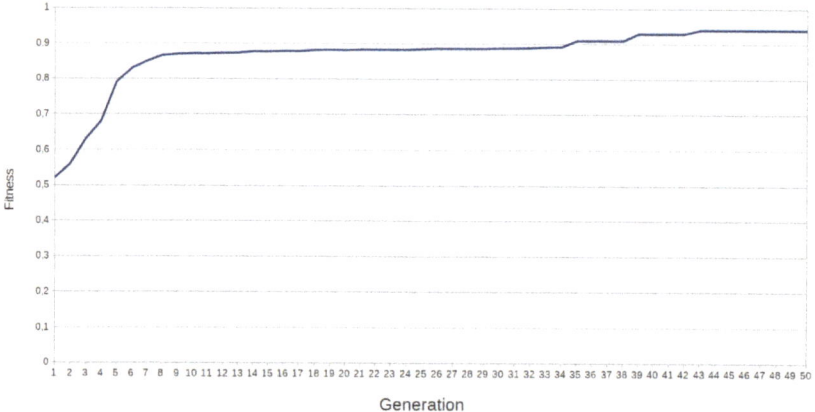

Figure 16. Progression of the fitness value during the XOR training for a 2 × 2 BbNN.

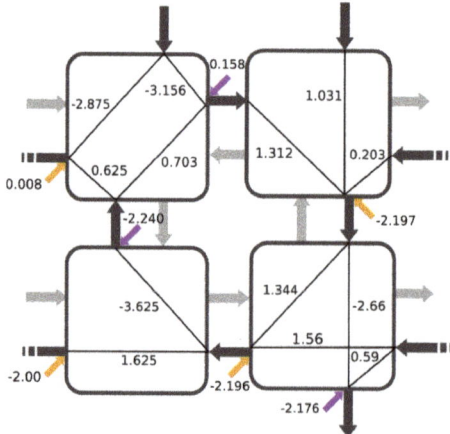

Figure 17. Solution for the XOR problem.

Table 7. Influence of the BbNN size on the training process for the XOR problem. Average stats from 100 convergent training processes.

Performance Indicator	2 × 2 BbNN	3 × 2 BbNN	4 × 2 BbNN	5 × 2 BbNN
Best fitness	0.95	0.97	0.98	0.95
Average tested configurations	19,954	13,434	13,036	20,090
Average generations	133	91	87	140

If the complexity of the classification problem is unknown at run-time, the dynamic scalability of the BbNN may take an essential role in the search for solutions. This situation is shown for the

XOR problem in Figure 19. The system starts by searching for a solution with a 1 × 2 BbNN structure. After a period with the fitness stalled completely, the system dynamically adds a new row of PEs to the BbNN (at generation 211, in Figure 19). After a few iterations with the new size, the neuroevolutionary system is able to find a solution. The EA does not support population where chromosomes encode BbNN of different sizes, but it can recompose a new BbNN architecture and reset the evolution process if the fitness does not show any improvement.

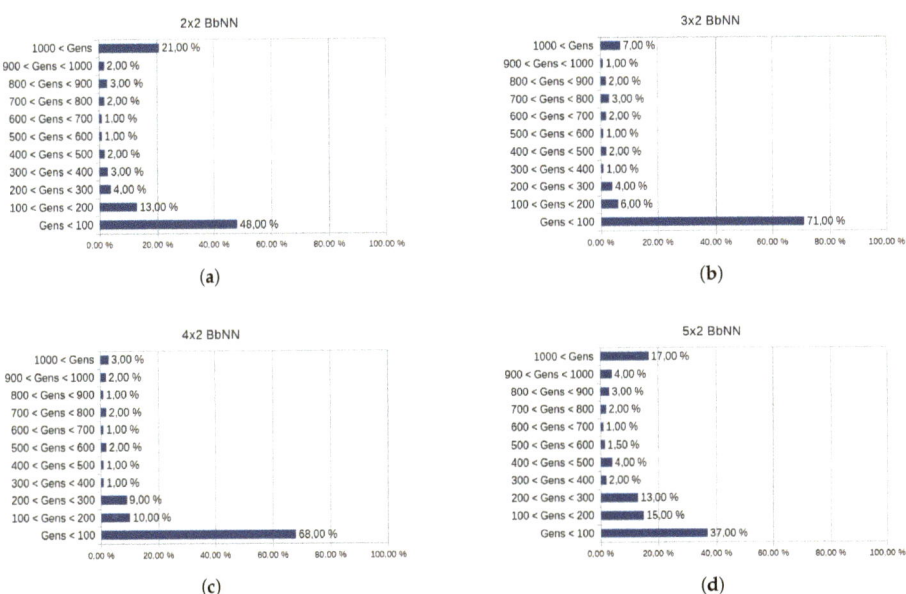

Figure 18. Influence of the BbNN size in the convergence of the algorithm for XOR problem. Each graph exposes the data from 100 executions of the EA. The generations needed to achieve a solution are segmented in intervals, from 0 to 1000 generations. Executions over 1000 generations are stopped. Convergence of different BbNN sizes is analyzed: 2 × 2 BbNN (**a**), 3 × 2 BbNN (**b**), 4 × 2 BbNN (**c**) and 5 × 2 BbNN (**d**).

Figure 19. Resolution of the XOR problem using the dynamic scalability feature. At generation 211 the Evolutionary Algorithm (EA) increases the BbNN size and resets evolution. At generation 249 the EA converges towards a solution.

7.2.2. Control Domain: Mountain Car

The Mountain Car is a standard control problem. It involves a car whose starting position is at the bottom of a valley. The car must reach the top of the hill at the right. The engine of the car is not powerful enough to reach the goal position by accelerating up the slope. Therefore, the car needs to gain momentum to reach it by oscillating from left to right.

A simulation environment for the Mountain Car problem is included in the Gym OpenAI [14] toolkit (Figure 20). The observation space of the environment has two variables: the position of the car and the speed. Both variables are float type that are transformed to the fixed-point representation before being processed by the network. Three possible actions can be performed on the car: push left, push right or do not push. The force of the engine is constant.

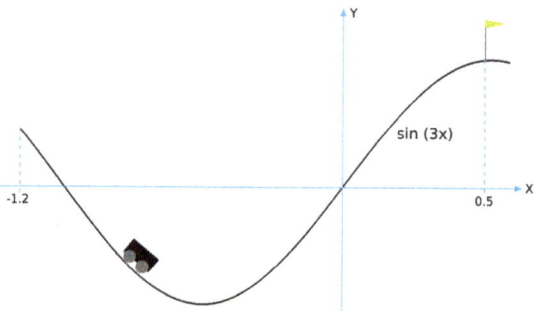

Figure 20. OpenAI Mountain Car environment and coordinate system used to determine the position of the car. The hills are generated with the sin(3x) function.

The BbNN is evolved to find a controller for this problem directly by interacting with the environment. The Zynq-7020 SoC FPGA device in which the neuroevolvable hardware system runs has been integrated as a hardware-in-the-loop platform with the OpenAI simulator running on a PC. The evaluation of each candidate circuit is called an episode. Each episode finishes when the car reaches the goal position, or after 200 control actions (steps). This value has been obtained experimentally after observing that beyond this number of actions, the likelihood that an unsuccessful candidate circuit reaches the final position decreases.

A specific fitness function has been developed for this environment, which is shown in Equation (6). This fitness function rewards circuits able to drive the car close to the desired position with the fewest possible number of steps. Position of the car is its X coordinate according to Figure 20. It can vary in the range $(-1.2, 0.5)$, the fitness expression presents three possible scenarios:

- Fitness score in the range $(-0.12, 0)$: the *steps* component in the fitness function is equal to zero since the circuit performs 200 control actions without any success. The car is far from the goal position at the end of the episode.
- Fitness score in the range $(0, 0.05)$: the *steps* component is also null because all control actions were consumed, but the circuit can drive up the car near the desired position.
- Fitness score over 0.05: circuits scored in this range can drive the car to the goal position in less than 200 *steps*. The fewer control actions needed, the higher the score is. We consider that achieving the top of the hill with 150 *steps* can be considered good behavior. This corresponds to a fitness score over 0.4, which is set as the threshold to consider a problem as solved.

Fitness computation for this problem takes 41 µs. Fitness is computed once at the end of each episode and hence once per chromosome. An example of the evolution of fitness in an episode is shown in Figure 21.

Table 8 exposes the influence of the BbNN size on the training process. We only consider topologies with two columns since this is the number of observable variables in the environment. The number of rows varies from 2 to 4. First, we can see that all the considered BbNNs can solve the problem, even with a single row. However, the size has a direct effect on the performance of the EA. Small network architectures need fewer generations to solve the problem since chromosomes have fewer parameters to be optimized. A 1×2 BbNN needs 323 generations on average to converge to a solution; meanwhile, 2×2 BbNN increases the number of generations needed. Although networks over 1×2 size need more generations to be optimized, they enhance the quality of the solution. A 2×2 BbNN achieves a good compromise between the best fitness and evaluated circuits.

Figure 22 provides the convergence of the EA for different BbNN sizes similar to the previous problem. In this case, the smallest BbNN architecture ensures the convergence of the 81% executions below 100 generations and has a low rate of non-convergent executions. Moreover, this BbNN size presents the lowest average generations in Table 8. Therefore, 1×2 BbNN is the most suitable size in this case.

$$fitness = \left(1 - \frac{steps}{200}\right) + \frac{finalPosition}{10} \qquad (6)$$

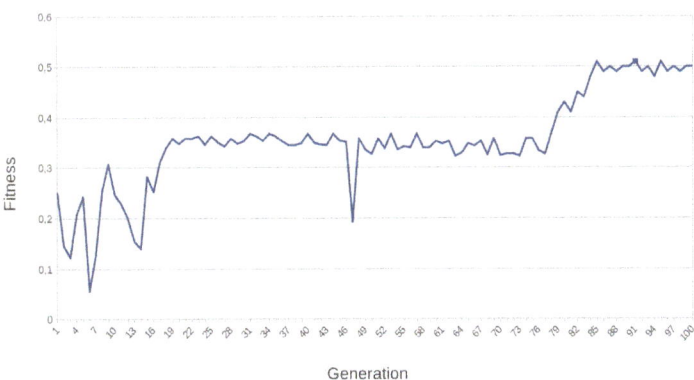

Figure 21. Example of progression of the fitness value during the Mountain Car training for 2×2 BbNN.

Table 8. Influence of the BbNN size on the training process for Mountain Car problem. Average stats from 100 training processes.

Performance Indicator	1×2 BbNN	2×2 BbNN	3×2 BbNN	4×2 BbNN
Best fitness	0.41	0.46	0.45	0.43
Average tested configurations	323	1.156	3.899	984
Average generations	3	8	26	7

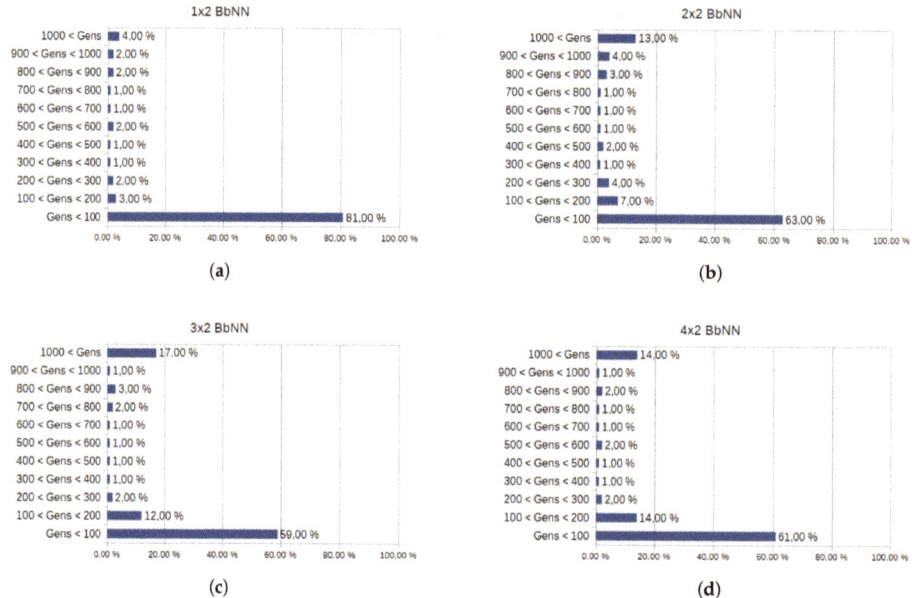

Figure 22. Influence of the BbNN size in the convergence of the algorithm for Mountain Car problem. Each graph exposes the data from 100 executions of the EA. The generations needed to achieve a solution are segmented in intervals, from 0 to 1000 generations. Executions over 1000 generations are stopped. Convergence of different BbNN sizes is analyzed: 1×2 BbNN (**a**), 2×2 BbNN (**b**), 3×2 BbNN (**c**) and 4×2 BbNN (**d**).

7.2.3. Control Domain: Cart Pole

Cart Pole or Inverted pendulum is a staple problem in the control domain. The center of mass of the pendulum is above its pivot point. Therefore, the pendulum is unstable if no control actions are performed on it. OpenAI also provides a python-based simulation environment for this problem, whose graphical representation is shown in Figure 23.

Figure 23. Cart Pole environment.

Four variables are observed in the environment: the position and speed of the cart, the angle of the pole and the speed at the end of the pole. All of them are float type variables with different ranges. The system must keep the pole in a balanced position. Two actions can be performed on the simulation environment: push the cart left or right.

In this case, an episode finishes if the angle of the pole is over $12°$ or the position of the cart exceeds the scenario boundaries. In those cases, the pole is considered to be unbalanced. After each control action on the pole, a partial error value is calculated. This value represents the instability of the pole after the control action. The partial error involves the four parameters of the observation space and their maximum value, as shown in Equation (7). If the pole falls, global fitness is calculated as the addition of all partial error. Not performed steps are scored with the highest partial error value, as shown in Equation (8):

$$partialerror_j = \frac{1}{4}\frac{1}{200}\left(\sum_{i=1}^{4}\frac{x_i}{max_i}^2\right) \quad (7)$$

$$fitness = 1 - \left(\sum_{j=1}^{200} partialerror_j + \frac{200 - steps}{200}\right) \quad (8)$$

where:

- x_i: is the i_{th} parameter in the observation space.
- max_i: is the maximum value in the range of i_{th} parameter in the observation space.
- $partialerror_j$: represents the instability of the pole after the j_{th} control action.

Fitness function showed in Equation (8) is designed to assign high scores to those chromosomes that complete 200 control actions in balance and low partial error. Fitness computation for this problem takes 46 µs. Fitness is computed after each control action since it involves an accumulation of the partial error. The ultimate fitness would be 1 in case the pole last for 200 control actions in a balanced and static position. However, two chromosomes able to balance the pole during 200 control actions can have different fitness scores since every *partial error* value depends on the value of the four variables of the observation space. The problem is solved if a fitness value over 0.95 is achieved. An example of the progression of fitness during a Cart Pole training experiment for 3 × 4 BbNN is shown in Figure 24.

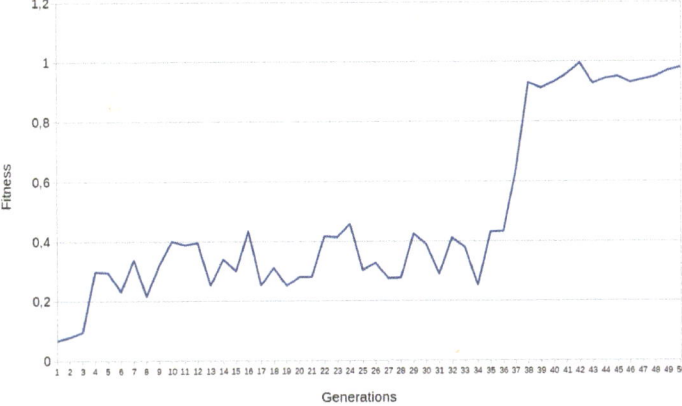

Figure 24. Example of progression of the fitness value during the Cart Pole training for 3 × 4 BbNN.

The minimum BbNN width for this problem is four: one column for each variable in the observation space. The minimum network size compatible with this control problem is, therefore, 1 × 4 BbNN. Networks with an additional row to 2 × 4 BbNN broaden the design space exploration, and the EA evaluates more configurations to encounter a solution. Additional rows on the architecture have the same effect. Table 9 and graphs in Figure 25 exposes the influence of the BbNN size on the training process. These data have been gathered similarly to former case studies. In this case, increasing the size of the network leads to higher rates of non-convergent executions. Therefore, the most suitable size for this problem is 1 × 4 BbNN, which has the lowest rate of non-convergent executions (Figure 25) and the lowest average generations needed to solve the problem (Table 9).

Table 9. Influence of the BbNN size on the training process for Cart Pole problem. Average stats from 100 training processes.

Performance Indicator	1 × 4 BbNN	2 × 4 BbNN	3 × 4 BbNN	4 × 4 BbNN
Best fitness	0.977	0.973	0.970	0.978
Average tested configurations	518	2101	8651	2051
Average generations	4	14	58	14

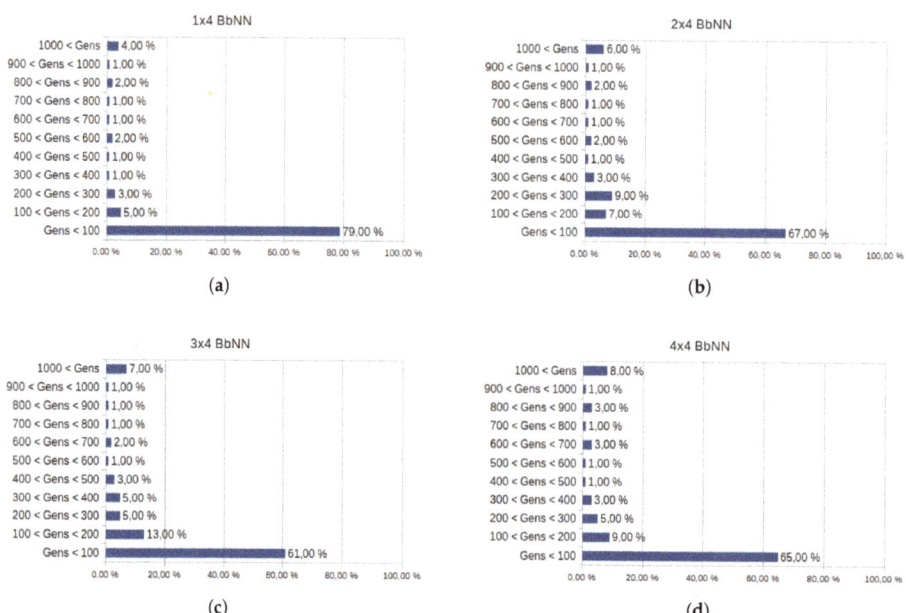

Figure 25. Influence of the BbNN size in the convergence of the algorithm for Cart Pole problem. Each graph exposes the data from 100 executions of the EA. The generations needed to achieve a solution are segmented in intervals, from 0 to 1000 generations. Executions over 1000 generations are stopped. Convergence of different BbNN sizes is analyzed: 1 × 4 BbNN (**a**), 2 × 4 BbNN (**b**), 3 × 4 BbNN (**c**) and 4 × 4 BbNN (**d**).

Figure 24 contains the fitness progression of 3 × 4 BbNN during the training process of the Cart Pole problem. The initial unbalanced condition of the pole is different from each generation. Therefore, the same BbNN configuration varies its fitness value depending on the initial state. Figure 26 presents a solution to this problem in which the evolutionary algorithm has created two feedback loops.

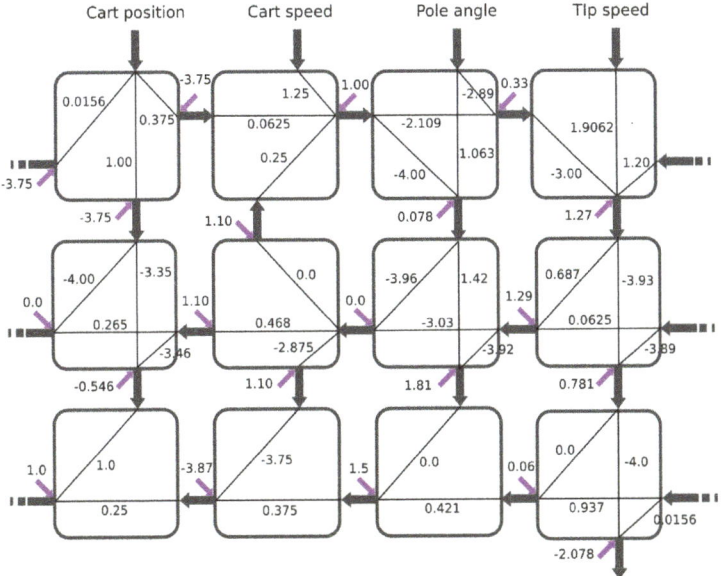

Figure 26. BbNN solution for Cart Pole problem.

7.3. Online Adaptation for Control in Dynamic Environments

As proof of the online adaptation capability of the proposed system, two examples based on the previous control problems are provided. Both online training examples are tackled following the same approach. First, the system is trained under normal conditions, and once it is capable of controlling the problem for at least 10 generations, physical parameters are changed. This change hampers the capability of the trained BbNN to solve the initial problem. Table 10 exhibits the initial conditions for each problem and their modified values.

Table 10. Initial and modified conditions for online training.

Problem	Parameter	Normal Value	Modified Value
Cart Pole	Gravity	9.8 m/s	20.0 m/s
	Pole length	0.5 m	0.1 m
	Cart mass	1.0 Kg	1.5 Kg
Mountain Car	Engine power	0.001	0.0008

Some of these modifications to the problem conditions emulate changing the environment. For instance, the modified value of the engine power of the car in the Mountain Car problem emulates a loss of power in the engine. Other changes emulate conditions that harden the problem resolution. For instance, an increment of the gravity over the pole seems unrealistic but creates a handicap for the problem resolution.

Both control problems exhibit similar behavior. After the change in the conditions, a drop in the fitness can be observed. The re-training stage has better average fitness than the first training stage. This means that the system has prior knowledge about the problem, creating a nice basis to solve it when harder conditions appear. Figures 27 and 28 show the evolution of the fitness when conditions change for both control problems.

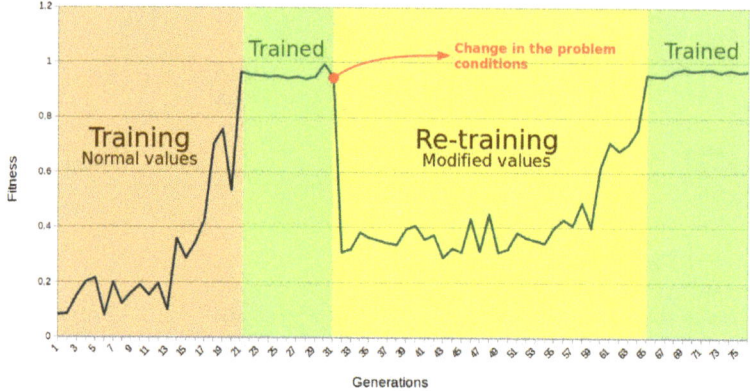

Figure 27. Cart Pole training and re-train for 3 × 4 BbNN.

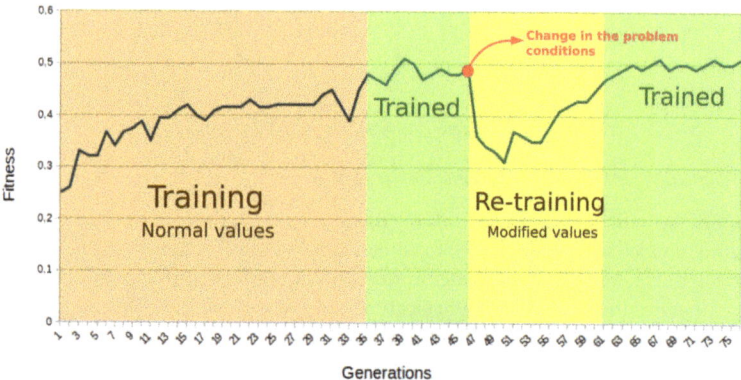

Figure 28. Mountain Car training and re-train for 2 × 2 BbNN.

8. Conclusions and Future Work

In this paper, we propose a dynamically scalable hardware implementation of the Block-based Neural Network model, which, under the control of an evolutionary algorithm, enables continuous system adaptation. The proposed neuroevolvable hardware system integrates advanced reconfiguration features that allow to (1) compose the BbNN at run-time by stitching together individual PEs and (2) providing the inputs and changing each PE configuration with reduced reconfiguration times. The result is a scalable BbNN whose size can be adapted to the computational demands required by a given application. Experimental results show how scalability allows changing the number of logic resources occupied by the network depending on the complexity of the problem or the expected quality of the results. The proposed system has been implemented in an SoC FPGA and integrated using a hardware-in-the-loop scheme with the OpenAI toolkit to show its efficiency in reinforcement learning problems, such as the cart pole and the mountain car problem.

Regarding resource utilization, each PE uses 473 LUTs, 163 FFs and 1 DSP. Compared to other state-of-the-art solutions, our proposal uses more LUTs but reduces the number of FFs or DSPs. Fine-grain reconfiguration has been proven to be a valid solution to train the BbNN online as all the parameters of a 3 × 3 BbNN can be reconfigured in just 41.7 µs. In real applications, it is not necessary to change all the parameters at the same time, which further reduces the total time needed to configure the network. The inputs of the network are also provided using fine-grain reconfiguration in 6.1 µs while the outputs are transferred using an AXI full interface in 4.3 µs. The time needed to compute the fitness is application-dependent and ranges from 21 µs to 46 µs for the use cases provided in this paper.

Further research will be carried out to extend the reinforcement learning capabilities of the proposed solution in more complex scenarios and other applications. Different variants of the evolutionary algorithm will also be explored to increase the capacity of the system to deal with more complex problems. Moreover, the evolutionary algorithm will be modified to use the size of the BbNN as an additional parameter subject to evolution, which will allow selecting the most appropriate BbNN size for a given application without user intervention. The fixed-point data encoding of the network can be an obstacle when solving complex problems. Therefore, more precise encoding schemes, like dynamic fixed-point or wider bit width of registers, will be studied. This improvement in data representation may cause an increment in FPGA resource consumption. Other optimization algorithms, such as gradient descend based or multi-threaded EAs will be analyzed, as an alternative to EAs.

Author Contributions: A.G. has contributed to the conceptualization, methodology, investigation, validation, writing—original draft preparation and writing—review and editing. R.Z. has contributed to the conceptualization, methodology, investigation, validation and writing—original draft preparation. A.O. has contributed to the conceptualization, methodology, investigation and writing—original draft preparation. E.d.l.T. has contributed to the investigation and writing—original draft preparation. All authors have read and agreed to the published version of the manuscript.

Funding: This research was partially funded by the European Union's Horizon 2020 research and innovation programme under grant agreement No 732105 (CERBERO Project).

Conflicts of Interest: The authors declare no conflict of interest. The funding sponsors had no role in the design of the study; in the collection, analyses, or interpretation of data; in the writing of the manuscript, and in the decision to publish the results.

References

1. Goldberg, D.E. *Genetic Algorithms in Search, Optimization and Machine Learning*, 1st ed.; Addison-Wesley Longman Publishing Co., Inc.: Boston, MA, USA, 1989.
2. Alattas, R.J.; Patel, S.; Sobh, T.M. Evolutionary modular robotics: Survey and analysis. *J. Intell. Robot. Syst.* **2019**, *95*, 815–828. [CrossRef]
3. Kriegman, S.; Blackiston, D.; Levin, M.; Bongard, J. A scalable pipeline for designing reconfigurable organisms. *Proc. Natl. Acad. Sci. USA* **2020**, *117*, 1853–1859, doi:10.1073/pnas.1910837117. [CrossRef] [PubMed]
4. Zebulum, R.S.; Pacheco, M.A.; Vellasco, M. Comparison of different evolutionary methodologies applied to electronic filter design. In Proceedings of the 1998 IEEE International Conference on Evolutionary Computation Proceedings, IEEE World Congress on Computational Intelligence (Cat. No. 98TH8360), Anchorage, AK, USA, 4–9 May 1998; pp. 434–439.
5. Hornby, G.; Globus, A.; Linden, D.; Lohn, J. Automated antenna design with evolutionary algorithms. In *Space 2006*; American Institute of Aeronautics and Astronautics: Reston, VA, USA, 2006; p. 7242.
6. Sekanina, L. Virtual Reconfigurable Circuits for Real-World Applications of Evolvable Hardware. In Proceedings of the 5th International Conference on Evolvable Systems: From Biology to Hardware, Wuhan, China, 21–23 September 2007; pp. 186–197, doi:10.1007/3-540-36553-2_17. [CrossRef]
7. Stanley, K.O.; Clune, J.; Lehman, J.; Miikkulainen, R. Designing neural networks through neuroevolution. *Nat. Mach. Intell.* **2019**, *1*, 24–35. [CrossRef]
8. Stanley, K.O.; Miikkulainen, R. Evolving Neural Networks through Augmenting Topologies. *Evol. Comput.* **2002**, *10*, 99–127, doi:10.1162/106365602320169811. [CrossRef] [PubMed]
9. Stanley, K.O.; D'Ambrosio, D.B.; Gauci, J. A Hypercube-Based Encoding for Evolving Large-Scale Neural Networks. *Artif. Life* **2009**, *15*, 185–212, doi:10.1162/artl.2009.15.2.15202. [CrossRef] [PubMed]
10. Such, F.P.; Madhavan, V.; Conti, E.; Lehman, J.; Stanley, K.O.; Clune, J. Deep neuroevolution: Genetic algorithms are a competitive alternative for training deep neural networks for reinforcement learning. *arXiv* **2017**, arXiv:1712.06567.

11. Moon, S.W.; Kong, S.G. Block-based neural networks. *IEEE Trans. Neural Netw.* **2001**, *12*, 307–317. [CrossRef] [PubMed]
12. Zamacola, R.; Martínez, A.G.; Mora, J.; Otero, A.; de La Torre, E. IMPRESS: Automated Tool for the Implementation of Highly Flexible Partial Reconfigurable Systems with Xilinx Vivado. In Proceedings of the 2018 International Conference on ReConFigurable Computing and FPGAs (ReConFig), Cancun, Mexico, 3–5 December 2018; pp. 1–8. [CrossRef]
13. Zamacola, R.; García Martínez, A.; Mora, J.; Otero, A.; de la Torre, E. Automated Tool and Runtime Support for Fine-Grain Reconfiguration in Highly Flexible Reconfigurable Systems. In Proceedings of the 2019 IEEE 27th Annual International Symposium on Field-Programmable Custom Computing Machines (FCCM), San Diego, CA, USA, 28 April–1 May 2019; p. 307. [CrossRef]
14. Brockman, G.; Cheung, V.; Pettersson, L.; Schneider, J.; Schulman, J.; Tang, J.; Zaremba, W. OpenAI Gym. *arXiv* **2016**, arXiv:1606.01540.
15. Yanling, Z.; Bimin, D.; Zhanrong, W. Analysis and study of perceptron to solve XOR problem. In Proceedings of the 2nd International Workshop on Autonomous Decentralized System, Beijing, China, 7 November 2002; pp. 168–173. [CrossRef]
16. Merchant, S.; Peterson, G.D.; Park, S.K.; Kong, S.G. FPGA Implementation of Evolvable Block-based Neural Networks. In Proceedings of the 2006 IEEE International Conference on Evolutionary Computation, Vancouver, BC, Canada, 16–21 July 2006; pp. 3129–3136. [CrossRef]
17. Merchant, S.; Peterson, G.; Kong, S. Intrinsic Embedded Hardware Evolution of Block-based Neural Networks. In Proceedings of the 2006 International Conference on Engineering of Reconfigurable Systems & Algorithms, ERSA 2006, Las Vegas, NV, USA, 26–29 June 2006; pp. 211–214.
18. Lee, K.; Hamagami, T. Performance Oriented Block-Based Neural Network Model by Parallelized Neighbor's Communication. In Proceedings of the 2018 IEEE International Conference on Systems, Man, and Cybernetics (SMC), Miyazaki, Japan, 7–10 October 2018; pp. 1623–1628. [CrossRef]
19. Merchant, S.; Peterson, G. Evolvable Block-Based Neural Network Design for Applications in Dynamic Environments. *VLSI Design* **2010**, *2010*, 251210. [CrossRef]
20. Jewajinda, Y.; Chongstitvatana, P. FPGA-based online-learning using parallel genetic algorithm and neural network for ECG signal classification. In Proceedings of the ECTI-CON2010: The 2010 ECTI International Confernce on Electrical Engineering/Electronics, Computer, Telecommunications and Information Technology, Chiang Mai, Thailand, 19–21 May 2010; pp. 1050–1054.
21. Nambiar, V.P.; Khalil-Hani, M.; Sahnoun, R.; Marsono, M. Hardware implementation of evolvable block-based neural networks utilizing a cost efficient sigmoid-like activation function. *Neurocomputing* **2014**, *140*, 228–241. [CrossRef]
22. Jiang, W.; Kong, S. A Least-Squares Learning for Block-based Neural Networks. *Adv. Neural Netw. A Suppl. (DCDIS)* **2007**, *14*, 242–247.
23. Nambiar, V.P.; Khalil-Hani, M.; Marsono, M.; Sia, C. Optimization of structure and system latency in evolvable block-based neural networks using genetic algorithm. *Neurocomputing* **2014**, *145*, 285–302. [CrossRef]
24. Kong, S. Time series prediction with evolvable block-based neural networks. In Proceedings of the 2004 IEEE International Joint Conference on Neural Networks, Budapest, Hungary, 25–29 July 2004; Volume 2, pp. 1579–1583. [CrossRef]
25. Jiang, W.; Kong, S.G.; Peterson, G.D. ECG signal classification using block-based neural networks. In Proceedings of the 2005 IEEE International Joint Conference on Neural Networks, Montreal, QC, Canada, 31 July–4 August 2005; Volume 1, pp. 326–331. [CrossRef]
26. Nambiar, V.P.; Khalil-Hani, M.; Marsono, M.N. Evolvable Block-based Neural Networks for real-time classification of heart arrhythmia From ECG signals. In Proceedings of the 2012 IEEE-EMBS Conference on Biomedical Engineering and Sciences, Langkawi, Malaysia, 17–19 December 2012; pp. 866–871. [CrossRef]
27. Nambiar, V.P.; Khalil-Hani, M.; Sia, C.W.; Marsono, M.N. Evolvable Block-based Neural Networks for classification of driver drowsiness based on heart rate variability. In Proceedings of the 2012 IEEE International Conference on Circuits and Systems (ICCAS), Kuala Lumpur, Malaysia, 3–4 October 2012; pp. 156–161. [CrossRef]

28. San, P.; Ling, S.H.; Nguyen, H. Block based neural network for hypoglycemia detection. In Proceedings of the Annual International Conference of the IEEE Engineering in Medicine and Biology Society, Boston, MA, USA, 30 August–3 September 2011; pp. 5666–5669. [CrossRef]
29. Karaköse, M.; Akin, E. *Dynamical Fuzzy Control with Block Based Neural Network*; Technical Report; Department of Computer Engineering, Fırat University: Elazığ, Turkey, 2006.
30. Tran, Q.A.; Jiang, F.; Ha, Q.M. Evolving Block-Based Neural Network and Field Programmable Gate Arrays for Host-Based Intrusion Detection System. In Proceedings of the 2012 Fourth International Conference on Knowledge and Systems Engineering, Danang, Vietnam, 17–19 August 2012; pp. 86–92. [CrossRef]
31. Samajdar, A.; Mannan, P.; Garg, K.; Krishna, T. GeneSys: Enabling Continuous Learning through Neural Network Evolution in Hardware. In Proceedings of the 2018 51st Annual IEEE/ACM International Symposium on Microarchitecture (MICRO), Fukuoka, Japan, 20–24 October 2018.
32. Upegui, A.; Pena-Reyes, C.A.; Sanchez, E. An FPGA platform for on-line topology exploration of spiking neural networks. *Microprocess. Microsyst.* **2005**, *29*, 211–223. [CrossRef]
33. Miller, J.F. *Cartesian Genetic Programming. Natural Computing Series*; Springer: Berlin/Heidelberg, Germany, 2011. [CrossRef]
34. Gallego, A.; Mora, J.; Otero, A.; de la Torre, E.; Riesgo, T. A scalable evolvable hardware processing array. In Proceedings of the 2013 International Conference on Reconfigurable Computing and FPGAs (ReConFig), Cancun, Mexico, 9–11 December 2013; pp. 1–7. [CrossRef]
35. Miller, J.; Job, D.; Vassilev, V. Principles in the Evolutionary Design of Digital Circuits—Part I. *Genet. Program. Evolvable Mach.* **2000**, *1*, 7–35. [CrossRef]
36. Torroja, Y.; Riesgo, T.; de la Torre, E.; Uceda, J. Design for reusability: Generic and configurable designs. In *Proceedings of System Modeling and Code Reusability*; Springer: Boston, MA, USA, 1997; pp. 11–21.
37. Jiang, Y.; Pattichis, M.S. A dynamically reconfigurable architecture system for time-varying image constraints (DRASTIC) for motion JPEG. *J. Real-Time Image Process.* **2014**, *14*, 395–411. [CrossRef]
38. Jiang, Y.; Pattichis, M. A dynamically reconfigurable deblocking filter for H.264/AVC codec. In Proceedings of the 2012 Conference Record of the Forty Sixth Asilomar Conference on Signals, Systems and Computers (ASILOMAR), Pacific Grove, CA, USA, 4–7 November 2012; pp. 2036–2040. [CrossRef]
39. Jacoby, A.; Llamocca, D. Dynamic Dual Fixed-Point CORDIC Implementation. In Proceedings of the 2017 IEEE International Parallel and Distributed Processing Symposium Workshops (IPDPSW), Orlando, FL, USA, 29 May–2 June 2017; pp. 235–240. [CrossRef]
40. Khraisha, R.; Lee, J. A Bit-Rate Aware Scalable H.264/AVC Deblocking Filter Using Dynamic Partial Reconfiguration. *Signal Process. Syst.* **2012**, *66*, 225–234. [CrossRef]
41. Koch, D.; Torresen, J.; Beckhoff, C.; Ziener, D.; Dennl, C.; Breuer, V.; Teich, J.; Feilen, M.; Stechele, W. Partial reconfiguration on FPGAs in practice—Tools and applications. In Proceedings of the Architecture of Computing Systems (ARCS 2012), Munich, Germany, 28 February–2 March 2012; pp. 1–12.
42. Hannachi, M.; Rabah, H.; Ben Abdelali, A.; Mtibaa, A. Dynamic reconfigurable architecture for adaptive DCT implementation. In Proceedings of the 2016 2nd International Conference on Advanced Technologies for Signal and Image Processing (ATSIP), Monastir, Tunisia, 21–23 March 2016; pp. 189–193. [CrossRef]
43. Huang, J.; Lee, J. A Self-Reconfigurable Platform for Scalable DCT Computation Using Compressed Partial Bitstreams and BlockRAM Prefetching. In Proceedings of the 2009 IEEE Computer Society Annual Symposium on VLSI, Tampa, FL, USA, 13–15 May 2009; pp. 67–72. [CrossRef]
44. Sudarsanam, A.; Barnes, R.; Carver, J.; Kallam, R.; Dasu, A. Dynamically reconfigurable systolic array accelerators: A case study with extended Kalman filter and discrete wavelet transform algorithms. *IET Comput. Digit. Tech.* **2010**, *4*, 126–142. [CrossRef]
45. Cervero, T.; Otero, A.; Lopez, S.; de la Torre, E.; Marrero Callico, G.; Riesgo, T.; Sarmiento, R. A scalable H.264/AVC deblocking filter architecture. *J. Real-Time Image Process.* **2016**, *12*, 81–105. [CrossRef]
46. Otero, A.; de la Torre, E.; Riesgo, T. Dreams: A tool for the design of dynamically reconfigurable embedded and modular systems. In Proceedings of the 2012 International Conference on Reconfigurable Computing and FPGAs, Cancun, Mexico, 5–7 December 2012; pp. 1–8. [CrossRef]
47. Kulkarni, A.; Stroobandt, D. How to efficiently reconfigure tunable lookup tables for dynamic circuit specialization. *Int. J. Reconfig. Comput.* **2016**, *2016*, 5340318. [CrossRef]
48. Mora, J.; de la Torre, E. Accelerating the evolution of a systolic array-based evolvable hardware system. *Microprocess. Microsyst.* **2018**, *56*, 144–156. [CrossRef]

49. Jewajinda, Y. An Adaptive Hardware Classifier in FPGA based-on a Cellular Compact Genetic Algorithm and Block-based Neural Network. In Proceedings of the 2008 International Symposium on Communications and Information Technologies, Lao, China, 21–23 October 2008; pp. 658–663.
50. Hansen, S.G.; Koch, D.; Torresen, J. High Speed Partial Run-Time Reconfiguration Using Enhanced ICAP Hard Macro. In Proceedings of the 2011 IEEE International Symposium on Parallel and Distributed Processing Workshops and Phd Forum, Shanghai, China, 16–20 May 2011; pp. 174–180. [CrossRef]

© 2020 by the authors. Licensee MDPI, Basel, Switzerland. This article is an open access article distributed under the terms and conditions of the Creative Commons Attribution (CC BY) license (http://creativecommons.org/licenses/by/4.0/).

Article

Performance of Two Approaches of Embedded Recommender Systems

Francisco Pajuelo-Holguera [1], Juan A. Gómez-Pulido [1,*] and Fernando Ortega [2]

[1] Department of Tecnología de Computadores y Comunicaciones, Escuela Politécnica, Universidad de Extremadura, 10003 Cáceres, Spain; franciscoph@unex.es
[2] Department of Sistemas Informáticos, ETSI Sistemas Informáticos, Universidad Politécnica de Madrid, 28031 Madrid, Spain; fernando.ortega@upm.es
* Correspondence: jangomez@unex.es

Received: 22 February 2020; Accepted: 21 March 2020; Published: 25 March 2020

Abstract: Nowadays, highly portable and low-energy computing environments require programming applications able to satisfy computing time and energy constraints. Furthermore, collaborative filtering based recommender systems are intelligent systems that use large databases and perform extensive matrix arithmetic calculations. In this research, we present an optimized algorithm and a parallel hardware implementation as good approach for running embedded collaborative filtering applications. To this end, we have considered high-level synthesis programming for reconfigurable hardware technology. The design was tested under environments where usual parameters and real-world datasets were applied, and compared to usual microprocessors running similar implementations. The performance results obtained by the different implementations were analyzed in computing time and energy consumption terms. The main conclusion is that the optimized algorithm is competitive in embedded applications when considering large datasets and parallel implementations based on reconfigurable hardware.

Keywords: embedded systems; collaborative filtering; recommender systems; parallelism; reconfigurable hardware; high-level synthesis

1. Introduction

Nowadays, in the framework of the information society, a large amount of information is being generated from multiple and heterogeneous data sources. The own interaction of the user who generates or uses this information is added to the same. Representative examples can be found in areas such as e-commerce (users who buy and value products) and the entertainment industry (users who value series and movies). This information is usually stored in large databases, permanently and dynamically growing and updating, which constitute a source of knowledge regarding user behavior, so that predictions and recommendations can be made. This is where recommendation systems emerge.

Recommender Systems (RS) [1] are algorithmic techniques that allow users to obtain recommendations and predictions after an intelligent processing of the data of large databases. RS give personalized recommendations to the users according to their behavior when requesting and handling information [2,3]. In this sense, RS are also known as filters because they block the data not connected to the users' behavior.

Besides the analysis and recommendation of information, an important application of RS is the prediction of the users' behavior. For example, in the *Predicting Student Performance* (PSP) problem [4], the score of an evaluation task in the academic environment for a particular student can be predicted when RS considers it as a ranking prediction problem. Nevertheless, the most popular implementation of RS is *Collaborative Filtering* (CF) [5,6], where users with similar preferences in the past will have similar preferences in the future [7]. For example, if two users have rated the same movies as positive, new movies that either rates as positive might be liked by the other user.

A matrix defines the relationship between users and items in CF. This matrix stores the ratings (explicit or implicit) of the users to the items, and has a high level of sparsity, because users only rate a small number of available items. Popular online applications, such as e-commerce websites or movies databases, generate rating matrices composed of thousands of million ratings, where hundreds of thousands of users have rated hundreds of thousands of items.

The way to fill the gaps of the sparse ratings matrix [8] considers the *Matrix Factorization* (MF) technique [9]. MF generates a scalable model for prediction purposes [10] composed of two matrices. The prediction is a combination of factors as result of multiplying the row corresponding to a user in the user-latent space with the column corresponding to an item in the item-latent matrix. In addition, MF assumes that users' ratings are conditioned by K latent factors describing the items of the system. MF algorithms try to find these hidden factors through the rating matrix.

We would like to highlight the interest in implementing a CF algorithm in hardware for running embedded applications due to several reasons. Firstly, we must bear in mind that CF involves large amount of data because of the number of users and items in databases. The needs of predictions and data handling involve high computational efforts, especially if real time constraints are required. Therefore, the design of hardware circuits that accelerate some processes of the algorithm is especially interesting. Besides, possible embedded applications of CF require fast algorithms if they should be performed on small, low-power computing environments. Therefore, we focus the research on implementing embedded applications of CF by considering *Field Programmable Gate Array* (FPGA) devices [11], under the *Reconfigurable Computing* (RC) [12] and System-On-Chip (SoC) [13] concepts.

We propose using FPGA devices for designing accelerated CF algorithms because this technology combines software flexibility with hardware performance by exploiting parallelism. Thus, if an embedded implementation is designed carefully by following these advantages, it can provide excellent results, even surpassing the performance delivered by usual microprocessors or *Central Processing Units* (CPU) in similar experimental conditions [14]. Other design approaches based on different hardware technologies can also be explored. In this sense, *Graphical Processing Units* (GPUs) can be programmed by using OpenCL for similar purposes, although their high power consumption could be a constraint when using them for embedded applications.

In summary, our proposal is to design an embedded, low-energy implementation of an efficient CF algorithm in order to perform applications on highly-portable light computing environments. Our approach was successfully tested considering several state-of-the-art datasets.

The remainder of this paper is structured as follows. We present some related works in Section 2. In Section 3, we discuss the basis of two approaches, basic and enhanced, of CF algorithms. Next, Section 4 explains the design and implementation of both algorithms, emphasizing on the parallelization strategy considered for improving the performance results. Section 5 shows a performance comparison between the two approaches and usual microprocessors, detailing the state-of-the-art datasets considered, the experimental procedure followed, and the timing and power results. Finally, the conclusions of this paper are summarized in Section 6.

2. Related Works

RS are a good opportunity to provide advanced services to Internet users. Some classic examples of heterogeneous successful applications are PHOAKS [15] (it helps users to locate useful information on the *World Wide Web* (WWW) examining USenet news messages), Referral Web [16] (it combines social networks and collaborative filtering), Fab [17] (it combines content-based information with collaborative filtering), Siteseer [18] (a conceptual recommender system for CiteSeerX), and many others. However, currently growing concepts in the Internet domain, such as Internet of Things, autonomous driving, and augmented reality, among many others, are pushing to consider new applications of the RS. For example, we can find novel and advanced applications of RS in vehicles [19], voice-enabled devices [20], smartphones [21], and multimedia data for robustness [22], diversification [23], and real-time [24] recommendation aims, among many other examples.

In the context of an increasing application of the RS, many research efforts are focused on improving the accuracy and reducing their limitations. In this regard, RS have some limitations, especially related to their complexity and difficulty in understanding them. They represent black boxes that require personalized explanations related to the individuals' mental models [25], which has consequences in many areas, such as computer vision [26].

Computing systems based on low-performance and low-consumption microprocessors may be involved in some of these new fields of application of RS. Thus, there are environments where RS could run on such computer systems, for example smartphones and IoT devices. In fact, the demand of computing resources by RS may have limited their application in these areas and devices. Particularly, mobile RS are an interesting area for online applications (social networks, e-commerce, and streaming platforms) in situations where the data volume can produce overload. These situations may occur more and more frequently, given the rapid increase in the use of mobile devices in a context of continuous growth and improvement of network infrastructure. The links between web and mobile RS are identified in [27] to provide guidelines for embedded RS in mobile domain. We find some examples of mobile RS in recommending different types of media to its users using a context-aware approach [28] or in recommending photos by means of current contextual data in combination with information found in the photos [29]. Other examples of mobile RS can be found in the mobile news based on the current context and format [30], the recommendation of music depending on the daily activities of a person [31], or the passengers of a car [32].

For all the above reasons, the tools and technologies for designing and implementing embedded computing systems based on low-consumption devices can lead to the application of RS for many purposes in novel fields. Our proposal considers the reconfigurable technology based on FPGA devices for implementing fast, low-power collaborative filtering algorithms for embedded applications. This proposal is in line with other works where ML functions and features have been implemented using similar technology, for different purposes, mainly for acceleration tasks. Thus, we can find FPGA technology applied for *Convolutional Neural Networks* (CNN) [33], *Deep Learning* (DL) [34], K-Means clustering [35–37], and kernel density estimation [38], among others.

It is particularly interesting to explore the application of FPGAs for CF, especially for acceleration purposes. In this regard, there are some attempts to accelerate tasks involved in cloud services and large databases, such as Amazon [39]. We can find some examples of FPGA implementations of different aspects of RS algorithms, rather than the whole system itself. For example, a *Stochastic Gradient Descent* (SGD) algorithm [40] used for training some RS models is implemented on FPGA considering single-precision floating-point [41]. In this sense, our proposal takes a step forward, as we undertake the complete implementation of two CF algorithms, which are capable of handling real datasets.

3. Recommender Systems: Two Approaches

In this section, we present two approaches of CF algorithms, detailing their mathematical descriptions and how they work.

3.1. Basic Algorithm

In the context of machine learning, MF technique represents a well known family of algorithms that split a matrix $X \in \mathbb{R}^{n \times m}$ into two matrices $U \in \mathbb{R}^{n \times k}$ and $V \in \mathbb{R}^{k \times m}$, in such a way that $X \approx U \cdot V$ [42]. Note that the rank of the matrices U and V is much smaller than the rank of X, since $k \ll n$ and $k \ll m$. Therefore, the factorized matrices U and V contain a compact representation of the original matrix X.

Applied to CF, MF based RS factorize the sparse rating matrix $R \in \mathbb{R}^{n \times m}$ that contains the set of known ratings of n users to m items [43]. The fundamental assumption of these kinds of algorithms is that the ratings of the users to the items are conditioned by a subset of latent factors intrinsic to the users and items. For example, in a movies' RS, it is assumed that the rating a user provides to a movie is conditioned by the genre of that movie. As consequence of the factorization process, two new matrices are generated: $P \in \mathbb{R}^{n \times k}$, which represents the k-latent factors of the n users; and $Q \in \mathbb{R}^{m \times k}$, which represents the k-latent factors of the m items. Once the factorization is performed, the rating predictions ($\hat{r}_{ui}$) of a user u to an item i can be computed by the dot product of the row vector of the matrix P that contains the latent factors of the user u ($\vec{p}_u$) and the column vector of the matrix Q that contains the latent factors of the item i ($\vec{q}_i$):

$$\hat{r}_{ui} = \vec{p}_u \cdot \vec{q}_i^T. \tag{1}$$

Hence, the learning process consists on find the optimal parameters for the matrices P and Q that verifies

$$R \approx P \cdot Q^T. \tag{2}$$

This process is usually raised as an optimization problem in which the quadratic difference between the known ratings ($r_{u,i}$) of the matrix R and the predicted ones ($\vec{p}_u \cdot \vec{q}_i^T$) must be minimized:

$$\min_{\vec{p}_u, \vec{q}_i} \sum_{(u,i) \in R} (r_{u,i} - \vec{p}_u \cdot \vec{q}_i^T)^2. \tag{3}$$

The most popular implementation of MF applied to CF is Probabilistic Matrix Factorization (PMF) [44]. PMF performs the factorization thorough a probabilistic model that represents interaction between the users and items in a CF context. Figure 1 contains a graphical representation of this probabilistic model. The figure contains three representational elements: circles that symbolize random variables; arrows between two variables that indicate dependence between that random variables; and rectangles that indicate repetitions of the random variables. The color of the circles indicates if the random variables are observed (black) or must be learned (white). As we can observe, there exists three random variable: R_{ui} that symbolizes the rating of the user u to the item i; P_u that symbolizes the latent factors of each user u; and Q_i that symbolizes the latent factors of each item i. The arrows between P_u and Q_i with R_{ui} denote that there exists dependency between the rating of user u to item i and the latent factors of user u and item i. PMF assumes a Gaussian distribution for all the random variables. σ_R, σ_P and σ_Q denotes model hyper-parameters.

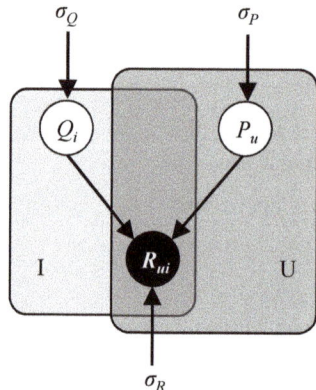

Figure 1. Graphical representation of PMF model.

Algorithm 1 summarizes PMF. The inputs are the rating matrix R, the number of latent factors K, and the hyper-parameters to control the learning process λ and γ. The outputs are the latent factors matrices P and Q learned from the rating matrix.

Algorithm 1: PMF algorithm.

---
input : R, K, λ, γ
output: P, Q
Create a random matrix P with U rows and K columns
Create a random matrix Q with I rows and K columns
repeat
    for *each user u* **do** // This loop can me parallelized for each user
        for *each item i rated by user u* **do**
            error = $R[u][i]$ - dotProduct($P[u], Q[i]$)
            for *each factor k* **do**
                $P[u][k]+ = \gamma \cdot (error \cdot P[u][k] - \lambda \cdot Q[i][k])$

    for *each item i* **do** // This loop can be parallelized for each item
        for *each user u that has rated the item i* **do**
            error = $R[u][i]$ - dotProduct($P[u], Q[i]$)
            for *each factor k* **do**
                $Q[i][k]+ = \gamma \cdot (error \cdot Q[i][k] - \lambda \cdot P[u][k])$

until *convergence*
return P, Q

3.2. BNMF Algorithm

Bayesian Non-negative Matrix Factorization (BNMF) [9] model is another factorization model designed for CF based RS. BNMF model has demonstrated its superiority by providing more accurate predictions and recommendations than PMF model. As PMF, BNMF factorizes the rating matrix in a probabilistic way.

The main objective of BNMF is to provide an understandable probabilistic meaning of the latent factors space generated as consequence of the factorization process. To achieve this, the model has been designed in such a way that it better represents the interaction between users and items. Instead of assuming a continuous distribution to represent ratings, such as Gaussian distribution, a discrete distribution is used. This coincides with the reality of most CF systems, where users must rate items on a pre-set scale (e.g., 1–5 stars).

Figure 2 contains a graphical representation of BNMF model. The model is composed by the following random variables:

- $\vec{\theta}_u$ is a K dimensional vector from a Dirichlet distribution. This random variables are used to represent the probability that a user belongs to each group.
- κ_{ik} from the Beta distribution used to represent the probability that a user in the group k likes the item i.
- Z_{ui} from the Categorical distribution used to represents that the user u rates the item i as if he or she belongs to the group k.
- ρ_{ui} from the Binomial distribution used to represent the observable rating of the user u to the item i.

The model also contains the following hyper-parameters:

- α is related to the possibility of obtaining overlapping groups of users sharing the same preferences.
- β is related to the amount of evidences required to belong to a group.

- K is related to the number of groups (i.e., number of latent factors) that exists in the dataset.
- R is related to the Binomial distribution which take values from 0 to R.

To be able to compute predictions with the BNMF model, we must determine the conditional probability distribution of the non-observable random variables given a set of observations (i.e., the known ratings). Applying the variational inference technique [45], we can obtain the algorithm to perform this task. Algorithm 2 contains a detailed explanation about the training phase of BNMF model. For further information about the inference process, see [9].

Algorithm 2: BNMF algorithm. The algorithm returns the latent factors for each user and item. Input ratings (r_{ui}) must be normalized.

---

input : r_{ui}, α, β, K, R
output: p_{uk}, q_{ik}
temp : γ_{uk}, ϵ_{ik}^-, ϵ_{ik}^+, λ_{uik}, λ'_{uik}
Initialize γ_{uk}
Initialize ϵ_{ik}^-
Initialize ϵ_{ik}^+
repeat
    for *each user u* **do**
        for *each item i rated by user u* **do**
            for *each factor k* **do**
                $\lambda'_{uik} \leftarrow exp(\Psi(\gamma_{uk}) + r_{ui}^+ \cdot \Psi(\epsilon_{ik}^+) + r_{ui}^- \cdot \Psi(\epsilon_{ik}^-) - R \cdot \Psi(\epsilon_{ik}^+ + \epsilon_{ik}^-))$
            for *each factor k* **do**
                $\lambda_{uik} \leftarrow \frac{\lambda'_{uik}}{\lambda'_{ui1} + \cdots + \lambda'_{uiK}}$
    for *each item i* **do**
        $\epsilon_{ik}^+ \leftarrow \beta$
        $\epsilon_{ik}^- \leftarrow \beta$
    for *each user u* **do**
        $\gamma_{uk} \leftarrow \alpha$
        for *each item i rated by user u* **do**
            for *each factor k* **do**
                $\gamma_{uk} \leftarrow \gamma_{uk} + \lambda_{uik}$
                $\epsilon_{ik}^+ \leftarrow \epsilon_{ik}^+ + \lambda_{uik} \cdot R \cdot r_{ui}$
                $\epsilon_{ik}^- \leftarrow \epsilon_{ik}^- + \lambda_{uik} \cdot R \cdot (1 - r_{ui})$
until *convergence*
for *each factor k* **do**
    for *each user u* **do**
        $p_{uk} \leftarrow \frac{\gamma_{uk}}{\sum_{f=1..K} \gamma_{uf}}$
    for *each item i* **do**
        $q_{ik} \leftarrow \frac{\epsilon_{ik}^+}{\epsilon_{ik}^+ + \epsilon_{ik}^-}$

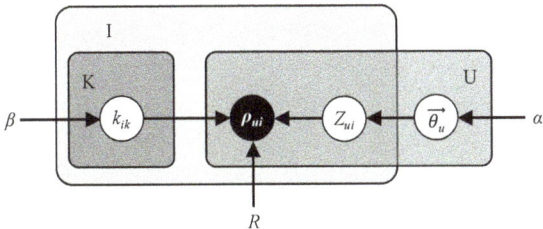

Figure 2. Graphical representation of BNMF model.

4. Hardware Designs for Embedded Applications

In this section, we present the hardware implementations of PMF and BNMF. The purpose of both implementations is twofold. On the one hand, the operations of the algorithms are accelerated by using the parallelism that hardware provides; on the other hand, the energy consumption is reduced in comparison with usual microprocessors.

4.1. PMF Design

PMF was parallelized by considering *High-Level Synthesis* (HLS) technology [46]. HLS transforms C specifications (C, C++, SystemC, or OpenCL code) into a *Register Transfer Level* (RTL) implementation, which allows us to synthesize the design to any Xilinx FPGA. This way, HLS facilitates the fast design of efficient circuits by parallelizing code automatically. Specifically, for this work, we considered Vivado HLS tool [47], which was deeply analyzed by O'Loughlin *et al.* [48].

The main parallelization strategy for PMF is described in [49]. As we can see in Algorithm 1, two consecutive loops can be parallelized after initialization in order to update the corresponding factorized matrices for each user/item. These loops are sequentially performed several times.

4.2. BNMF Design

In this section, we show how we implemented the BNMF algorithm on a reconfigurable hardware platform. Previously, we implemented two versions of PMF on FPGA. The first version was a simple design without parallelism in order to check the viability of using an embedded operating system for running a full recommender system and analyze its performance. The second version was a parallelized design in order to accelerate the operations. Therefore, next, we focused our efforts just on implementing a parallelized design of BNMF, once checked the viability of using the same hardware platforms and software tools applied to PMF. In this section, we detail how we designed the BNMF algorithm for a high-performance implementation on FPGA.

The main tools used for the design of the BNMF algorithm in an FPGA are summarized in Table 1. Zedboard is a low-energy and low-cost prototyping board that mounts a programmable System-on-Chip (SoC) including an ARM processing architecture. Furthermore, there are many elements and features to design any computing system based on Linux, Windows, and Android operating systems, among others, and interact with the user's needs.

Table 1. Main tools for implementing BNMF in FPGA.

Hardware	Zedboard Zynq-7000	*SoC*: *Elements*: *Memory*: *Oscillators*:	Xilinx Zynq XC7Z020 HDMI, VGA, audio, Ethernet, SD, USB ... 512 MB DDR3 100 MHz and 33.3 MHz
Operating System	Linaro OS		
Software	Xilinx Vivado HLS		

Figure 3 shows the architecture where BNMF is implemented and executed. This architecture basically consists of three elements, mutually communicated along an AXI bus: external memory, multiprocessor system, and programmable logic.

- The memory of type DDR3 can store up to 512 MB. It hosts the datasets that provide the users and items to the RS, as well as the main program to control the BNMF flow. Storing the datasets in the external memory instead of in the internal memory blocks of the FPGA frees up space in the programmable logic to implement the BNMF core. In addition, an AXI interface was chosen to implement parallel access to memory so as not to limit bandwidth excessively. However, very large datasets may exceed the available memory capacity; in this case, the dataset is hosted on the SD card together with Linaro OS.
- The multiprocessor system is based on an ARM Dual Cortex-A9. It just runs the main control program: basic operations for initializing and starting the BNMF core implemented in the FPGA, as well as getting and displaying the results returned by it.
- The SoC block implements the BNMF core. The main advantage of this block is the high parallelization level of the operations described in Algorithm 2. Thus, the expected performance of this design would be higher than the performance given by a simple sequential code in the same main control program.

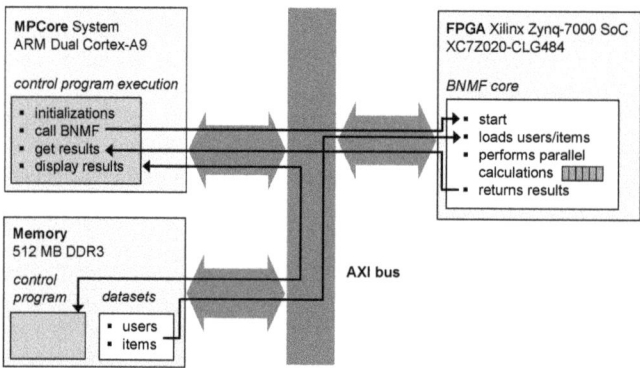

Figure 3. Basic architecture for BNMF on the Zynq Zedboard 7000.

As we did in PMF, we installed an embedded Linux OS (Linaro distribution) on the board in order to allow running the BNMF on the FPGA. This OS is launched from a separated partition in the SD card, thus the changes made by the program are written in that partition. The Linaro filesystem is a complete Ubuntu-based Linux distribution with graphical desktop. The advantage of using the Linaro is that we can work with the ZedBoard just as if we used a commercial processor. Thus, the code executed both in ZedBoard and in CPU is exactly the same.

4.3. Parallelization Strategy

In this section, we detail how the parallel implementation of the BNMF algorithm was designed. The results obtained in PMF encouraged us to improve the performance by designing a more accurate parallel design in BNMF.

The parallel design was developed mainly by programming with HLS. However, we also modified the design manually by including different optimization directives provided by HLS in order to increase the fine-grained parallelism without the need to modify the C code, in order to obtain a higher performance circuit. Thanks to these directives, we managed the way of parallelizing certain loops and operations. The most used directives were those for unrolling loops or functions, which allow us to work with arrays in parallel. Additionally, other directives to later transfer data to the BNMF algorithm were used too.

Figure 4 allows explaining easily the parallelization strategy followed by the design. First, according to Algorithm 2, we perform random initializations of γ, e^+ and e^- in parallel, since they are matrices and are highly parallelizable.

Next, four consecutive blocks implement parallel operation for calculating some sections of the algorithm. These four blocks are executed sequentially because there is a clear data dependency between them.

The update of λ requires a great computational cost, since we could define it as a matrix vector. Basically, the parallelization consists in updating each of the elements of that matrix vector in parallel. Then, we also perform the update of e^+ and e^- in parallel. Finally, we calculate the user factors a and b in parallel.

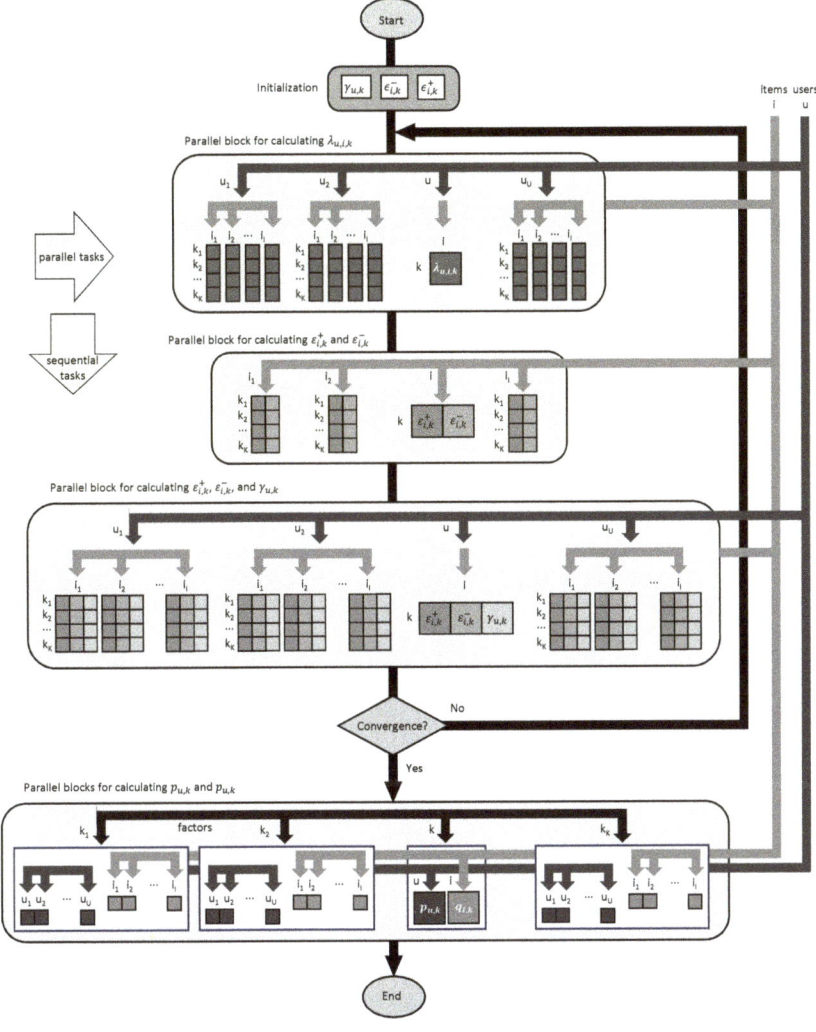

Figure 4. Strategy for parallelizing BNMF.

5. Performance Comparison

In this section, we highlight the different results obtained by PMF and BNMF. First, we explain the datasets considered for the experiments. Next, we show the performance results in terms of computing time and energy consumption.

5.1. Datasets

Both PMF and BNMF were tested using four state-of-the-art datasets of different characteristics, widely used for this purpose: The Movies Dataset (Kaggle), Movielens-100K, Movielens-1M, and Netflix-100M (Table 2). These datasets gather the activity of many users when rating movies with scores from 1 to 5, where each user rates at least 20 movies.

We chose datasets of very different sizes to check the impact of the matrix calculations in the performance given by the FPGA implementation. To get a rough idea, the product Users × Items goes from 6.3M in Kaggle to 8495M in Netflix-100M.

Table 2. Datasets used to test PMF and BNMF algorithms.

Dataset	Kaggle	Movielens-100k	Movielens-1M	Netflix-100M
Ratings	100,000	100,000	1,000,000	10,000,000
Users	700	943	6,000	480,188
Items	9000	1682	4000	17,691

5.2. Experimental Procedure

Figure 5 shows the phases of the experimental procedure followed in our research. First, we studied in depth the best way to parallelize BNMF, looking for those operations that can be parallelized without altering the right calculation of the remaining ones. Once the parallelizaton strategy was determined, we generated the parallel core using Xilinx Vivado HLS. The BNMF design was exported as IP core, which can be reached by the processor and memory in the architecture described in Figure 3. Next, this core was exported as bitstream into the Linaro OS, and the aforementioned datasets were added to perform the tests. Finally, the BNMF algorithm was executed and the results are validated.

This experimental procedure was performed as many times as different datasets available for performance purposes.

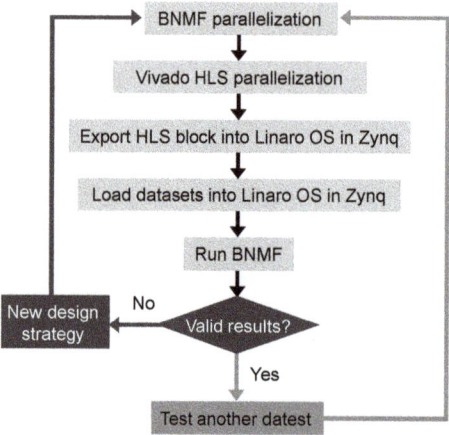

Figure 5. Experimental procedure.

5.3. Timing Results

In this section we show the computing time obtained by the hardware implementations of BNMF and PMF algorithms, and by an up-to-date microprocessor for comparison purposes.

With regard to the FPGA implementation, we measured the elapsed time by using HLS, considering the same FPGA device and the required operational frequency. Once the design is synthesized, HLS allows us to know whether the given frequency can be supported by the FPGA device, as well as the number of clock cycles used by the hardware. Hence, we calculated the elapsed computing time.

We considered for the CPU experiments an Intel i7-950 with clock frequency of 3 GHz. Note that the RS implemented on the FPGA reached a very low frequency compared to the CPU: 667 MHz. The CPU runs codes that implement the same operations described in the PMF and BNMG algorithms, considering the same parameters and datasets.

Table 3 shows the computing time in seconds of the PMF and BNMF algorithms for the CPU and FPGA implementations, considering the four datasets. We deduce two interesting conclusions.

Table 3. Computing time (s) and FPGA speedup of PMF and BNMF algorithms for the CPU and FPGA implementations.

Dataset	Kaggle		Movielens-100k		Movielens-1M		Netflix-100M	
Algorithm	PMF	BNMF	PMF	BNMF	PMF	BNMF	PMF	BNMF
CPU (s)	76.12	284.38	33.62	152.22	113.41	504.01	96,381.80	405,843.84
FPGA (s)	1129.70	313.82	831.04	163.72	2934.57	105.93	98,649.80	50,625.32
FPGA speedup	×0.07	×0.91	×0.04	×0.93	×0.04	**×4.76**	×0.98	**×8.02**

First, comparing both algorithms, we can observe that BNMF takes more computing time than PMF in CPU, although much less in FPGA. The reason is simply that BNMF provides the greatest parallelization degree in the FPGA implementation. Second, we can observe that, the larger is the dataset, the better are the results we obtain in the parallel implementation of BNMF in FPGA. In both the Kaggle dataset and the Movielenes-100k dataset, the time results are very similar. However, the two largest datasets begin to show a greater computing time difference between FPGA and CPU. Thus, for the Movielens-1M dataset, the FPGA gets a speedup of almost ×5, while this speedup increases to ×8 for the Netflix-100M dataset.

In conclusion, a FPGA implementation is more attractive for the BNMF algorithm and larger datasets. As a proposal, it would be interesting to experiment with larger sets corresponding to other types of data.

5.4. Power Results

Energy consumption is another important metric for computing systems performance. The RS algorithms have a certain energy impact on the hardware platforms. Knowing this impact is important because it helps us to optimize energy-aware designs of embedded RS. We keep in mind that embedded RS can be demanded for computing-intensive cases when performing many predictions over time.

Xilinx Vivado provides the total on-chip power of the FPGA implementations. Table 4 shows the power in watts of the PMF and BNMF algorithms for the CPU and FPGA implementations, considering the four datasets. We observe that the power reduction in any FPGA implementation is very high (more than 80% on average). Therefore, a clear advantage of implementing RS in FPGA is the low energy consumption with regard to current CPUs.

Under the algorithmic point of view, we can check in Table 4 that BNMF gives a more significant power reduction than PMF. This fact, along with the computing time reduction for large datasets deduced from Table 3, encourage us to consider BNMF as the best algorithmic option for building embedded RS applications.

Table 4. Power (w) and FPGA power reduction of PMF and BNMF algorithms for the CPU and FPGA implementations.

Dataset	Kaggle		Movielens-100k		Movielens-1M		Netflix-100M	
Algorithm	PMF	BNMF	PMF	BNMF	PMF	BNMF	PMF	BNMF
CPU (w)	8.21	11.33	7.33	10.81	12.31	16.26	32.21	41.20
FPGA (w)	0.95	2.52	0.82	2.24	1.64	4.41	3.03	7.37
FPGA power reduction	88%	78%	89%	80%	87%	73%	91%	83%

6. Conclusions

We researched the performance of two different approaches of collaborative filtering based recommender systems for embedded applications. For this purpose, we parallelized some operations by considering high-level synthesis technology for FPGA devices. Regarding computing time, the FPGA implementation of the Bayesian non-negative matrix factorization algorithm provided good speedups compared to general-purpose microprocessors when dealing with large datasets, and it surpassed clearly the results obtained by the probabilistic matrix factorization approach. Furthermore, the low power consumption of FPGA devices makes interesting the line of exploring computing solutions for embedded applications of collaborative filtering. In summary, the proposed approach allows running efficient embedded collaborative filtering applications when using low-energy computing systems based on FPGAs, taking advantage of the opportunity provided by reconfigurable computing to exploit parallelism.

Author Contributions: F.O. proposed the recommender systems algorithms and provided the datasets. F.P.-H. and J.A.G.-P. proposed the methodology and tools for designing the embedded architectures. F.P.-H. programmed the parallel codes, implemented the circuits, and measured the timing and energy behaviors. All authors analyzed the results, suggested the conclusions, and revised the manuscript. All authors have read and agreed to the published version of the manuscript.

Funding: This research was funded by the Government of Extremadura (Spain) grant number IB16002 and by the AEI (State Research Agency, Spain) and the ERDF (European Regional Development Fund, EU) grant number TIN2016-76259-P. The APC was funded by the Government of Extremadura (Spain) grant number IB16002.

Conflicts of Interest: The authors declare no conflict of interest. The founding sponsors had no role in the design of the study; in the collection, analyses, or interpretation of data; in the writing of the manuscript, and in the decision to publish the results.

Abbreviations

The following abbreviations are used in this manuscript:

BNMF	Bayesian Non-negative Matrix Factorization
CF	Collaborative Filtering
CNN	Convolutional Neural Networks
DL	Deep Learning
FPGA	Field-Programmable Gate Array
HLS	High-Level Synthesis
MF	Matrix Factorisation
ML	Machine Learning
PMF	Probabilistic Matrix Factorization
RC	Reconfigurable Computing
RMSE	Root Mean Squared Error
RS	Recommender Systems
RTL	Register Transfer Level
SGD	Stochastic Gradient Descent
SoC	System-on-Chip
WWW	World Wide Web

References

1. Jannach, D.; Felfernig, A.; Zanker, M.; Friedrich, G. *Recommender Systems. An Introduction*; Cambridge University Press: Cambridge, UK, 2011.
2. Bobadilla, J.; Ortega, F.; Hernando, A.; Gutiérrez, A. Recommender systems survey. *Knowl. Based Syst.* **2013**, *46*, 109–132. [CrossRef]
3. Adomavicius, G.; Tuzhilin, A. Context-aware recommender systems. In *Recommender Systems Handbook*; Springer: Berlin/Heidelberg, Germany, 2015; pp. 191–226.
4. Thai-Nghe, N.; Drumond, L.; Horvath, T.; Krohn-Grimberghe, A.; Nanopoulos, A.; Schmidt-Thieme, L. Factorization Techniques for Predicting Student Performance. In *Educational Recommender Systems and Technologies: Practices and Challenges*; IGI-Global: Hershey, PA, USA, 2012; pp. 129–153.
5. Adomavicius, G.; Tuzhilin, A. Toward the next generation of recommender systems: A survey of the state-of-the-art and possible extensions. *IEEE Trans. Knowl. Data Eng.* **2005**, *17*, 734–749. [CrossRef]
6. Ricci, F.; Rokach, L.; Shapira, B. Introduction to recommender systems handbook. In *Recommender Systems Handbook*; Springer: Berlin/Heidelberg, Germany, 2011; pp. 1–35. [CrossRef]
7. Bobadilla, J.; Serradilla, F.; Bernal, J. A new collaborative filtering metric that improves the behavior of recommender systems. *Knowl. Based Syst.* **2010**, *23*, 520–528.
8. Herlocker, J.L.; Konstan, J.A.; Terveen, L.G.; Riedl, J.T. Evaluating collaborative filtering recommender systems. *ACM Trans. Inf. Syst. TOIS* **2004**, *22*, 5–53. [CrossRef]
9. Hernando, A.; Bobadilla, J.; Ortega, F. A non negative matrix factorization for collaborative filtering recommender systems based on a Bayesian probabilistic model. *Knowl. Based Syst.* **2016**, *97*, 188–202. [CrossRef]
10. Rendle, S.; Schmidt-Thieme, L. Online-updating regularized kernel matrix factorization models for large-scale recommender systems. In Proceedings of the 2008 ACM Conference on Recommender Systems, Lousanne, Switzerland, 23–25 October 2008; pp. 251–258. [CrossRef]
11. Unsalan, C.; Tar, B. *Digital System Design with FPGA: Implementation Using Verilog and VHDL*; McGraw-Hill: New York, NY, USA, 2017.
12. Tessier, R.; Pocek, K.; DeHon, A. Reconfigurable Computing Architectures. *Proc. IEEE* **2015**, *103*, 332–354.
13. Goeders, J.; Holland, G.M.; Shannon, L.; Wilton, S.J.E. Systems-on-Chip on FPGAs. In *FPGAs for Software Programmers*; Koch, D., Hannig, F., Ziener, D., Eds.; Springer International Publishing: Cham, Switzerland, 2016; pp. 261–283. doi:10.1007/978-3-319-26408-0_15. [CrossRef]
14. Vestias, M.; Neto, H. Trends of CPU, GPU and FPGA for high-performance computing. In Proceedings of the IEEE 24th International Conference on Field Programmable Logic and Applications, Munich, Germany, 2–4 September 2014; pp. 1–6. [CrossRef]
15. Terveen, L.; Hill, W.; Amento, B.; McDonald, D.; Creter, J. PHOAKS: A system for sharing recommendations. *Commun. ACM* **1997**, *40*, 59–62. [CrossRef]
16. Kautz, H.; Selman, B.; Shah, M. Referral Web: Combining Social Networks and Collaborative Filtering. *Commun. ACM* **1997**, *40*, 63–65. [CrossRef]
17. Balabanovic, M.; Shoham, Y. Fab: Content-Based, Collaborative Recommendation. *Commun. ACM* **1997**, *40*, 66–72. [CrossRef]
18. Pudhiyaveetil, A.K.; Gauch, S.; Luong, H.P.; Eno, J. Conceptual recommender system for CiteSeerX. In Proceedings of the 2009 ACM Conference on Recommender Systems, RecSys 2009. New York, NY, USA, 23–25 October 2009; Bergman, L.D., Tuzhilin, A., Burke, R.D., Felfernig, A., Schmidt-Thieme, L., Eds.; ACM: New York, NY, USA, 2009; pp. 241–244. [CrossRef]
19. Luettin, J.; Rothermel, S.; Andrew, M. Future of In-Vehicle Recommendation Systems @ Bosch. In *Proceedings of the 13th ACM Conference on Recommender Systems*; RecSys '19; Association for Computing Machinery: New York, NY, USA, 2019; p. 524. [CrossRef]
20. Ostuni, V.C. "Just Play Something Awesome": The Personalization Powering Voice Interactions at Pandora. In *Proceedings of the 13th ACM Conference on Recommender Systems*; RecSys '19; Association for Computing Machinery: New York, NY, USA, 2019; p. 523. [CrossRef]

21. Verma, R.; Ghosh, S.; Saketh, M.; Ganguly, N.; Mitra, B.; Chakraborty, S. Comfride: A Smartphone Based System for Comfortable Public Transport Recommendation. In *Proceedings of the 12th ACM Conference on Recommender Systems*; RecSys '18; Association for Computing Machinery: New York, NY, USA, 2018; p. 181–189. [CrossRef]
22. Tang, J.; Du, X.; He, X.; Yuan, F.; Tian, Q.; Chua, T. Adversarial Training Towards Robust Multimedia Recommender System. In *IEEE Transactions on Knowledge and Data Engineering*; IEEE: Piscataway, NJ, USA, 2019; pp. 1–1. [CrossRef]
23. Raja, D.R.K.; Pushpa, S. Diversifying personalized mobile multimedia application recommendations through the Latent Dirichlet Allocation and clustering optimization. *Multim. Tools Appl.* **2019**, *78*, 24047–24066. [CrossRef]
24. Amato, F.; Moscato, V.; Picariello, A.; Sperli'ì, G. Extreme events management using multimedia social networks. *Future Gen. Comput. Syst.* **2019**, *94*, 444–452. [CrossRef]
25. Kuhl, N.; Lobana, J.; Meske, C. Do you comply with AI? —Personalized explanations of learning algorithms and their impact on employees' compliance behavior. *arXiv* **2020**, arXiv:2002.087772020. [CrossRef]
26. Meske, C.; Bunde, E. Using Explainable Artificial Intelligence to Increase Trust in Computer Vision. *arXiv preprint* **2020**, arXiv:cs.HC/2002.01543.
27. Pimenidis, E.; Polatidis, N.; Mouratidis, H. Mobile recommender systems: Identifying the major concepts. *J. Inf. Sci.* **2019**, *45*, 387–397.
28. Zhiwen Yu.; Xingshe Zhou.; Daqing Zhang.; Chung-Yau Chin.; Xiaohang Wang.; Ji Men. Supporting Context-Aware Media Recommendations for Smart Phones. *IEEE Pervas. Comput.* **2006**, *5*, 68–75. [CrossRef]
29. Lemos, F.; Carmo, R.; Viana, W.; Andrade, R. Towards a context-aware photo recommender system. *CEUR Workshop Proc.* **2012**, *889*. [CrossRef]
30. Sotsenko, A.; Jansen, M.; Milrad, M. Using a rich context model for a news recommender system for mobile users. *CEUR Workshop Proc.* **2014**, *1181*, 13–16.
31. Wang, X.; Rosenblum, D.; Wang, Y. Context-Aware Mobile Music Recommendation for Daily Activities. In *Proceedings of the 20th ACM International Conference on Multimedia*; MM '12; Association for Computing Machinery: New York, NY, USA, 2012; p. 99–108.
32. Baltrunas, L.; Ludwig, B.; Peer, S.; Ricci, F. Context relevance assessment and exploitation in mobile recommender systems. *Perso. Ubiquit. Comput.* **2012**, *16*, 507–526. [CrossRef]
33. Ma, Y.; Suda, N.; Cao, Y.; Vrudhula, S.; sun Seo, J. ALAMO: FPGA acceleration of deep learning algorithms with a modularized RTL compiler. *Integration* **2018**, *62*, 14–23. [CrossRef]
34. Gankidi, P.R.; Thangavelautham, J. FPGA architecture for deep learning and its application to planetary robotics. In *Proceedings of the 2017 IEEE Aerospace Conference, Big Sky, MT, USA, 4–11 March 2017*; pp. 1–9. [CrossRef]
35. Canilho, J.; Véstias, M.; Neto, H. Multi-core for K-means clustering on FPGA. In *Proceedings of the 2016 26th International Conference on Field Programmable Logic and Applications (FPL), Lausanne, Switzerland, 29 August–2 September 2016*; pp. 1–4. [CrossRef]
36. Winterstein, F.; Bayliss, S.; Constantinides, G.A. FPGA-based K-means clustering using tree-based data structures. In *Proceedings of the 2013 23rd International Conference on Field programmable Logic and Applications, Porto, Portugal, 2–4 September 2013*; pp. 1–6. [CrossRef]
37. Lin, Z.; Lo, C.; Chow, P. K-means implementation on FPGA for high-dimensional data using triangle inequality. In *Proceedings of the 22nd International Conference on Field Programmable Logic and Applications (FPL), Oslo, Norway, 29–31 August 2012*; pp. 437–442. [CrossRef]
38. Nagarajan, K.; Holland, B.; George, A.D.; Slatton, K.C.; Lam, H. Accelerating Machine-Learning Algorithms on FPGAs using Pattern-Based Decomposition. *J. Signal Proc. Syst.* **2011**, *62*, 43–63. [CrossRef]
39. Amazon EC2 F1 Instances. 2019. Available online: https://aws.amazon.com/cn/ec2/instance-types/f1/ (accessed on 22 February 2020). [CrossRef]
40. Bottou, L. Large-Scale Machine Learning with Stochastic Gradient Descent. In *Proceedings of 19th International Conference on Computational Statistics*; Springer: Heidelberg, Germany, 2010; pp. 177–186.
41. Kara, K.; Alistarh, D.; Alonso, G.; Mutlu, O.; Zhang, C. FPGA-Accelerated Dense Linear Machine Learning: A Precision-Convergence Trade-Off. In *Proceedings of the 2017 IEEE 25th Annual International Symposium on Field-Programmable Custom Computing Machines (FCCM), Napa, CA, USA, 30 April–2 May 2017*; pp. 160–167.

42. Lee, D.D.; Seung, H.S. Unsupervised learning by convex and conic coding. In *Advances in Neural Information Processing Systems*; IEEE: Piscatawy, NJ, USA, 1997; pp. 515–521. [CrossRef]
43. Koren, Y.; Bell, R.; Volinsky, C. Matrix factorization techniques for recommender systems. *Computer* **2009**, *42*, 30–37.
44. Mnih, A.; Salakhutdinov, R.R. Probabilistic matrix factorization. In *Advances in Neural Information Processing Systems*; IEEE: Piscatawy, NJ, USA, 2008; pp. 1257–1264. [CrossRef]
45. Hoffman, M.D.; Blei, D.M.; Wang, C.; Paisley, J. Stochastic variational inference. *J. Mach. Learn. Res.* **2013**, *14*, 1303–1347.
46. Cong, J.; Liu, B.; Neuendorffer, S.; Noguera, J.; Vissers, K.; Zhang, Z. High-Level Synthesis for FPGAs: From Prototyping to Deployment. *IEEE Trans. Comput. Aided Des. Integr. Circ. Syst.* **2011**, *30*, 473–491.
47. Xilinx Inc. *Vivado Design Suite User Guide: High-Level Synthesis*; Technical Report UG902 (v2019.2); Xilinx Inc.: San Jose, CA, USA, 2020. [CrossRef]
48. O'Loughlin, D.; Coffey, A.; Callaly, F.; Lyons, D.; Morgan, F. Xilinx Vivado High Level Synthesis: Case studies. In Proceedings of the 25th IET Irish Signals Systems Conference 2014 and 2014 China-Ireland International Conference on Information and Communications Technologies (ISSC 2014/CIICT 2014), Limerick, Ireland, 26–27 June 2014; pp. 352–356.
49. Pajuelo-Holguera, F.; Gómez-Pulido, J.A.; Ortega, F.; Granado-Criado, J.M. Recommender system implementations for embedded collaborative filtering applications. *Microproce. Microsyst.* **2020**, *73*, 102997. [CrossRef]

© 2020 by the authors. Licensee MDPI, Basel, Switzerland. This article is an open access article distributed under the terms and conditions of the Creative Commons Attribution (CC BY) license (http://creativecommons.org/licenses/by/4.0/).

Article

High-Level Synthesis of Multiclass SVM Using Code Refactoring to Classify Brain Cancer from Hyperspectral Images

Abelardo Baez [1,*], Himar Fabelo [1], Samuel Ortega [1], Giordana Florimbi [2], Emanuele Torti [2], Abian Hernandez [1], Francesco Leporati [2], Giovanni Danese [2], Gustavo M. Callico [1] and Roberto Sarmiento [1]

1. Institute for Applied Microelectronics (IUMA), University of Las Palmas de Gran Canaria (ULPGC), 35017 Las Palmas de Gran Canaria, Spain; hfabelo@iuma.ulpgc.es (H.F.); sortega@iuma.ulpgc.es (S.O.); ahguedes@iuma.ulpgc.es (A.H.); gustavo@iuma.ulpgc.es (G.M.C.); roberto@iuma.ulpgc.es (R.S.)
2. Department of Electrical, Computer and Biomedical Engineering, University of Pavia, 27100 Pavia, Italy; giordana.florimbi01@universitadipavia.it (G.F.); emanuele.torti@unipv.it (E.T.); leporati@unipv.it (F.L.); gianni.danese@unipv.it (G.D.)
* Correspondence: abaez@iuma.ulpgc.es; Tel.: +34-928-451-220

Received: 29 October 2019; Accepted: 3 December 2019; Published: 6 December 2019

Abstract: Currently, high-level synthesis (HLS) methods and tools are a highly relevant area in the strategy of several leading companies in the field of system-on-chips (SoCs) and field programmable gate arrays (FPGAs). HLS facilitates the work of system developers, who benefit from integrated and automated design workflows, considerably reducing the design time. Although many advances have been made in this research field, there are still some uncertainties about the quality and performance of the designs generated with the use of HLS methodologies. In this paper, we propose an optimization of the HLS methodology by code refactoring using Xilinx SDSoC™ (Software-Defined System-On-Chip). Several options were analyzed for each alternative through code refactoring of a multiclass support vector machine (SVM) classifier written in C, using two different Zynq®-7000 SoC devices from Xilinx, the ZC7020 (ZedBoard) and the ZC7045 (ZC706). The classifier was evaluated using a brain cancer database of hyperspectral images. The proposed methodology not only reduces the required resources using less than 20% of the FPGA, but also reduces the power consumption −23% compared to the full implementation. The speedup obtained of 2.86× (ZC7045) is the highest found in the literature for SVM hardware implementations.

Keywords: high-level synthesis; HLS; SDSoC; support vector machines; SVM; code refactoring; Zynq; ZedBoard

1. Introduction

High-level synthesis (HLS) methodologies allow hardware (HW) designers to increase the abstraction level and accelerate the automation for the synthesis and verification of the design process. The current rise in the complexity of the applications and the increment of the capabilities of silicon technologies, as well as the so called *time to market* constrain, make HLS methodologies and tools of mandatory use in the near future [1]. Due to the multiple commercial solutions that can be found in the market for multiprocessor system-on-chips (MPSoCs) nowadays, it is strictly necessary to improve its techniques and methodologies [2] so that the technology is able to deal with the multiple implementation possibilities by using high-level design [3,4].

Some implementations of support vector machine (SVM) classifiers in field programmable gate arrays (FPGAs) have been released in different applications, such as image processing [5,6], automotive [7], medical [8,9], and data signal processing [10,11], among others. These implementations use different platforms depending on the application and the desired accuracy and timing. For readers who are interested in different implementations using diverse devices and including not only a training implementation but also a classification one, we recommend [12], where the authors review the state-of-arts of SVM implementations using different types of FPGAs. Another interesting research from the same authors is a SVM classifier for melanoma detection using a Zynq® device (ZC7020) and HLS methodology. The dataset employed is based on traditional RGB (red, green, and blue) images and the generation of a binary SVM model, having an output of the class as 1 (melanoma) and −1 (non-melanoma) [13]. The implementation depended on directives used directly in Vivado HLS without code refactoring. Finally, it is relevant to take into account that, in every implementation, the communication between the software (SW) and the hardware (HW) parts in an embedded system represents a relevant bottleneck to be solved, especially when using data with high storage and data transfer requirements, e.g., hyperspectral image processing. For example, in [14], the different stages of an Least-Squares Support Vector Machine (LS-SVM) implementation using a Zynq device is approached, separating the code of the algorithm into different parts, depending on the communications necessary for each part. In consequence, some parts are more suitable to be computed using the Advanced RISC Machines (ARM) processors than implementing them in the programmable logic (PL) part. For this reason, it is mandatory to know the code in detail, and to identify the parts (loops and sequential code) that are suitable to be accelerated in the embedded system.

Hyperspectral imaging (HSI) integrates conventional imaging and spectroscopy methods to obtain both spatial and spectral information of a scene [15]. While a conventional RGB (red, green, and blue) image only records three spectral bands in the visible spectrum (380–740 nm), HSI is able to obtain spectral information within and beyond the human eye [16]. Hyperspectral (HS) sensors are capable of capturing a very large number of contiguous spectral bands, measuring the radiation reflectance, absorbance, or emission of the material that is being captured. At the end, a vector of radiance values for each pixel of the image (called the *spectral signature*) is obtained [15], allowing the automatic identification of the materials presented in the scene through image processing algorithms [17]. HSI is a non-invasive and non-ionizing technique that supports the rapid acquisition and analysis of diagnostic information in several fields, such as remote sensing [18,19], drug identification [20,21], forensics [22–24], food safety inspection, and control [25–27], among many others. In the medical field, several studies can be found in the literature where HSI is applied to different medical applications [28–30]. Particularly, many research groups have investigated the use of HSI for surgical applications, especially for cancer analysis [31,32], such as laparoscopic HS imaging [33], the differentiation of breast cancerous and non-cancerous tissue [34], the identification of tongue cancer of in vivo human samples [35], intestinal ischemia identification [36], prostate cancer detection [37], gastric cancer delineation [38], head and neck cancer classification and delineation [39,40], among others.

In this paper, an evaluation of code refactoring and SDSoC™ (Software-Defined System-On-Chip) design methodology and implementation is performed, using both binary and multiclass SVM classifiers for hyperspectral imagery. To test the implementation design flow, the SVM codes were modified to increase the speed up and were tested in two different Zynq devices. Our proposed methodology could provide a reliable solution to accelerate the processing of hyperspectral data in several medical applications, in particular for the intraoperative brain cancer detection application.

This paper is organized as follows. In Section 2, the most relevant specifications of the research work are described, such as the devices (Zynq), the electronic design automation tool (SDSoC), and the basis of the SVM classifiers. In addition, a summary of the hyperspectral dataset employed in this work is detailed. In Section 3, a detailed explanation of the code refactoring of the binary and the multiclass SVM classifiers is provided, together with an explanation of the used methodology. This paper concludes including the experimental results in Section 4 and outlining the conclusions in Section 5.

2. Materials and Methods

This section is intended to briefly describe the tools and platforms employed for the development of this work, as well as the methodology followed for the implementation of the algorithms using HLS. Furthermore, the hyperspectral dataset employed for the experiments is described.

2.1. Zynq-7000 SoC Device from Xilinx

The Zynq is an SoC (system-on-chip) provided by Xilinx [41]. All versions have the same processing system (PS) features, a dual-core ARM Cortex A9 (ARMv7-A architecture), 32 KB Level 1 cache for instructions, and 32 KB Level 1 cache for data. The two cores share a 512 KB L2 cache and a 256 KB on-chip memory (OCM). The basic clock frequency for the PS part of this platform is 667 MHz, but some specific versions can reach 1 GHz. The programmable logic (PL) part can access the DDR memory, the OCM memory, and the L2 cache in the PS via AXI interfaces, with coherency behavior through the Accelerated Coherency Port (ACP). The resources of the PL part depend on the version selected. In this paper, two Zynq versions were selected: a ZC7020 in a ZedBoard™ Evaluation Kit [42] and the ZC7045 in a Xilinx Zynq-7000 SoC ZC706 Evaluation Kit [43]. These devices prevent the designer from wasting excessive HW or SW design time, increasing the communication performance between the two parts by using the provided communication interfaces, but sometimes some modifications are required to get an appropriate HLS implementation. The transactions between the PL and the PS parts suppose a relevant challenge for the designer and dramatically affect the final system performance.

The ZC706 board uses the XC7Z045 SOC and 1 GB DDR3 RAM among other resources. The XC7Z045 includes the standard SW configuration (PS part) for a generic Zynq device, and the PL part contains a Kintex-7 architecture with 350 K logic cells, 218.6 K LUTs (Look Up Tables), 437.2 K FFs (Flip Flops), 19.2 Mb BRAM (Block RAM), and 900 DSPs (Digital Signal Processors) (18 × 25). The ZedBoard uses the XC7Z020 SOC and 512 MB DDR3 RAM. The XC7Z020 contains an Artix-7 architecture with 85 K logic cells, 53.2 K LUTs, 106.4 K FF, 4.9 Mb BRAM, and 220 DSP (18 × 25). Both devices include the same SW part, but do not use the same architecture. In this work, both devices were used to check if it is worth using the most expensive SOC for the application.

In a data-intensive embedded system, the designer needs to deal with the communication bottleneck, not only with the HW implementation but also with the SW communication. The Zynq provides dedicated and well-defined data bus communications between both parts, including SW and HW parts, in one device. Moreover, the design tools created by the manufactures provide the designers with efficient mechanisms to save time in the final implementation. Such tools provide libraries and methods to communicate the two parts and create the final implementation in a reasonable amount of time.

2.2. SDSoC Development Environment by Xilinx

SDSoC is a tool developed by Xilinx that provides the designer with the possibility of creating complete embedded systems from C or C++ code using Zynq devices as the target system. This type of tools provides new features over the traditional HLS tools, which are of high interest in the research community [44,45]. SDSoC includes a system compiler that analyzes the code in order to determine the data flow between the PS and PL parts, and provides the designer with a complete system. SDSoC invokes Vivado to create the system and Vivado HLS to create the IPs for the desired accelerated functions. Then, SDSoC includes the accelerated functions and the Data Movers IP (Intellectual Property) for data transaction. In order to provide an efficient time implementation, the tool generates a thread for each accelerated function, ensuring synchronization between the software and hardware threads. The designer can configure the communication between PL and PS parts in the code with SDSoC pragma directives to meet the application and solution constraints and adds Vivado HLS directives to create the desired accelerated IP. The version used in this work is the 2018.2.

The methodology applied in this paper includes that proposed by Xilinx [46] with some modifications, thus creating a well-defined six-step design flow, as shown in 0. After the code is verified in the ARM, checking the results Figure 1a, the first step in the design flow is the *profiling stage* Figure 1b. In this step, a profiling tool is needed to detect the functions that must be accelerated. This step can be carried out with different profiling tools, such as Valgrind [47] for memory usage and gprof [48] for timing. This step lets the designer identify the relevant functions in the code for HW acceleration. Since SDSoC uses Vivado HLS, the second step shown in Figure 1c includes the *optimization* suggested by the Vivado HLS and SDSoC guidelines. The third step of the methodology Figure 1d consists of *code refactoring*, restructuring the source code for an improvement of the latency. In some cases, this phase is mandatory if a certain speedup is pursued. Moreover, without this code refactoring, the acceleration could not be affordable. The objective is to modify the code in such a way that the final implementation reuses the FPGA resources, makes the most of the FPGA embedded resources, e.g., DSP (digital signal processing) macros, or reflects a particular architecture to achieve the design constrains. Code refactoring for HLS performance improvement is the main contribution of this paper, and it will be further explained in Section 3.

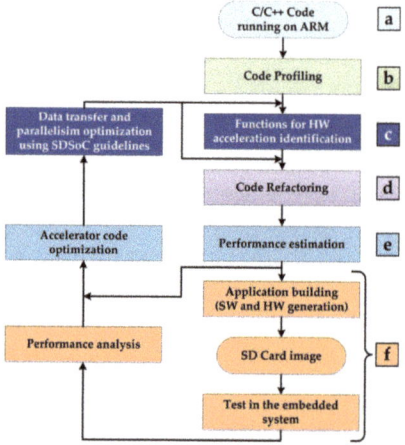

Figure 1. Proposed modification in the Software-Defined System-On-Chip (SDSoC) Design Flow.

The fourth step of the methodology Figure 1e is to obtain the *performance estimation* provided by the tool, and check if the results are the expected ones. In this stage, a detailed report of the resources and speedup of accelerated functions is provided, and a new iteration can be done to improve the expected performances. The final iteration of *performance estimation* depends on the resources of the PL part, and the resources used will be shown in the HLS report obtained in the next step. The constraints, the SDSoC compiler directives, and the code refactoring drive the *performance estimation*. This step has a high impact on the quality of the final implementation. The designer can also use Vivado HLS directives together with SDSoC directives. The directives provide instructions to the compiler to meet the characteristics of the HW architecture and the desired timing constrains, e.g., the use of pipelines to implement loops, the type of communication channels for data-flow implementations (Data Movers), FPGA resources to be used for variable storage, etc. To improve the results, it is necessary to take into account the inferred implementation of the compiler tool.

The final step of the methodology shown in Figure 1f lets the designer check the estimated performance in the selected board. The estimated performance is obtained during the performance estimation stage (before the synthesis) with the profiling tool included in the SDSoC software. This estimation does not allow the designer to know the critical functions (obtained in the profiling stage), but it shows the estimated speedup that will be achieved with the current implementation. Commonly, these results are different from the real speedup obtained in the final implementation. Here, the speedup can be computed by measuring the clock cycles taken by the accelerated solution compared to those taken by the serial execution in the ARM processors. SDSoC invokes Vivado HLS in order to generate the HDL implementation files for the accelerated functions in HDL (VHDL or Verilog) and provides several comprehensive synthesis reports. The information provided in the synthesis reports helps the designer meet the targeted performance and resource usage requirements for a specific application. SDSoC also generates all the files needed to run the application in the embedded system, the bitstream for the PL part, the connection between the PS and PL parts (Data Movers), and the files of the OS in Linux or FreeRTOS with the executable binary (ELF file) for running the application. This final step is mandatory due to the difference between the real and the estimated performance. The real performance usually is lower than the estimated one. In order to obtain the real performance, it is mandatory to check the clock used in the PS part.

2.3. Support Vector Machine Classifier

The SVM algorithm is a binary classification approach proposed by Vapnik in 1979 [49]. The main goal of this algorithm is to find a hyperplane that separates two classes according to their features with maximum margin. A set of data x_i ($x_i \in \mathbb{R}^d$) and labels associated to this data ($y_i \in \mathbb{R}$) are given. Each label provides information about data x_i; if $y_i = 1$, the class is positive, and if $y_i = -1$, the class is assumed to be negative. For example, if we are dealing with a diagnostic test, a positive class could mean 'disease' while a negative can represent 'non-disease'. According to the input data x_i, Equation (1) can be written.

$$\hat{y} = x_i \cdot w + b \tag{1}$$

In Equation (1), $\hat{y}$ is the predicted class for the instance x_i, and the parameters w and b define the maximum margin hyperplane ($w \in \mathbb{R}^d$ and $b \in \mathbb{R}$). These parameters, w and b, are learned from a training set, consisting of tuples of data and labels (x_i, y_i). One of the main features of the SVM algorithm is that it can be easily generalized for non-linear data [50], which is especially useful for complex data where a linear separation hyperplane is not capable of separating the data accurately. Similarly to other binary classifiers, SVM can be extended to a multiclass classifier by combining several binary classifiers [51].

SVMs are kernel-based supervised classifiers that have been widely used in the classification of HS images [52]. In the literature, SVMs achieve good performance for classifying HS data, even when a limited number of training samples are available [53]. Due to its strong theoretical foundation, good generalization capabilities, low sensitivity to the curse of dimensionality, and ability to find global classification solutions, many researchers usually prefer SVMs instead of other classification algorithms for classifying HS images [30].

SVM Multiclass Classifier

In this paper, we address the implementation of the multiclass SVM classification stage. For this purpose, we first employed an implementation of the basic binary SVM classifier to perform the experiments and optimizations. Then, a multiclass SVM classifier implementation based on the *one-vs-one* method was used to apply and evaluate the optimizations proposed with the binary algorithm. This allowed reusing some parts of the binary code modifications and copying the methodology used in this first implementation. The linear kernel with the hyperparameter cost equal to 1 was employed for the SVM classifier, since it has been demonstrated to produce accurate results for hyperspectral brain cancer detection applications [54].

The first version of binary and multiclass classification were written in C++ language and both final versions were written in plain C following a hardware-friendly way. Both codes were tested comparing results with the SVM implementation of the LIBSVM [55] implementation in MATLAB® 2019a (The MathWorks, Inc., Natick, MA, USA) software. To validate the implementation, gold standard results were obtained from the MATLAB SVM implementation in double precision and saved into binary files. Such data were used to compare the software and hardware implementations.

In this implementation, the multiclass SVM algorithm was split into four different stages:

(1) **Variables declaration and initialization.** Here, the inputs that represents the previously trained model of the algorithm (support vectors, the bias, and the sigmoid function parameters) as well as the samples to be classified are declared and initialized.

(2) **Distances computation**. In this step, the distances between the samples (i.e., the pixel) and the established hyperplane are computed.

(3) **Binary probability computation.** This step has the goal of estimating the binary probability of a certain pixel to belong to the two classes under study in the one-vs-one method, taking into account the distances computed in the previous step.

(4) **Multiclass probability computation**. This final step aims to obtain the multiclass probabilities for each pixel performing a *for* loop that iteratively refines the probabilities for each pixel associated to a certain class obtained in the previous step. The value of each probability is incrementally modified on the assumption that the difference with the value of the previous iteration is under a certain threshold or if the maximum error is reached (the user establishes both parameters). As soon as one of these two situations is confirmed, the multiclass probabilities of the pixel are computed, and the final classification map is generated.

This partition of the algorithm will allow performing two different implementations, one where the entire algorithm is implemented onto the PL part (full version) and another one where the stage with the most computational cost (modular version) is implemented onto the PL part and the remaining stages are executed in the PS part.

2.4. In Vivo HS Human Brain Cancer Database

In this work, the HS data employed to evaluate the performance of the implementations belong to an in vivo HS human brain cancer database [56]. This database was generated intraoperatively using an HS acquisition system developed during the execution of the HELICoiD project [56]. Particularly, three HS images that belonged to three adult patients undergoing craniotomy for resection of intra-axial brain tumors at the University Hospital Doctor Negrin of Las Palmas de Gran Canaria (Spain) were employed for the validation of the implementations. The patients had a grade IV glioblastoma tumor confirmed by histopathology. The study protocol and consent procedures were approved by the *Comité Ético de Investigación Clínica-Comité de Ética en la Investigación* (CEIC/CEI) of the University Hospital Doctor Negrin, and written informed consent was obtained from all subjects. HS data from these images were labeled into four classes as normal tissue, tumor tissue, hypervascularized tissue, and background, following the method explained in [56]. This method consisted of two main steps. First, the pathologists analyzed the biopsied tissue from the tumor area extracted during the surgical procedure after capturing the intraoperative HS image. Then, the neurosurgeon labeled certain pixels of the image where they were confident that the pixels belonged to one of the four classes. Normal tissue, hypervascularized tissue, and background were labeled according to the surgeon criteria and experience by visual inspection using the labeling tool based on the Spectral Angle Mapper (SAM) algorithm. Tumor tissue pixels were labeled with the same labeling tool, but taking into account the definitive diagnostic information provided by histopathological analysis. Normal and hypervascularized tissue samples were not pathologically analyzed due to ethical reasons. Figure 2a shows the information structure of an HS cube [31]. On one side, each pixel of the HS image contains a full spectral signature of length equal to the number of spectral bands of the HS cube. The reflectance value of a certain pixel in a certain wavelength is called a *voxel*. On the other side, a gray-scale image of the captured scene can be obtained using any of the spectral bands that display the spatial information provided by the image sensor at such a particular wavelength. The rubber ring markers presented in the image were employed for labeling purposes with the goal of identifying the pathological assessment of the brain tissue (normal or tumor).

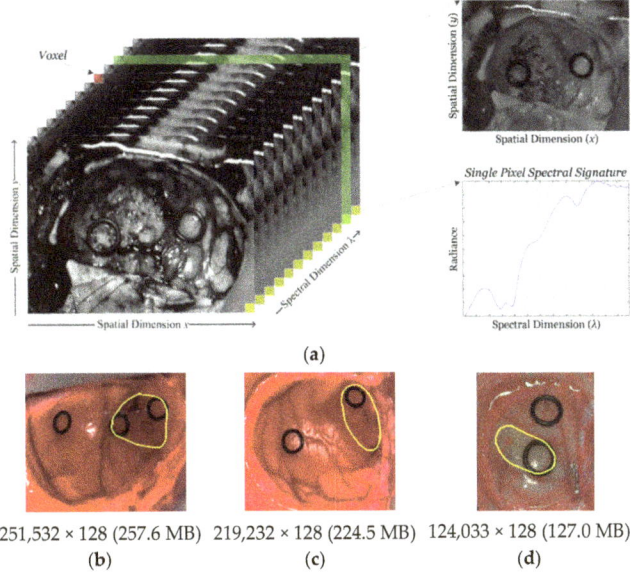

Figure 2. Hyperspectral (HS) in vivo brain human database. (**a**) Example of the HS cube basis [31]. (**b**–**d**) are synthetic red, green, and blue (RGB) representations of the HS images employed in this study for results validation (OP8C1, OP12C1, and OP20C1, respectively), where the tumor area is surrounded in yellow [56]. The size of the HS image in terms of pixels×bands and megabytes is shown below each RGB representation.

The HS data generated by the sensor was preprocessed following the preprocessing chain described in [54]. This chain was based on five main steps: (1) a white and dark calibration employed to perform a radiometric calibration of the HS image using a white tile that reflects 99% of the incident light and a dark reference image that remove the effect of the dark currents produced by the HS sensor; (2) an extreme band removal applied due to the low performance of the HS sensor in these bands; (3) a band averaging process where the redundant information provided by the high spectral resolution of the camera is eliminated; (4) a smooth filter employed to remove the spectral noise in the spectral signatures; and (5) a normalization of the spectral signatures between 0 and 1 to avoid differences in the amplitude of the signatures produced by the non-uniform illumination. Finally, the HS dataset consists of 128 spectral bands, covering the spectral range between 450 and 900 nm (visible and near-infrared spectra). Figure 2b–d show the synthetic RGB representations of the HS cubes selected for this study and their corresponding size. These synthetic RGB images were generated only for visualization purposes using three wavelengths directly extracted from the original HS cube to conform the RGB image (R = 708.97 nm, G = 539.44 nm, B = 479.06 nm).

3. Code Refactoring

The reference code was modified until the final implementation showed clear indications of reaching the performance objectives. After each change or restructuration in the code, a serial verification was performed in order to check the results. These modifications were applied to the binary classifier code. Once the optimal modifications were reached, the same methodology was applied to the multiclass classifier code.

3.1. Use of Directives and Memory Allocation

The first modification in the code was to include the minimal directives in order to avoid dependences of the tool. In this case, only the HLS pragma for pipelining (the number of pragma HLS pipeline) was used. For memory allocation, only the sds_alloc function was used. This function is defined in a SDSoC library (sds_lib.h), and allocates physically contiguous memory, which can affect system performance in the data transfer between the PS and the PL part. Since the accelerated function receives a considerable amount of data, normally more than 8 MB, the AXI DMA scatter gather was selected using the related SDSoC directives (#pragma SDS data zero_copy and #pragma SDS data data_mover (Var1:AXIDMA_SG ...)).

3.2. Improvement in Data Transfer

If the accelerated function only processes one pixel at each iteration, no speedup is obtained even with the pragma directives. In order to improve the acceleration of the classification function, several pixels are transferred between the PS and PL parts in the same clock cycle. Due to the 533-MHz DDR3 SODIMM bandwidth constraint, an optimal amount of data must be selected in order to avoid wasted data cycles. Since the implemented system is not always able to reach the entire bandwidth, it is necessary to determine the highest data transfer near the bandwidth constrain. It is necessary to take into account that the amount of pixels is not always an integer multiple of the optimal amount of pixels for a data cycle, so zero padding is a good option to avoid calculating non-existent values. Figure 3a shows the original code of the SVM binary software implementation. Figure 3b shows the re-factored code applied in order to improve the transferred data using the proposed modification, where BLOCKSIZE is the amount of pixels in each data transfer, BANDS is the number of bands values for each pixel, PIXELS is the number of pixels in the image, and inputInter/outputInter are the arrays for intermediate input/output data transfers.

```
for( int i = 0; i < PIXELS; i++){
    outputVector[i] = bias;
}

for (int j = 0; j < BANDS; j++){
    for (int k = 0; k < PIXELS; k++){
        outputVector[k] += inputData[ k * BANDS + j] * weights[j];
    }
}
```

(a)

```
int nElemBlocks = BLOCKSIZE * BANDS;
int lastElement = BANDS * PIXELS;
int currentPixel = 0;

for (int currentElement = 0;
     currentElement < lastElement;
     currentElement += nElemBlocks){

    for (int element = 0;
         element < nElemBlocks;
         element++){

        if(currentElement+element<lastElement){
            inputInter[element] =
                inputData[currentElement + element];
        }else{
            inputInter[element] = 0;
        }
    }

    svmClassifyHW(inputInter, bias, weights,
                  outputInter);
    for(int pixelIndex = 0;
        pixelIndex < BLOCKSIZE;
        pixelIndex++){

        if(currentPixel + pixelIndex < PIXELS){
            output[currentPixel + pixelIndex] =
                outputInter[pixelIndex];
        }
    }
    currentPixel += BLOCKSIZE;
}
```

(b)

```
for( int i = 0; i < BLOCKSIZE; i++){
    for (int k = 0; k < 8; k++){
        #pragma HLS pipeline
        inter[k] = 0;
    }
    for (int m=0; m < BANDS/8; m++){
        for (int j=0; j<8; j++){
            #pragma HLS pipeline
            inter[j] += inputData[i*BANDS + m*8 +j]
                        * weights[m*8 + j];
        }
    }
    outputVector[i] = biasData + inter[0] +
                      inter[1] + inter[2] +
                      inter[3] + inter[4] +
                      inter[5] + inter[6] +
                      inter[7];
}
```

(c)

Figure 3. Support vector machine (SVM) binary code refactoring. (**a**) Original code. (**b**) Refactorized code for transferring a block of pixels. (**c**) Refactorized code for parallelizing the data processing in groups of eight elements.

3.3. Improvement in Data Processing

The classification function features a temporal dependency because the actual value on each iteration depends on its value in the previous iteration. Each classification value for a pixel (*clValue*) is calculated adding the *bias* data and then accumulating the result of multiplying the weight of every band obtained in the training classification (*bandWeight*) by the value of the pixel in that band (*bandWeight*). So pipelining is not possible to be used in the function given in Equation (2).

$$clValue+ = bandValue \cdot bandWeight \qquad (2)$$

To improve the execution of this function in order to calculate *clValue*, instead of using just one accumulator, we propose the use of several intermediate accumulators. At the end, the final value for *clValue* is the sum of the intermediate accumulators. 0 3c shows the refactored code, where the proposed modification is applied in order to improve the data processing. This refactorization allows the pipelining implementation to use eight accumulators, where BLOCKSIZE is the number of pixels for each data transfer, BANDS is the amount of bands for each pixel, intputData[n] is the array with the pixel values, outputVector[n] is the array with the classification results, weights[n] is the array with the weights for the classification, and inter[m] is the array for intermediate accumulators.

Figure 4 shows a diagram of the improvement in data transferring and processing, where P is the number of pixels, P_n is the block of pixels processed in each data transfer, B_n is the block of bands in which it is divided into the total bands value for each pixel, A_n represent the intermediate accumulators, and A is the final accumulator for that pixel.

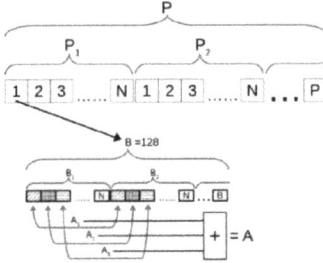

Figure 4. Diagram of the improving on transferring and processing data.

3.4. Including Redundant Data inside Accelerated Function

Every time the classification is called, bias and weights values are transferred via the data-mover IP to the accelerated function in the PL part. The classification data type is double (8 bytes, 64 bits); therefore, every time Equation (2) is called, the bias and the corresponding weight need to be transferred for computation. If the SVM training is done before, the weights will not change, hence, weights and bias values can be included in the IP, reducing the data transfer and improving the speedup.

3.5. Data Type Reduction

Reducing the data type from double to float decreases the bus bandwidth required for the data transfer between the PS and PL parts. It is necessary to take into account that it is not possible in every application to change the data type due to the precision needed. In this work, the HS images were processed in double and float precision, comparing the classification results. In this application, it was verified that the precision lost did not change the classification results. This data change reduced the bus bandwidth from 64 bits (8 bytes) to 32 bits (4 bytes).

4. Experimental Results and Discussion

All the results presented in this section were obtained through the elaboration of the designed architecture straight on the boards, i.e., no estimated performance was used in these results. In summary, about 70 implementations were tested in order to obtain accurate results. Each implementation was iterated 100 times per classification on board to obtain a reliable average values. Linux was used as the OS in all the implementations for controlling and verification purposes. The speedup was calculated calling the classification twice, the first one in software without any modification at all, and the second one in hardware, with all the modifications incorporated.

The preliminary results obtained without applying code refactoring shows a speedup factor of 0.67× (in fact, the implementation showed a slowdown situation); this result was the main reason to change the code in order to find a better implementation. Once the code was modified by changing the amount of pixels per clock cycle, parallelizing the processing data with several accumulators and selecting 100 MHz for the Data Movers IP, a speedup factor between 1.15× and 1.41× was obtained, depending on the block size.

Once the optimal number of pixels per clock cycle was established, we optimized the other parameters of the HS design. First, increasing the frequency for data movers and for the accelerated function to 200 MHz showed a speedup of 1.61×. Second, including weights and bias inside the accelerated function and keeping the 200 MHz for data movers and the accelerated IP showed a speedup of 2.35×. Finally, keeping all the configurations shown in Figure 5, 200 MHz for data movers and accelerated function, including weights and bias in the accelerated function, and changing the data type from double to float showed a speedup of 2.89×. It is worth noticing that the speedup decreases once the block size (number of pixels per clock cycle) increases above 128 pixels. This speedup decrease is due to the wasted space in each transfer to the PL part, since the block size exceeds the amount of data that the PS part can send to the PL part in each clock cycle.

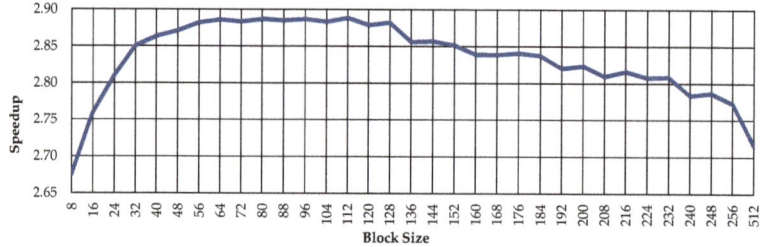

Figure 5. Speedup obtained varying the amount of pixels per clock cycle (100 MHz for data movers and accelerated function).

Figure 6 shows a speedup comparison applying all the above modifications, using different pixels per data cycle and different partitions for bands value. In the best case, with the code refactoring and changing the data type, the highest speedup achieved is 2.89× with a block size of 64 pixels per data cycle and partitioning the bands value using 16 accumulators.

Finally, the same methodology was applied to the multiclass SVM classifier. In this case, the code was divided into four stages (see Section 2.3), and once the performance analysis was obtained, two versions were implemented, the *full* one (including all the stages in the PL part) and the *modular* one, implementing only the most intensive computational stage (the distance computation, stage number 2) in the PL part. This difference allows us to compare the speedup versus the resources occupied in the PL part and the power consumption. As well as in the binary classification, the classification results obtained were validated with the gold standard results provided by the LIBSVM implementation in MATLAB. In this case, for the multiclass classification, Figure S1 of the supplementary material shows the four-class classification maps obtained for each HS cube employed in this study. The red color indicates tumor pixels, the green color indicates normal pixels, the blue color indicates hypervascularized pixels, and the background pixels are represented in black. These gold standard classification results were previously published in [57] and exactly match with the results obtained by the proposed multiclass SVM implementation.

Figure 7 shows the time consumption and speedup obtained using both the ZedBoard (ZC7020) and the ZC706 (ZC7045) for both cases, full (F) and modular (M) implementations, as well as the SW implementation results. These results show that the obtained speedup is the best when the modularization of the SVM stage is performed, considering both platforms. In addition, it is clear that the ZC706 platform outperforms the results obtained with the ZedBoard. In all cases, the selected frequency for the PL part was 100 MHz. On the other hand, Figure 8 shows the resources occupied using both platforms for both implementations, where it is possible to observe that the modular version is more efficient than the full version in terms of resources usage. Finally, Table 1 shows the power consumption for the two platforms using both implementations. As it can be observed, comparing all the results, the separation of the code offers better performance, since it consumes less power than the full one, uses fewer resources, and obtains better latency values.

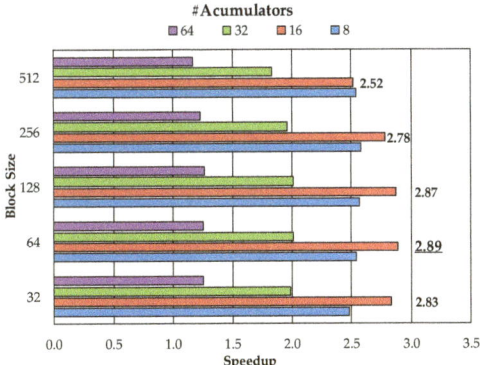

Figure 6. Speedup obtained varying the amount of pixels per clock cycle and accumulators (200 MHz for data movers and accelerated function).

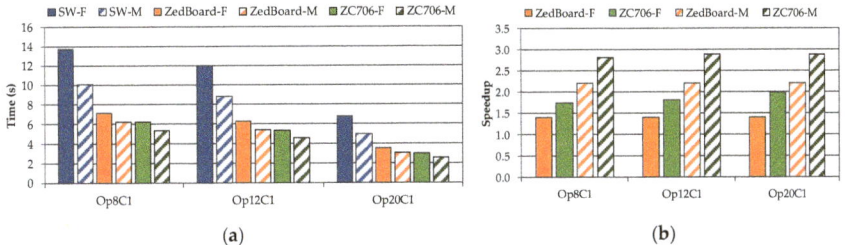

Figure 7. Execution time (**a**) and speedup (**b**) results respect to the software (SW) implementation of both hardware (HW) implementations (F = full, M = modular) in each processing platform.

Table 1. Power consumption for both implementations (F = full, M = modular).

	ZedBoard (ZC7020)		ZC706 (ZC7045)	
Type	F	M	F	M
Dynamic Power (W)	2.42	1.89	2.61	1.91
Static Power (W)	0.17	0.15	0.22	0.21
Total (W)	2.59	2.04	2.84	2.13

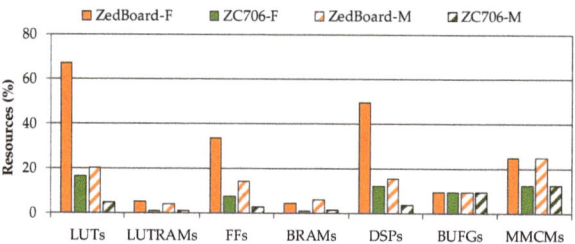

Figure 8. Resources consumption for both implementations (F = full, M = modular) in both platforms.

As it was mentioned in the introduction, other hardware implementations have been performed [12]. In some cases, the implementations have increased the speedup; in other cases, they have reduced the resources needed or they have reduced the power consumption for different types of FPGAs. In all cases, a stand-alone FPGA was used. Only one work used a Zynq device [58], although a binary SVM classifier was implemented, and for that reason it is not included in this comparison. On all cases, the SDSOC was not used in any such implementations. In this comparison, only Xilinx devices have been taken into account for resources assessment, due to the different architectures used between Xilinx and Altera devices. In summary, the implementations used for comparison have been [59–62]. As different FPGAs have different types of resources, even using only Xilinx devices, some resources cannot be comparable. In those cases, the resources were omitted. Table 2 presents the comparison of the speedup, power consumption, and resources employed among the state-of-the-art implementations and our proposed solution. Notice that some of the articles did not provide all the necessary information for this comparison. In this table, bold values refer to the best result for each feature or resource.

Table 2. Comparison of the speedup, power consumption, and resources employed among the different implementations. Bold values represent the best results for the specific resource or feature.

Reference Method	[59]	[60]	[61]	[62]	Proposed (M Version)	
Device	Xilinx Virtex-4	Xilinx Virtex-6	Xilinx Virtex-II	Xilinx Virtex-7	ZC7020 (ZedBoard)	ZC7045 (ZC706)
Tool	System Generator	Xilinx ISE	n/a	Xilinx XPE 14.1	SDSOC 2018.2	SDSOC 2018.2
Clock rate (MHz)	202.84	n/a	42.012	n/a	200	200
Speedup factor	n/a	n/a	2.53	n/a	2.20	**2.86**
Power (W)	n/a	2.02	n/a	**1.70**	2.04	2.13
Slice Registers (%)	5.00	**0.15**	21.00	11.00	n/a	n/a
Slice LUTs (%)	2.00	**0.35**	20.00	11.00	n/a	n/a
LUTs (%)	n/a	n/a	n/a	n/a	20.22	**4.84**
LUTRAM (%)	n/a	n/a	n/a	n/a	4.30	**1.00**
FF (%)	4.00	32.00	**2.00**	100.00	14.18	2.76
IOBs (%)	37.00	37.00	20.00	**4.00**	n/a	n/a
DSP (%)	14.00	**0.91**	n/a	0.00	15.45	3.78
BUFG (%)	**3.00**	**3.00**	n/a	n/a	9.38	9.38
BRAM (%)	n/a	n/a	n/a	n/a	6.07	**1.56**
MMCM (%)	n/a	n/a	n/a	n/a	25.00	**12.50**

n/a: Data not available, LUTs: Look Up Tables, LUTRAM: LUTs used as RAM, FFs: Flip Flops, IOBs: Input/Output Blocks, DSPs: Digital Signal Processors, BUFG: Global Clock Buffer, BRAM: Block RAM, MMCM: Mixed-Mode Clock Manager.

Although all the compared implementations address SVM multiclass classification, to the best of our knowledge, none of the implementations use medical images. Furthermore, none of such works used HSI. In [59], binary images were used for Persian handwritten digits detection [63]. In [60], Patil et al. employed RGB images to develop a facial expression recognition system using the Cohn-Kanade database [64]. In [61], a phoneme recognition system was tested using the DARPA TIMIT Acoustic-Phonetic Continuous Speech Corpus database [65]. Finally, Mandal et al. [62] employed the setosa and non-setosa data of Fisher's Iris database available in MATLAB®. Furthermore, it is worth noticing that different techniques for data reduction were employed in each work. For example, in [59,60], fixed point and truncation methods were used. In this work, the only data reduction performed was a conversion from double to float data type. For these reasons, a fair comparison is not possible because the types of data used for the SVM classifier are different. However, the superiority of our implementation is demonstrated using HSI data, which imposes relevant challenges due to their high dimensionality and data throughput. As it can be seen in Table 2, our proposed implementation achieved the best speedup factor (2.86×) using the ZC7045 (ZC706 board) device. Regarding the power consumption, the implementation performed in [62] obtained the lower value. However, our proposed solutions provide similar values, having only an increment of 0.34 and 0.43 W in the ZC7020 (ZedBoard) and ZC7045 (ZC706) devices, respectively. In contrast, the use of the FPGA resources is lower than [62], especially in the ZC7045 device. Furthermore, it is worth noticing that in the ZC706, the designer has also extra space for other applications; for example, if the designer wants to use the output of the SVM to another machine learning algorithm, or if extra space is required to execute other algorithms in parallel.

5. Conclusions

The results obtained in this work demonstrate the major benefits of writing efficient code for HLS tools, in this case SDSoC, to accelerate a binary SVM classifier. This methodology can be easily replicated in other HLS tools to validate the inferred system, as only a few specific tool directives have been used. It is recommended to include all the redundant data in the accelerated function in order to decrease the interfaces between PS and PL, thus significantly improving the speedup of the system by reducing the transferred data. Moreover, the modular version (M), the one that only implements the binary probability computation, not only obtains better speedup compared to the full version (F), but also uses less resources, consuming less power. In summary, it is advisable to reduce as much as possible the implemented functions in HLS, taking into account the transferred data between the SW and HW parts, fitting each chunk of data to the bus data-width plus the control data. On the other hand, looking at the resources used in the (ZC7045) ZC706, this implementation allows the designer to add other algorithms in the SOC, for example, to reuse the output of the SVM in other applications, or to parallelize the computation of the inputs in other types of algorithms. Finally, it is worth noticing that the power consumption of the ZC706 is similar to the one obtained with the ZedBoard. However, the speedup achieved by the ZC706 is higher than the one achieved by the ZedBoard. In summary, in this paper, the following methodology is proposed. First, a profiling stage is mandatory in order to identify the functions to accelerate. Second, we make use only of the basic pragmas in the HLS tool. With these two basic steps, we create a basic project in order to check the preliminary results. If the results meet the requirements, it will be necessary to modify the loops to create small arrays instead of passing to the hardware part large amounts of data, trying to fit the data size to the bandwidth of the bus used in the communication. Next, check for the data dependencies inside the loop, trying to remove the dependencies, as the accumulators could be if they suppose additional dependencies. Once all these steps have been committed, the designer should create the final project and check the results. In case it was not possible to avoid the dependencies inside the loop, the obtained speedup will represent the time variations in the transmission stage. Future works will contemplate the automation of code refactoring in order to provide a reliable tool that facilitates the implementation of the original code, obtaining an improved speedup.

Supplementary Materials: The following are available online at http://www.mdpi.com/2079-9292/8/12/1494/s1, Figure S1: Classification results of the SVM multiclass classifier for the employed HS cubes. (a), (c) and (e) are the synthetic RGB representations of the HS images, where the tumor area is surrounded in yellow [34]. (b), (d) and (f) Classification maps generated by the SVM multiclass classifier implementation. Normal, tumor, hypervascularized and background classes are represented in green, red, blue, and black color, respectively.

Author Contributions: Conceptualization, A.B., H.F., S.O., F.L., and G.M.C.; methodology, A.B., G.F., and E.T.; software, A.B., S.O., G.F., and A.H.; validation, A.B., S.O., G.F., and A.H.; formal analysis, A.B., H.F. and G.M.C.; investigation, A.B., H.F., and S.O; resources, F.L., G.D., G.M.C., and R.S.; data curation, H.F. and S.O.; writing—original draft preparation, A.B. and H.F.; writing—review and editing, S.O., G.F., E.T., A.H., F.L., and G.M.C.; supervision, F.L. and G.M.C.; project administration, F.L., G.D., G.M.C., and R.S.; funding acquisition, F.L., G.D., G.M.C., and R.S.

Funding: This work has been supported by the Canary Islands Government through the ACIISI (Canarian Agency for Research, Innovation and the Information Society), ITHACA project "Hyperspectral Identification of Brain Tumors" under Grant Agreement ProID2017010164, and it has been partially supported also by the Spanish Government and European Union (FEDER funds) as part of support program in the context of Distributed HW/SW Platform for Intelligent Processing of Heterogeneous Sensor Data in Large Open Areas Surveillance Applications (PLATINO) project, under contract TEC2017-86722-C4-1-R. This work has been also supported in part by the European Commission through the FP7 FET (Future and Emerging Technologies) Open Programme ICT-2011.9.2, European Project HELICoiD "HypErspectraL Imaging Cancer Detection" under Grant Agreement 618080. This work was completed while Samuel Ortega was beneficiary of a pre-doctoral grant given by the "*Agencia Canaria de Investigacion, Innovacion y Sociedad de la Información (ACIISI)*" of the "*Conserjería de Economía, Industria, Comercio y Conocimiento*" of the "*Gobierno de Canarias*", which is part-financed by the European Social Fund (FSE) (*POC 2014-2020, Eje 3 Tema Prioritario 74 (85%)*).

Conflicts of Interest: The authors declare no conflict of interest. The funders had no role in the design of the study; in the collection, analyses, or interpretation of data; in the writing of the manuscript, or in the decision to publish the results.

References

1. Coussy, P.; Gajski, D.D.; Meredith, M.; Takach, A. An Introduction to High-Level Synthesis. *IEEE Des. Test Comput.* **2009**, *26*, 8–17. [CrossRef]
2. Nane, R.; Sima, V.-M.; Pilato, C.; Choi, J.; Fort, B.; Canis, A.; Chen, Y.T.; Hsiao, H.; Brown, S.; Ferrandi, F.; et al. A Survey and Evaluation of FPGA High-Level Synthesis Tools. *IEEE Trans. Comput. Des. Integr. Circuits Syst.* **2016**, *35*, 1591–1604. [CrossRef]
3. Saha, R.; Banik, P.P.; Kim, K.-D.D. HLS Based Approach to Develop an Implementable HDR Algorithm. *Electronics* **2018**, *7*, 332. [CrossRef]
4. Liu, Z.; Chow, P.; Xu, J.; Jiang, J.; Dou, Y.; Zhou, J. A Uniform Architecture Design for Accelerating 2D and 3D CNNs on FPGAs. *Electronics* **2019**, *8*, 65. [CrossRef]
5. Kyrkou, C.; Theocharides, T. A parallel hardware architecture for real-time object detection with support vector machines. *IEEE Trans. Comput.* **2012**, *61*, 831–842. [CrossRef]
6. Jallad, A.H.M.; Mohammed, L.B. Hardware support vector machine (SVM) for satellite on-board applications. In Proceedings of the 2014 NASA/ESA Conference on Adaptive Hardware and Systems (AHS 2014), Leicester, UK, 14–18 July 2014; IEEE Computer Society: Washington, DC, USA, 2014; pp. 256–261.
7. Anguita, D.; Carlino, L.; Ghio, A.; Ridella, S. A FPGA core generator for embedded classification systems. *J. Circuits Syst. Comput.* **2011**, *20*, 263–282. [CrossRef]
8. Hussain, H.M.; Benkrid, K.; Seker, H. Reconfiguration-based implementation of SVM classifier on FPGA for Classifying Microarray data. In Proceedings of the Annual International Conference of the IEEE Engineering in Medicine and Biology Society EMBS, Osaka, Japan, 3–7 July 2013; pp. 3058–3061.
9. Pan, X.; Yang, H.; Li, L.; Liu, Z.; Hou, L. FPGA implementation of SVM decision function based on hardware-friendly kernel. In Proceedings of the 2013 International Conference on Computational and Information Sciences (ICCIS 2013), Shiyang, China, 21–23 June 2013; pp. 133–136.
10. Papadonikolakis, M.; Bouganis, C.S. A novel FPGA-based SVM classifier. In Proceedings of the 2010 International Conference on Field-Programmable Technology (FPT'10), Beijing, China, 8–10 December 2010; pp. 283–286.
11. Vranjković, V.S.; Struharik, R.J.R.; Novak, L.A. Reconfigurable hardware for machine learning applications. *J. Circuits Syst. Comput.* **2015**, *24*, 1550064. [CrossRef]
12. Afifi, S.M.; Gholamhosseini, H.; Sinha, R. Hardware Implementations of SVM on FPGA: A State-of-the-Art Review of Current Practice. *Int. J. Innov. Sci. Eng. Technol.* **2015**, *2*, 733–752.

13. Afifi, S.; GholamHosseini, H.; Sinha, R. A low-cost FPGA-based SVM classifier for melanoma detection. In Proceedings of the IECBES 2016-IEEE-EMBS Conference on Biomedical Engineering and Sciences, Kuala Lumpur, Malaysia, 4–8 December 2016; IEEE: Piscataway, NJ, USA, 2016; pp. 631–636.
14. Ning, M.; Shaojun, W.; Yeyong, P.; Yu, P. Implementation of LS-SVM with HLS on Zynq. In Proceedings of the 2014 International Conference on Field-Programmable Technology (FPT), Shanghai, China, 10–12 December 2014; IEEE: Piscataway, NJ, USA, 2014; pp. 346–349.
15. Kamruzzaman, M.; Sun, D.-W. Introduction to Hyperspectral Imaging Technology. In *Computer Vision Technology for Food Quality Evaluation*, 2nd ed.; Academic Press: Cambridge, MA, USA, 2016; pp. 111–139.
16. Starr, C.; Evers, C.A.; Starr, L. *Biology: Concepts and Applications without Physiology*; Cengage Learning: Boston, MA, USA, 2010; ISBN 9780538739252.
17. Manolakis, D.; Shaw, G. Detection algorithms for hyperspectral imaging applications. *IEEE Signal Process. Mag.* **2002**, *19*, 29–43. [CrossRef]
18. Govender, M.; Chetty, K.; Bulcock, H. A review of hyperspectral remote sensing and its application in vegetation and water resource studies. *Water SA* **2009**, *33*, 145–152. [CrossRef]
19. van der Meer, F.D.; van der Werff, H.M.A.; van Ruitenbeek, F.J.A.; Hecker, C.A.; Bakker, W.H.; Noomen, M.F.; van der Meijde, M.; Carranza, E.J.M.; de Smeth, J.B.; Woldai, T. Multi-and hyperspectral geologic remote sensing: A review. *Int. J. Appl. Earth Obs. Geoinf.* **2012**, *14*, 112–128. [CrossRef]
20. de Carvalho Rocha, W.F.; Sabin, G.P.; Março, P.H.; Poppi, R.J. Quantitative analysis of piroxicam polymorphs pharmaceutical mixtures by hyperspectral imaging and chemometrics. *Chemom. Intell. Lab. Syst.* **2011**, *106*, 198–204. [CrossRef]
21. de Moura França, L.; Pimentel, M.F.; da Silva Simões, S.; Grangeiro, S.; Prats-Montalbán, J.M.; Ferrer, A. NIR hyperspectral imaging to evaluate degradation in captopril commercial tablets. *Eur. J. Pharm. Biopharm.* **2016**, *104*, 180–188. [CrossRef] [PubMed]
22. Edelman, G.J.; Gaston, E.; van Leeuwen, T.G.; Cullen, P.J.; Aalders, M.C.G. Hyperspectral imaging for non-contact analysis of forensic traces. *Forensic Sci. Int.* **2012**, *223*, 28–39. [CrossRef] [PubMed]
23. Silva, C.S.; Pimentel, M.F.; Honorato, R.S.; Pasquini, C.; Prats-Montalbán, J.M.; Ferrer, A. Near infrared hyperspectral imaging for forensic analysis of document forgery. *Analyst* **2014**, *139*, 5176–5184. [CrossRef] [PubMed]
24. Fernández de la Ossa, M.Á.; Amigo, J.M.; García-Ruiz, C. Detection of residues from explosive manipulation by near infrared hyperspectral imaging: A promising forensic tool. *Forensic Sci. Int.* **2014**, *242*, 228–235. [CrossRef]
25. Wu, D.; Sun, D.-W. Advanced applications of hyperspectral imaging technology for food quality and safety analysis and assessment: A review—Part II: Applications. *Innov. Food Sci. Emerg. Technol.* **2013**, *19*, 15–28. [CrossRef]
26. Feng, Y.-Z.; Sun, D.-W. Application of Hyperspectral Imaging in Food Safety Inspection and Control: A Review. *Crit. Rev. Food Sci. Nutr.* **2012**, *52*, 1039–1058. [CrossRef]
27. Lorente, D.; Aleixos, N.; Gomez-Sanchis, J.; Cubero, S.; Garcia-Navarrete, O.L.; Blasco, J.; Gómez-Sanchis, J.; Cubero, S.; García-Navarrete, O.L.; Blasco, J. Recent Advances and Applications of Hyperspectral Imaging for Fruit and Vegetable Quality Assessment. *Food Bioprocess Technol.* **2011**, *5*, 1121–1142. [CrossRef]
28. Lu, G.; Fei, B. Medical hyperspectral imaging: A review. *J. Biomed. Opt.* **2014**, *19*, 10901. [CrossRef]
29. Calin, M.A.; Parasca, S.V.; Savastru, D.; Manea, D. Hyperspectral imaging in the medical field: Present and future. *Appl. Spectrosc. Rev.* **2014**, *49*, 435–447. [CrossRef]
30. Li, Q.; He, X.; Wang, Y.; Liu, H.; Xu, D.; Guo, F. Review of spectral imaging technology in biomedical engineering: Achievements and challenges. *J. Biomed. Opt.* **2013**, *18*, 100901. [CrossRef] [PubMed]
31. Halicek, M.; Fabelo, H.; Ortega, S.; Callico, G.M.; Fei, B. In-Vivo and Ex-Vivo Tissue Analysis through Hyperspectral Imaging Techniques: Revealing the Invisible Features of Cancer. *Cancers* **2019**, *11*, 756. [CrossRef] [PubMed]
32. Akbari, H.; Kosugi, Y. Hyperspectral imaging: A new modality in surgery. In *Recent Advances in Biomedical Engineering*; IntechOpen: London, UK, 2009.
33. Baltussen, E.J.M.; Kok, E.N.D.; Brouwer de Koning, S.G.; Sanders, J.; Aalbers, A.G.J.; Kok, N.F.M.; Beets, G.L.; Flohil, C.C.; Bruin, S.C.; Kuhlmann, K.F.D.; et al. Hyperspectral imaging for tissue classification, a way toward smart laparoscopic colorectal surgery. *J. Biomed. Opt.* **2019**, *24*, 016002. [CrossRef] [PubMed]

34. Pourreza-Shahri, R.; Saki, F.; Kehtarnavaz, N.; Leboulluec, P.; Liu, H. Classification of ex-vivo breast cancer positive margins measured by hyperspectral imaging. In Proceedings of the 2013 IEEE International Conference on Image Processing (ICIP 2013), Melbourne, VIC, Australia, 15–18 September 2013; pp. 1408–1412.
35. Liu, Z.; Wang, H.; Li, Q. Tongue tumor detection in medical hyperspectral images. *Sensors* **2012**, *12*, 162–174. [CrossRef] [PubMed]
36. Akbari, H.; Kosugi, Y.; Kojima, K.; Tanaka, N. Detection and Analysis of the Intestinal Ischemia Using Visible and Invisible Hyperspectral Imaging. *IEEE Trans. Biomed. Eng.* **2010**, *57*, 2011–2017. [CrossRef] [PubMed]
37. Akbari, H.; Halig, L.V.; Schuster, D.M.; Osunkoya, A.; Master, V.; Nieh, P.T.; Chen, G.Z.; Fei, B. Hyperspectral imaging and quantitative analysis for prostate cancer detection. *J. Biomed. Opt.* **2012**, *17*, 0760051. [CrossRef]
38. Akbari, H.; Uto, K.; Kosugi, Y.; Kojima, K.; Tanaka, N. Cancer detection using infrared hyperspectral imaging. *Cancer Sci.* **2011**, *102*, 852–857. [CrossRef]
39. Halicek, M.; Lu, G.; Little, J.V.; Wang, X.; Patel, M.; Griffith, C.C.; El-Deiry, M.W.; Chen, A.Y.; Fei, B. Deep convolutional neural networks for classifying head and neck cancer using hyperspectral imaging. *J. Biomed. Opt.* **2017**, *22*, 060503. [CrossRef]
40. Halicek, M.; Fabelo, H.; Ortega, S.; Little, J.V.; Wang, X.; Chen, A.Y.; Callicó, G.M.; Myers, L.; Sumer, B.; Fei, B. Cancer detection using hyperspectral imaging and evaluation of the superficial tumor margin variance with depth. In *Medical Imaging 2019: Image-Guided Procedures, Robotic Interventions, and Modeling*; Fei, B., Linte, C.A., Eds.; SPIE: Bellingham, WA, USA, 2019; Volume 10951, p. 45.
41. APU, A.P.U. Zynq-7000 All Programmable SoC Overview. Available online: https://cdn.hackaday.io/files/19354828041536/ds190-Zynq-7000-Overview.pdf (accessed on 27 October 2019).
42. Zedboard.org ZedBoard (Zynq Evaluation and Development) Hardware User's Guide. Available online: http://www.zedboard.org/sites/default/files/documentations/ZedBoard_HW_UG_v2_2.pdf (accessed on 27 October 2019).
43. Xilinx Documentation ZC706 Evaluation Board for the Zynq-7000 XC7Z045 SoC-User Guide. Available online: https://www.xilinx.com/support/documentation/boards_and_kits/zc706/ug954-zc706-eval-board-xc7z045-ap-soc.pdf (accessed on 27 October 2019).
44. Cacciotti, M.; Camus, V.; Schlachter, J.; Pezzotta, A.; Enz, C. Hardware Acceleration of HDR-Image Tone Mapping on an FPGA-CPU Platform Through High-Level Synthesis. In Proceedings of the 2018 31st IEEE International System-on-Chip Conference (SOCC), Arlington, VA, USA, 4–7 September 2018; IEEE: Piscataway, NJ, USA, 2018; pp. 158–162.
45. Kowalczyk, M.; Przewlocka, D.; Krvjak, T. Real-Time Implementation of Contextual Image Processing Operations for 4K Video Stream in Zynq UltraScale+ MPSoC. In Proceedings of the Conference on Design and Architectures for Signal and Image Processing (DASIP), Porto, Portugal, 10–12 October 2018; pp. 37–42.
46. Xilinx Documentation SDSoC Environment User Guide UG1027. Available online: https://www.xilinx.com/support/documentation/sw_manuals/xilinx2017_4/ug1027-sdsoc-user-guide.pdf (accessed on 27 October 2019).
47. Nethercote, N.; Seward, J. Valgrind: A framework for heavyweight dynamic binary instrumentation. *ACM Sigplan Not.* **2007**, *42*, 89–100. [CrossRef]
48. Graham, S.L.; Kessler, P.B.; Mckusick, M.K. Gprof: A call graph execution profiler. *ACM Sigplan Not.* **1982**, *17*, 120–126. [CrossRef]
49. VAPNIK, V. *Estimation of Dependences Based on Empirical Data*; Springer: Cham, Switzerland, 2006; ISBN 9780387342399.
50. Boser, B.E.; Guyon, I.M.; Vapnik, V.N. A training algorithm for optimal margin classifiers. In Proceedings of the Fifth Annual Workshop on Computational Learning Theory, Pittsburgh, PA, USA, 27–29 July 1992; pp. 144–152.
51. Hsu, C.-W.; Lin, C.-J. A comparison of methods for multiclass support vector machines. *IEEE Trans. Neural Netw.* **2002**, *13*, 415–425. [PubMed]
52. Mountrakis, G.; Im, J.; Ogole, C. Support vector machines in remote sensing: A review. *ISPRS J. Photogramm. Remote Sens.* **2011**, *66*, 247–259. [CrossRef]
53. Camps-Valls, G.; Bruzzone, L. Kernel-based methods for hyperspectral image classification. *IEEE Trans. Geosci. Remote Sens.* **2005**, *43*, 1351–1362. [CrossRef]

54. Fabelo, H.; Ortega, S.; Lazcano, R.; Madroñal, D.M.; Callicó, G.; Juárez, E.; Salvador, R.; Bulters, D.; Bulstrode, H.; Szolna, A.; et al. An Intraoperative Visualization System Using Hyperspectral Imaging to Aid in Brain Tumor Delineation. *Sensors* **2018**, *18*, 430. [CrossRef]
55. Chang, C.-C.; Lin, C.-J. LIBSVM: A library for support vector machines. *ACM Trans. Intell. Syst. Technol.* **2011**, *2*, 1–27. [CrossRef]
56. Fabelo, H.; Ortega, S.; Szolna, A.; Bulters, D.; Pineiro, J.F.; Kabwama, S.; J-O'Shanahan, A.; Bulstrode, H.; Bisshopp, S.; Kiran, B.R.; et al. In-Vivo Hyperspectral Human Brain Image Database for Brain Cancer Detection. *IEEE Access* **2019**, *7*, 39098–39116. [CrossRef]
57. Fabelo, H.; Ortega, S.; Ravi, D.; Kiran, B.R.; Sosa, C.; Bulters, D.; Callicó, G.M.; Bulstrode, H.; Szolna, A.; Piñeiro, J.F.; et al. Spatio-spectral classification of hyperspectral images for brain cancer detection during surgical operations. *PLoS ONE* **2018**, *13*, e0193721. [CrossRef]
58. Kelly, C.; Siddiqui, F.M.; Bardak, B.; Woods, R. Histogram of oriented gradients front end processing: An FPGA based processor approach. In Proceedings of the IEEE Workshop on Signal Processing Systems (SiPS: Design and Implementation), Belfast, UK, 20–22 October 2014; IEEE: Piscataway, NJ, USA, 2014.
59. Mahmoodi, D.; Soleimani, A.; Khosravi, H.; Taghizadeh, M. FPGA Simulation of Linear and Nonlinear Support Vector Machine. *J. Softw. Eng. Appl.* **2011**, *4*, 320–328. [CrossRef]
60. Patil, R.A.; Gupta, G.; Sahula, V.; Mandal, A.S. Power aware hardware prototyping of multiclass SVM classifier through reconfiguration. In Proceedings of the IEEE International Conference on VLSI Design, Hyderabad, India, 7–11 January 2012; pp. 62–67.
61. Cutajar, M.; Gatt, E.; Grech, I.; Casha, O.; Micallef, J. Hardware-based support vector machine for phoneme classification. In Proceedings of the IEEE EuroCon 2013, Zagreb, Croatia, 1–4 July 2013; pp. 1701–1708.
62. Mandal, B.; Sarma, M.P.; Sarma, K.K.; Mastorakis, N. Implementation of Systolic Array Based SVM Classifier Using Multiplierless Kernel. In Proceedings of the 16th International Conference on Automatic Control, Modelling & Simulation (ACMOS'14), Brasov, Romania, 26–28 June 2014; ISBN 9789604743834.
63. Khosravi, H.; Kabir, E. Introducing a very large dataset of handwritten Farsi digits and a study on their varieties. *Pattern Recognit. Lett.* **2007**, *28*, 1133–1141. [CrossRef]
64. Lucey, P.; Cohn, J.F.; Kanade, T.; Saragih, J.; Ambadar, Z.; Matthews, I. The extended Cohn-Kanade dataset (CK+): A complete dataset for action unit and emotion-specified expression. In Proceedings of the 2010 IEEE Computer Society Conference on Computer Vision and Pattern Recognition-Workshops (CVPRW 2010), San Francisco, CA, USA, 13–18 June 2010; pp. 94–101.
65. Garofolo, J.S.; Lamel, L.F.; Fisher, W.M.; Fiscus, J.G.; Pallett, D.S. *DARPA TIMIT Acoustic-Phonetic Continous Speech Corpus CD-ROM. NIST Speech Disc 1-1.1*; NASA STI/Recon Technical Report N: Gaithersburg, MD, USA, 1993; Volume 93.

© 2019 by the authors. Licensee MDPI, Basel, Switzerland. This article is an open access article distributed under the terms and conditions of the Creative Commons Attribution (CC BY) license (http://creativecommons.org/licenses/by/4.0/).

 *electronics*

Article

The Design of a 2D Graphics Accelerator for Embedded Systems

Hyun Woo Oh, Ji Kwang Kim, Gwan Beom Hwang and Seung Eun Lee *

Department of Electronic Engineering, Seoul National University of Science and Technology, Seoul 01811, Korea; ohhyunwoo@seoultech.ac.kr (H.W.O.); jikwang.kim@seoultech.ac.kr (J.K.K.); hwanggwanbeom@seoultech.ac.kr (G.B.H.)
* Correspondence: seung.lee@seoultech.ac.kr; Tel.: +82-2-970-9021

Citation: Oh, H.W.; Kim, J.K.; Hwang, G.B.; Lee, S.E. The Design of a 2D Graphics Accelerator for Embedded Systems. *Electronics* **2021**, *10*, 469. https://doi.org/10.3390/electronics10040469

Academic Editor: Jorge Portilla

Received: 21 December 2020
Accepted: 10 February 2021
Published: 15 February 2021

Publisher's Note: MDPI stays neutral with regard to jurisdictional claims in published maps and institutional affiliations.

Copyright: © 2021 by the authors. Licensee MDPI, Basel, Switzerland. This article is an open access article distributed under the terms and conditions of the Creative Commons Attribution (CC BY) license (https://creativecommons.org/licenses/by/4.0/).

Abstract: Recently, advances in technology have enabled embedded systems to be adopted for a variety of applications. Some of these applications require real-time 2D graphics processing running on limited design specifications such as low power consumption and a small area. In order to satisfy such conditions, including a specific 2D graphics accelerator in the embedded system is an effective method. This method reduces the workload of the processor in the embedded system by exploiting the accelerator. The accelerator assists the system to perform 2D graphics processing in real-time. Therefore, a variety of applications that require 2D graphics processing can be implemented with an embedded processor. In this paper, we present a 2D graphics accelerator for tiny embedded systems. The accelerator includes an optimized line-drawing operation based on Bresenham's algorithm. The optimized operation enables the accelerator to deal with various kinds of 2D graphics processing and to perform the line-drawing instead of the system processor. Moreover, the accelerator also distributes the workload of the processor core by removing the need for the core to access the frame buffer memory. We measure the performance of the accelerator by implementing the processor, including the accelerator, on a field-programmable gate array (FPGA), and ascertaining the possibility of realization by synthesizing using the 180 nm CMOS process.

Keywords: 2D graphics accelerator; embedded system; line-drawing; Bresenham's algorithm; alpha-blending; anti-aliasing

1. Introduction

Recently, as advances in computer technology and semiconductor process technology lead a processor to high performance and high integration density, the overall performance of an embedded system, such as computing performance and energy efficiency, has been increased [1,2]. Due to the progress of embedded systems, the demand for adopting embedded systems for a variety of applications is also increasing [3–9]. Some of these applications, such as user-centric applications, require communication with users through 2D graphics [10]. Therefore, an embedded system used in these applications requires the functions to process graphics data and write data on the display device. In order to perform these functions, an embedded system, which includes a general-purpose processor (GPP), generally utilizes the GPP or additional graphics processing units (GPUs) with a graphics library [3]. However, performing a graphics process in real-time using these methods requires a high-performance GPP or GPU due to the execution of a large number of instruction codes in a limited time. For this reason, these methods are not appropriate for applications that have limited design specifications such as low power consumption or a small area [10–12].

In order to solve these issues, 2D graphics accelerators, which perform 2D graphics processing implemented in hardware, were proposed for embedded systems [13,14]. These accelerators are connected to the processor in the embedded system through various kinds of interfaces such as PCI Express and memory bus. Unlike the core of a GPP, which requires a long execution time because it performs only simple operations with one instruction, a hardware accelerator can perform complex operations relatively fast [15–19]. Moreover, the accelerators have a relatively small area because of the limited and optimized execution logic [20–24]. Therefore, including and exploiting the 2D graphics accelerator allows for a variety of applications that require 2D graphics operations to be implemented with low power and small size. As applying architecture to the system that contains a specific accelerator is an efficient way to satisfy the design specifications of the embedded system, research to design the accelerator for image processing has been performed [25].

Line-drawing is one of the methods to visualize the graphics. As every image is represented as a collection of lines, line-drawing is a basic means of drawing an image [26,27]. Accordingly, the line-drawing operation can deal with various kinds of graphics processing [28,29]. Although this approach is not the most efficient way for all situations, this approach is significantly efficient when the data to be displayed are in the form of points and lines. In this point of view, some research was performed to utilize line-drawing for image processing [27]. Nevertheless, there is not a lot of research using line-drawing as a core algorithm for a graphics accelerator. Our research motivation starts with the idea to apply line-drawing for a graphics accelerator.

In this paper, we present a 2D graphics accelerator for embedded systems. The accelerator performs a 2D graphics process with a line-drawing operation based on Bresenham's algorithm. Furthermore, the accelerator provides anti-aliasing and alpha-blending features. The accelerator is directly connected to the memory bus to communicate with the core of the processor in the embedded system. Based on this structure, the accelerator can be controlled through reading or writing to certain memory addresses. Moreover, the accelerator is directly connected to the frame buffer, which has the memory to send 2D graphic data to a display device. This architectural characteristic reduces workloads by offloading the burden of the processor to have access to the frame buffer. We analyzed the performance of the accelerator by simulating and implementing the processor including the 2D graphics accelerator on a field-programmable gate array (FPGA). In addition, we ascertained the feasibility of the accelerator by synthesizing the accelerator with the Synopsys design compiler using the 180 nm CMOS process.

The paper consists of the following: Section 2 describes the preliminaries, which are essential to implement the features of the accelerator. The preliminaries are composed of Bresenham's algorithm, alpha-blending, and anti-aliasing. Section 3 explicates the architecture of the 2D graphics accelerator and explains the reasons for adopting the architecture. Section 4 describes the hardware implementation results, the analysis results of the accelerator through a sample application running on implemented hardware, and the synthesis results through the Synopsys design compiler. Section 5 summarizes our entire work and presents future work.

2. Preliminaries

A line-drawing algorithm is an essential element to implement the presented 2D graphics accelerator. As the algorithms vary according to the design architecture and resource usage of the hardware, choosing an appropriate algorithm is important. We chose Bresenham's algorithm and optimized it for the hardware accelerator [30]. Moreover, in order to provide advanced visualization, supporting additional features such as alpha-blending and anti-aliasing are needed.

2.1. Bresenham's Line Algorithm

Bresenham's line algorithm is one of the line-drawing algorithms and is typically used in raster graphics systems [31,32]. The algorithm calculates the position of the pixels to draw the lines. As this process performs only with integer arithmetic calculation, the process has low complexity and a fast calculation speed [33]. In raster graphics, lines are drawn as a way of painting pixels between the start point and end point. Figure 1 represents the various types of lines by Bresenham's algorithm. The two lines in Figure 1a are the type that the x coordinates of the painting pixels always increment by one while drawing lines, and the two lines in Figure 1b are the type that the y coordinates of the drawing pixels always increment. The type of the line depends on the slope of the line. The slope, marked as letter m, represents the y-coordinate change, marked as dy, compared to the x-coordinate change, marked as dx, of the line, expressed by dividing dy by dx. The expression of the line is as shown in expression (1) because of the slope attribute as m and the line including the start point (x_1, y_1).

$$m = \frac{dy}{dx}, \quad y = m(x - x_1) + y_1 \tag{1}$$

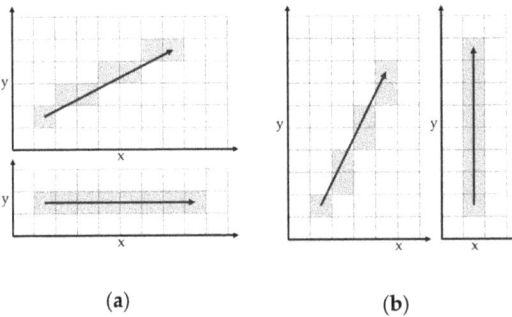

(a)   (b)

Figure 1. Various lines by Bresenham's algorithm. (**a**) Lines when dx > dy; (**b**) Lines when dx < dy.

Figure 2 presents the fundamentals of the algorithm for drawing each type of line. The algorithm proceeds by selecting the next point to paint based on the current point, marked as (x_i, y_i). Figure 2a shows the case of x coordinates of the points always increment while drawing lines. In this case, choosing the y coordinate of the next point between being changed and not being changed is needed. This job is executed by the following operations. Calculate where the real value y at point $(x_i + 1, y)$ is close to y_i or $y_i + 1$, change the y coordinate when y is close to $y_i + 1$. The algorithm repeats these operations until the current point reaches the end point. In the case of y coordinates of the points always increment, the algorithm proceeds by similar operations as shown in Figure 2b.

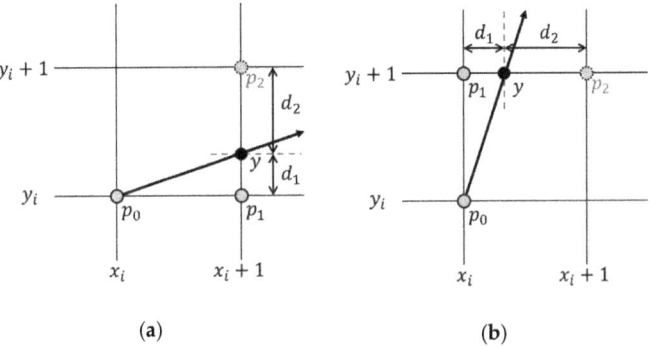

(a)   (b)

Figure 2. Bresenham's line algorithm according to the line type. (**a**) Lines when dx > dy; (**b**) Lines when dx < dy.

Although the algorithm can be implemented in hardware as it is, optimizing the algorithm for hardware reduces the resource usage. Accordingly, the algorithm should be optimized for hardware implementation by the transformation of the pseudo-code. The following pseudo-code can be obtained through the appropriate transformation of this process as shown in Algorithm 1. In order to optimize the algorithm, binary division, which has a high cost in hardware implementation, is fully excluded by the transformation. This optimization allows the implemented hardware of the algorithm to achieve the design specifications for embedded systems such as low power consumption and less area.

Algorithm 1: Bresenham's line algorithm pseudo-code

Input   : $P_s(x_s, y_s)$, $P_e(x_e, y_e)$
Output : $P = \{P_i(x_i, y_i)\}$

1 $i \leftarrow 0$, $x_i \leftarrow x_s$, $y_i \leftarrow y_s$;
2 $err \leftarrow dx - dy$, $e2 \leftarrow 2 \times err$;
3 **while** $x_i \neq x_e$ or $y_i \neq y_e$ **do**
4   **if** $e2 \geq -dy$ **then**
5        $err \leftarrow err - dy$;
6        $x_{i+1} \leftarrow x_i + sx$; $(sx \leftarrow +1 \text{ or } -1)$
7   **end**
8   **if** $e2 \leq +dx$ **then**
9        $err \leftarrow err + dx$;
10       $y_{i+1} \leftarrow y_i + sy$; $(sy \leftarrow +1 \text{ or } -1)$
11   **end**
12    $e2 \leftarrow 2 \times err$, $i \leftarrow i^{++}$;
13 **end**

2.2. Bresenham's Circle Algorithm

When the width of the line to draw is greater than one pixel's width, drawing the edge of the line to a certain shape increases the quality of the visualization. The circle shape is one of the proper choices. In order to draw circle shapes, we adopt Bresenham's circle algorithm. The algorithm proceedings are similar to Bresenham's line algorithm. Figure 3 shows the rough fundamentals of Bresenham's circle algorithm. Based on the current point (x_i, y_i), the algorithm selects the next painting point between $p_1(x_i, +1, y_i)$ and $p_2(x_i + 1, y_i - 1)$. In order to select the point, calculate the result of the expression (2) by input $(x_i + 1, y_i - 0.5)$. The next point is p_2 when the result is lower than 0. Otherwise, the next point is p_1.

$$f = x^2 + y^2 - r^2 \qquad (2)$$

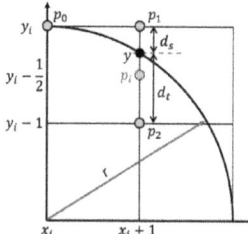

Figure 3. Bresenham's circle algorithm.

2.3. Alpha-Blending

In order to provide drawing graphics with transparency and blending with the original image, alpha-blending is needed. Figure 4 shows the description of alpha-blending. Each pixel's data in the image to draw has an alpha value α to express the transparency. Alpha-blending blends the graphics to draw and the original image by reading the color value of each pixel of the original image and graphics to draw, calculating the new pixel value of the image frame by expression (3). As the color of the digital image is composed of three color elements—red, green, and blue—the calculation of the new color of pixel p requires calculating each three-color axis.

$$p_{new} = \alpha p_{draw} + (1 - \alpha) p_{original} \qquad (3)$$

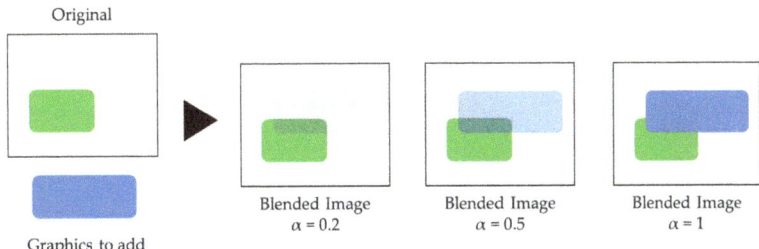

Figure 4. Description of alpha-blending.

2.4. Anti-Aliasing

When expressing a graphical object that has a higher pixel density than the target graphics system, aliasing can be generated because the raster graphics system has limited pixel density. As the line to draw is an ideal graphical object that has unlimited pixel density, the generation rate of aliasing is very high. Anti-aliasing is a technique to deal with this problem. Figure 5 shows the description of anti-aliasing. Anti-aliasing improves visualization of the aliasing-generated lines, such as the line shown in Figure 5a, by blurring the rough edges at the borders of the line. Blurring can be done by decrementing the alpha value of the rough edges sequentially as shown in Figure 5b.

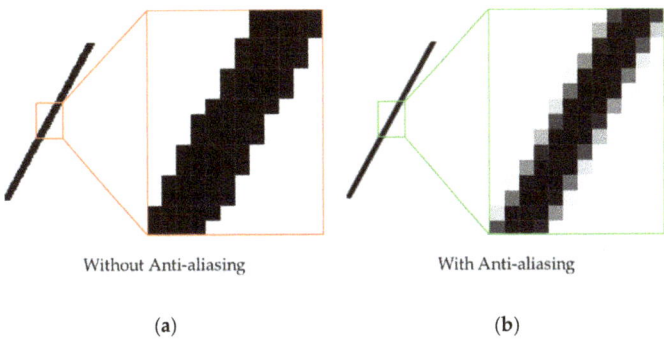

Figure 5. Description of anti-aliasing. (a) Line without anti-aliasing; (b) Line with anti-aliasing.

The anti-aliasing process starts with detecting the borders of the line. Akin to Bresenham's line algorithm, the anti-aliasing has two types of lines to process, which are related to the slope value. Figure 6 shows the progression of the anti-aliasing process. The anti-aliasing starts with detecting the start point and end point of each border segment. The detection is executed while drawing a line with Bresenham's line algorithm by checking the generated coordinates. Next, as the start point ends and the end point of the border segment is clarified, the process applies the decremental alpha value to each point of the border segment. The following pseudo-code presents the process to apply the alpha value when the slope is lower than or equal to one. The alpha value of the pixel is quantified by three bits, maximum of seven, to reduce the area of the circuit by minimizing the arithmetic calculation.

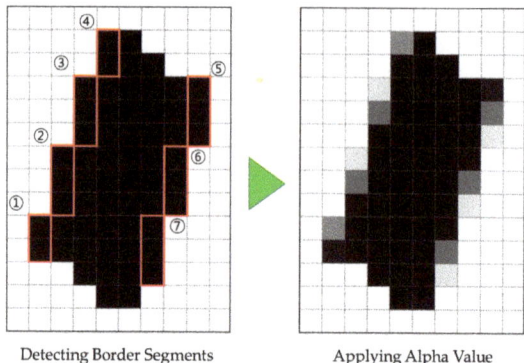

Figure 6. Progression of the anti-aliasing process.

3. 2D Graphics Accelerator

The 2D graphics accelerator provides the 2D graphic processing features including line-drawing, alpha-blending, and anti-aliasing. In order to perform the execution with those features, the accelerator receives setup data, such as start point, end point, the width of the line, bit per pixel (BPP), other configurations, and start flag, from the core of the processor. After the setup data are received and the start instruction is sent, the accelerator operates independently to the core during execution. When the line-drawing process is completed, the accelerator sends the interrupt signal to the interrupt handler of the processor, letting the core recognize the line-drawing process is completed. Based on this characteristic, the workload of the processor is reduced by making it unnecessary for the processor to continuously check what the accelerator completed.

3.1. Line-Drawing Process

Figure 7 presents the progression of the line-drawing process. The setup first receives the line configuration from the core, such as start point, end point, and line width. The module generates the aligned coordinate, slope, line width, and point of the edges from the line configuration and transfers to edge builder. The edge builder sets up the borders of the line by generating the coordinates. The accelerator has three cap modes called perpendicular, vertical, and circle for drawing line caps. Line caps are created by submodules in edge builder. The submodules transfer the minimum and maximum value of x and y coordinates to the line detector module. The line detector starts to process line-drawing by determining what coordinates are borders. The painter generates the coordinates to paint, which are inside the borders, and executes the anti-aliasing process when the anti-aliasing option is set. Finally, the blender paints the pixels with alpha-blending through options transferred from the setup and coordinates from the painter by writing the color to the frame buffer.

3.2. Optimized Architecture

Figure 8 shows the architecture of the processor including the proposed 2D graphics accelerator. As shown in Figure 8a, the accelerator is connected to the core through the memory bus of the processor. For this reason, the core controls the accelerator through memory access instructions. Moreover, the frame buffer is directly connected to the accelerator and connected to the memory bus. Based on this architecture, the core can deal with the conditions that line-drawing is inefficient to process 2D graphics, such as loading a bitmap image to the frame buffer. This characteristic enables the processor to respond flexibly and efficiently to various conditions. Figure 8b presents the architecture of the 2D graphics accelerator.

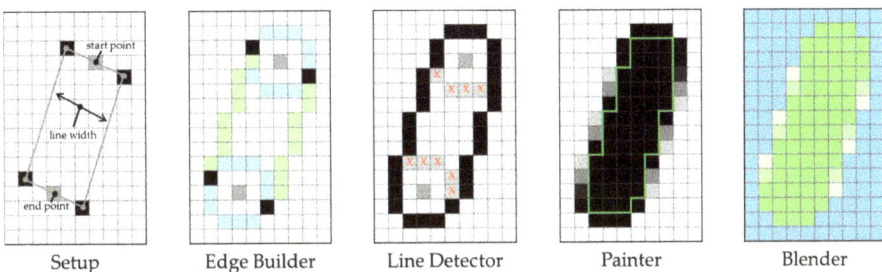

Figure 7. Progression of the line-drawing process.

The accelerator contains the following six modules, called config register, setup, edge builder, line detector, painter, and blender. Config register is a module to save the line configuration and options, such as anti-aliasing and cap mode, from the memory bus. The other modules perform the line-drawing process with options saved in the config register. The five modules, which perform the line-drawing process, operate as a pipelined architecture. Therefore, the accelerator provides high throughput.

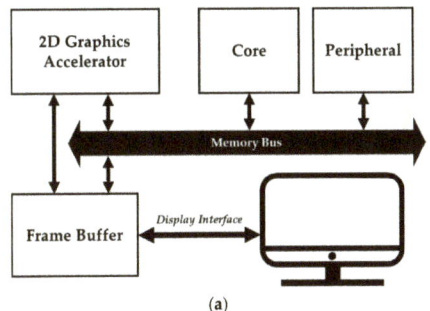

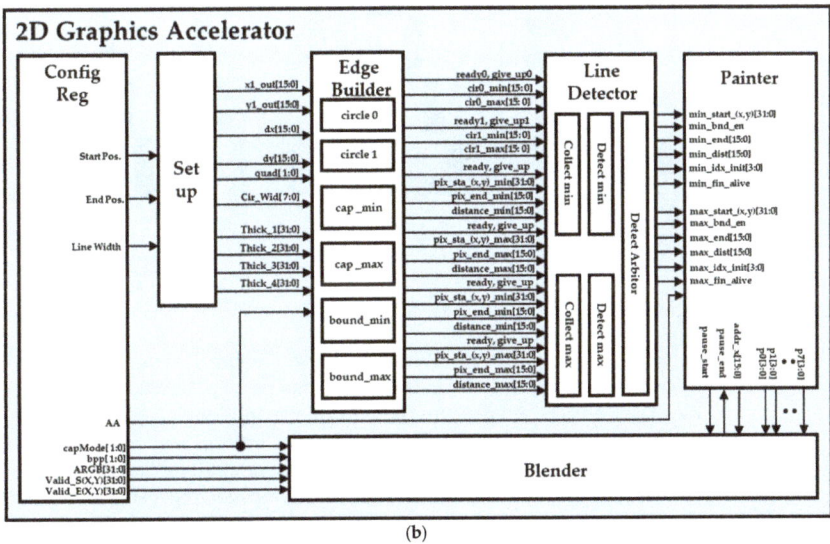

Figure 8. Architecture of the processor and 2D graphics accelerator. (**a**) Architecture of the processor with 2D graphics accelerator; (**b**) Architecture of the 2D graphics accelerator.

In the setup module, the operation to generate the coordinates of the four edges is executed based on the width of the line and the distance between the start point and end point. These coordinates are used for the edge builder module, which is the next pipelined stage. Figure 9 is a block diagram to explain the operations of the edge builder. The edge builder receives the following data signals: minimum and maximum (x, y) coordinates of the points, the distance between the start point and end point (dx, dy), width of the circle to paint when the cap mode is circle, line width, and cap mode. The module generates coordinates of the borders with these signals and submodules. Figure 10 shows all of the cap modes. The edge builder has three selectable cap modes, perpendicular, vertical, and circle, to paint the line caps. The circle submodule generates the coordinates to paint a pixel, which is circular-shaped on edges. The cap submodule generates the coordinates that are parallelogram-shaped, and rectangle-shaped. The line submodule generates borders of the line except for the edges. The entire submodule operates in parallel to provide fast execution. The generated coordinates are sent to the line detector module.

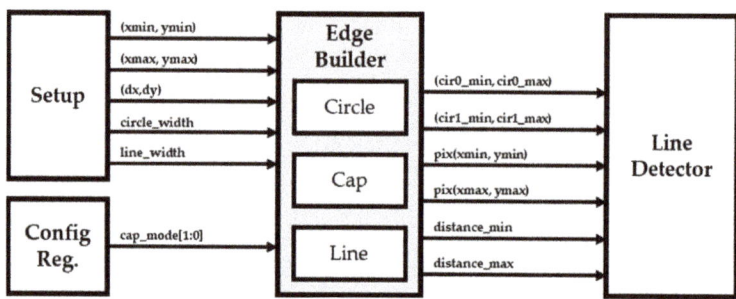

Figure 9. Block diagram of the edge builder.

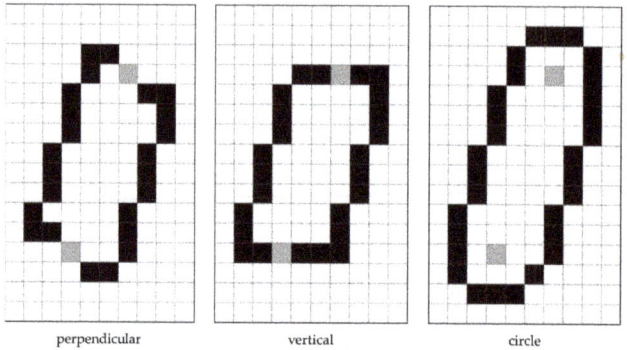

Figure 10. Cap modes of the edge builder.

As the circle submodule generates the whole circular edge, removing the coordinates that are inside the borders is required. This process is done by the line detector module. The line detector receives the coordinates from the edge builder and detects which coordinate is a valid border. Then, it transfers the valid borders, and the minimum and maximum value of the coordinates, to the painter module. The painter module generates the coordinates inside the borders and paints the pixels of generated coordinates by writing the RGBA data to the memory at a certain address. The address to write the RGBA data can be configured by writing the address to the config register through the memory bus. In addition, the module smooths the pixels at borders through the anti-aliasing when anti-aliasing mode is set on the config register. The written RGBA data are used by the blender module. The blender is a module to draw the line to the display device. As the frame buffer has the previous image drawn, blending the drawing line with the image is required. Therefore, the blender performs the alpha-blending with the previous image and the coordinates of the line to draw. Finally, the blender writes the updated image to the frame buffer, and provides the images to be shown to the display device.

4. Implementation and Analysis

In order to implement and verify the 2D graphics accelerator, we verified the algorithms that are required for the 2D graphics accelerator by programming software. We describe the scripts using MATLAB to verify the algorithms, which are line-drawing, anti-aliasing, alpha-blending, and drawing various line caps. As the algorithms are verified, we transformed the algorithms in accordance with the register-transfer level (RTL) and designed the accelerator with Verilog HDL.

In order to evaluate the 2D graphics accelerator, we integrated the accelerator into the processor, which includes Cortex M0 as a core, by interfacing the accelerator and the core with an AHB-Lite bus. Furthermore, the function that generates the interrupt request signal when the drawing of one line is complete is added. Next, before synthesizing the processor to hardware, we simulated the processor on Vivado 2020.1 version to verify the functionality of the accelerator by executing a customized testbench with a sample program included in the internal ROM of the processor. The embedded program performs the same work as previous MATLAB scripts. The interrupt request signal is generated when the accelerator completes the drawing of one line, and the next configuration of the line is performed by the program.

The synthesis and implementation were executed with the same Vivado tool with a Xilinx xc7z010clg400 FPGA. Table 1 shows the resource utilization of the 2D graphics accelerator and the processor. The result presents that the resource usage of the 2D graphics accelerator is suitable for embedded systems as the utilization of the processor containing the 2D graphics accelerator does not exceed eighty percent of the programmable logic.

Table 1. Resource utilization of the processor including 2D graphics accelerator.

	Resource	Synthesis	Utilization %
2D graphics Accelerator	LUTs [1]	5050	28.69
	Flip-Flops [2]	3087	8.77
	DSP [3]	3	3.75
Processor	LUTs	13,923	79.10
	Flip-Flops	4501	12.79
	DSP	4	5

[1] total of 17,600 [2] total of 35,200, [3] total of 80.

Table 2 presents the performance of the accelerator on 1024 × 768 resolution at 30 frames per second. In order to evaluate the line-drawing performance, we set up the start point and end point as (50, 50) and (700, 900), which are almost the top-left and bottom-right edges of the display, and tested for various conditions such as operating frequency and line width. The result shows that even if the width is as thick as 50 pixels, line-drawing can be performed with more than one line per frame when the operating frequency is more than 50 MHz. According to this result, the accelerator is suitable for a wide range of applications that have resource limitations and line-drawing-based features such as a real-time scope. However, as the results of Table 2 indicate that the drawing efficiency decreases when the width of the line is small, applying the accelerator to complex graphics applications that are not based on line-drawing can be a challenge.

Table 2. Performance of the 2D graphics accelerator.

1024 × 768 @ 30 fps	Width					
	1 px			50 px		
Clock cycles per line		21,634			246,613	
Operating frequency (MHz)	50	100	120	50	100	120
Times per line (ms/line)	0.43	0.22	0.18	4.93	2.47	2.06
Lines per frame (line/frame)	77	154	185	7	14	16

In order to test the features of the accelerator, line-drawing with various cap modes, anti-aliasing, and alpha-blending, we ran the test firmware on the processor that draws the various kinds of lines by controlling the 2D graphics accelerator with memory access. The processor contains the video graphics array (VGA) controller to display the image in the frame buffer to a display device through a VGA protocol. Consequently, the 2D graphics features, namely line-drawing, alpha-blending, and anti-aliasing, are visually identified by the display device as shown in Figure 11.

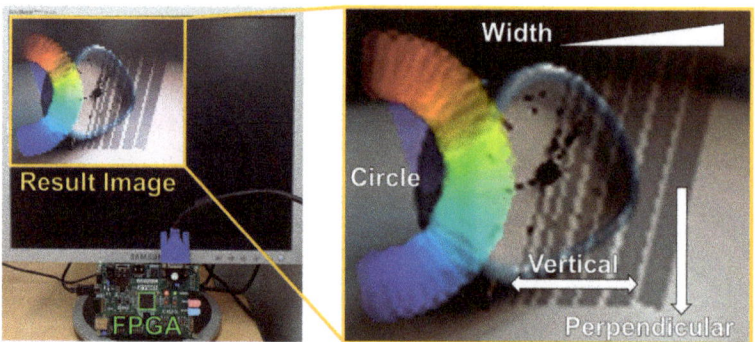

Figure 11. Experimental environment of the field-programmable gate array (FPGA) implementation.

One of the essential things in verifying the feasibility of the 2D graphics accelerator is to identify the area of the actual synthesized circuit. In order to identify the area, we synthesize the accelerator by Synopsys design compiler N-2017.09-SP2 version using the 180 nm CMOS process. Table 3 summarizes the synthesis result. The result shows that the total area of the accelerator is 742,494 um^2, which is around 75K gate counts. The results from Tables 2 and 3 show that the accelerator can be realized through a chip with acceptable performance, drawing more than one line per frame. Therefore, attaching the 2D graphics accelerator to the embedded processor can be a suitable solution to deal with design specifications when the application of the system can effectively be composed with line-drawing features.

Table 3. Synthesis result of the 2D graphics accelerator.

Process Technology	180 nm CMOS
Operating frequency (MHz)	100
Area (um^2)	742,494.25
Estimated gate count	75,406

5. Conclusions

In this paper, we proposed a 2D graphics accelerator, based on line-drawing, for embedded systems. As line-drawing can be a basic element of image drawing in specific applications, defining required 2D graphics as a set of multiple lines is an effective way to implement graphic features rather than other methods. The accelerator provides the basic line-drawing features and user-centric features that improve visualization, such as alpha-blending and anti-aliasing. In order to implement these 2D graphics features, we analyzed the line-drawing algorithm and required functions. Moreover, we optimized the algorithm and functions for hardware realization. By transforming the binary division and reducing the size of arithmetic calculation in the algorithm, the algorithm can be implemented with fewer arithmetic units and enables the hardware to operate with low power and few resources. We also constructed a system-on-a-chip including the accelerator for embedded systems. We also included the designed accelerator in the processor, which is used for embedded systems. The accelerator is connected to the core through the memory bus of the processor to receive line configuration and start signals from the core. As the accelerator is directly connected to the frame buffer, the accelerator works independently of the core while performing the line-drawing process. Based on these characteristics of the architecture, the core can execute other jobs while the accelerator performs graphics processes. As a result, the overall performance of the processor with applications using 2D graphics can be improved. In addition, the results of the FPGA implementation and the synthesis using the 180 nm CMOS process show that the accelerator is feasible to realize.

In future work, we will apply our 2D graphics accelerator to a variety of applications that are implemented on embedded systems, compare the performance of the accelerator with other methods, such as implementation with a GPP or GPU. As the drawing performance of the accelerator is not suitable for complex, microscopic graphic processes, classifying and finding the applications that have appropriate conditions to apply the accelerator is necessary. We expect that applying the 2D graphics accelerator based on line-drawing to the processor can be effective in a variety of embedded systems.

Author Contributions: Conceptualization, H.W.O., J.K.K., and G.B.H.; methodology, J.K.K.; software, G.B.H.; validation, H.W.O., J.K.K., and G.B.H.; investigation, H.W.O. and J.K.K.; writing—original draft preparation, H.W.O.; writing—review and editing, H.W.O. and S.E.L.; visualization, H.W.O. and G.B.H.; supervision, S.E.L. All authors have read and agreed to the published version of the manuscript.

Funding: This research was funded by the National Research Foundation of Korea (NRF) grant funded by the Korean government (MSIT). No. 2019R1F1A1060044, 'Multi-core Hardware Accelerator for High-Performance Computing (HPC)'. This research was also funded by the Ministry of Trade, Industry & Energy (MOTIE, Korea) under the Industrial Technology Innovation Program. No. 10076314, 'Development of lightweight SW-SoC solution for respiratory medical device'.

Conflicts of Interest: The authors declare no conflict of interest.

References

1. Yoon, Y.H.; Hwang, D.H.; Yang, J.H.; Lee, S.E. Intellino: Processor for Embedded Artificial Intelligence. *Electronics* **2020**, *9*, 1169. [CrossRef]
2. Guo, F.; Wan, W.; Zhang, W.; Feng, X. Research of Graphics Acceleration Based on Embedded System. In Proceedings of theInternational Conference on Audio, Language and Image Processing, Shanghai, China, 16–18 July 2012; pp. 1120–1124.
3. Cheng, K.; Wang, Y. Using mobile GPU for general-purpose computing—A case study of face recognition on smartphones. In Proceedings of the 2011 International Symposium on VLSI Design, Automation and Test, Hsinchu, Taiwan, 25–28 April 2011; pp. 1–4.
4. Reddy, B.; Kim, Y.; Yun, S.; Seo, C.; Jang, J. Real-Time Driver Drowsiness Detection for Embedded System Using Model Compression of Deep Neural Networks. In Proceedings of the IEEE Conference on Computer Vision and Pattern Recognition (CVPR) Workshops, Honolulu, HI, USA, 21–26 July 2017; pp. 121–128.
5. Duffau, C.; Grabiec, B.; Blay-Fornarino, M. Towards Embedded System Agile Development Challenging Verification, Validation and Accreditation: Application in a Healthcare Company. In Proceedings of the IEEE International Symposium on Software Reliability Engineering Workshops, Toulouse, France, 23–26 October 2017; pp. 82–85.
6. Chen, Y.L.; Chiang, H.H.; Chiang, C.Y.; Liu, C.M.; Yuan, S.M.; Wang, J.H. A vision-based driver nighttime assistance and surveillance system based on intelligent image sensing techniques and a heterogamous dual-core embedded system architecture. *Sensors* **2012**, *12*, 2373–2399. [CrossRef] [PubMed]

7. Marchesan, G.C.; Carara, E.A.; Zanetti, M.S.; de Oliveira, L.L. Exploring the Training and Execution Acceleration of a Neural Network in a Reconfigurable General-purpose Processor for Embedded Systems. In Proceedings of the 17th IEEE International New Circuits and Systems Conference, Munich, Germany, 23–26 June 2019; pp. 1–4.
8. Arslan, S.; Gündüzalp, M.; Türk, E. An embedded system vehicle tracking system application. In Proceedings of the National Conference on Electrical, Electronics and Biomedical Engineering, Bursa, Turkey, 1–3 December 2016; pp. 447–451.
9. Yazgaç, B.G.; Kırcı, M. Embedded system application for sunn pest detection. In Proceedings of the 6th International Conference on Agro-Geoinformatics, Fairfax, VA, USA, 7–10 August 2017; pp. 1–6.
10. Kim, J.K.; Oh, J.H.; Yang, J.H.; Lee, S.E. 2D Line Draw Hardware Accelerator for Tiny Embedded Processor in Consumer Electronics. In Proceedings of the IEEE International Conference on Consumer Electronics, Las Vegas, NV, USA, 11–13 January 2019; pp. 1–2.
11. Huang, H.; Liu, Z.; Chen, T.; Hu, X.; Zhang, Q.; Xiong, X. Design Space Exploration for YOLO Neural Network Accelerator. *Electronics* **2020**, *9*, 1921. [CrossRef]
12. Yoo, J.; Krishnadasan, S.; Shin, T.; Lee, W.; Ryu, S. Accelerating vector graphics on low-end device. In Proceedings of the IEEE International Conference on Consumer Electronics, Las Vegas, NV, USA, 8–10 January 2017; pp. 180–181.
13. Pinto, A.; Harish, Y.S. Maximizing Efficiency in Reference Model Based Verification of 2D Graphics Engine. In Proceedings of the Fourth International Conference on Emerging Trends in Engineering & Technology, Port Louis, Mauritius, 18–20 November 2011; pp. 290–295.
14. Tsiktsiris, D.; Ziouzios, D.; Dasygenis, M. A portable image processing accelerator using FPGA. In Proceedings of the 7th International Conference on Modern Circuits and Systems Technologies, Thessaloniki, Greece, 7–9 May 2018; pp. 1–4.
15. Gogte, V.; Kolli, A.; Cafarella, M.J.; D'Antoni, L.; Wenisch, T.F. HARE: Hardware accelerator for regular expressions. In Proceedings of the 49th Annual IEEE/ACM International Symposium on Microarchitecture, Taipei, Taiwan, 15–19 October 2016; pp. 1–12.
16. Moini, S.; Alizadeh, B.; Emad, M.; Ebrahimpour, R. A Resource-Limited Hardware Accelerator for Convolutional Neural Networks in Embedded Vision Applications. *IEEE Trans. Circuits Syst. II Express Briefs* **2017**, *64*, 1217–1221. [CrossRef]
17. Lyons, M.J.; Brooks, D. The Design of a Bloom Filter Hardware Accelerator for Ultra Low Power Systems. In Proceedings of the 2009 ACM/IEEE International Symposium on Low Power Electronics and Design, San Francisco, CA, USA, 19–21 August 2009; pp. 371–376.
18. Dennl, C.; Ziener, D.; Teich, J. On-the-fly Composition of FPGA-Based SQL Query Accelerators Using a Partially Reconfigurable Module Library. In Proceedings of the IEEE 20th International Symposium on Field-Programmable Custom Computing Machines, Toronto, ON, Canada, 29 April–1 May 2012; pp. 45–52.
19. Tumeo, A.; Monchiero, M.; Palermo, G.; Ferrandi, F.; Sciuto, D. A Pipelined Fast 2D-DCT Accelerator for FPGA-based SoCs. In Proceedings of the IEEE Computer Society Annual Symposium on VLSI (ISVLSI '07), Porto Alegre, Brazil, 9–11 May 2007; pp. 331–336.
20. Cardarilli, G.C.; Di Nunzio, L.; Fazzolari, R.; Re, M.; Silvestri, F.; Spanò, S. Energy Consumption Saving in Embedded Microprocessors Using Hardware Accelerators. *Telkomnika* **2018**, *16*, 1019–1026. [CrossRef]
21. Zhou, Y.; Lyu, Y.; Huang, X. RoadNet: An 80-mW Hardware Accelerator for Road Detection. *IEEE Embed. Syst. Lett.* **2019**, *11*, 21–24. [CrossRef]
22. Melpignano, D.; Benini, L.; Flamand, E.; Jego, B.; Lepley, T.; Haugou, G.; Clermidy, F.; Dutoit, D. Platform 2012, a many-core computing accelerator for embedded SoCs: Performance evaluation of visual analytics applications. In Proceedings of the 49th Annual Design Automation Conference (DAC '12), New York, NY, USA, 3–7 June 2012; pp. 1137–1142.
23. Hegde, G.; Siddhartha; Ramasamy, N.; Kapre, N. CaffePresso: An optimized library for Deep Learning on embedded accelerator-based platforms. In Proceedings of the International Conference on Compliers, Architectures, and Sythesis of Embedded Systems (CASES), Pittsburgh, PA, USA, 2–7 October 2016; pp. 1–10.
24. Simon, W.A.; Qureshi, Y.M.; Levisse, A.; Zapater, M.; Atienza, D. BLADE: A BitLine Accelerator for Devices on the Edge. In Proceedings of the 2019 on Great Lakes Symposium on VLSI (GLSVLSI '19), 2019, New York, NY, USA, 9–11 May 2019; pp. 207–212.
25. Li, Y.; Liu, Z.; Xu, K.; Yu, H. A GPU-Outperforming FPGA Accelerator Architecture for Binary Convolutional Neural Networks. *ACM J. Emerg. Technol. Comput. Syst.* **2018**, *14*, 1–16. [CrossRef]
26. Freeman, H. Computer Processing of Line-Drawing Images. *ACM Comput. Surv.* **1974**, *6*, 57–97. [CrossRef]
27. Ismae, S.; Tareq, O.; Qassim, T. Hardware/software co-design for a parallel three-dimensional bresenham's algorithm. *Int. J. Electr. Comput. Eng.* **2019**, *9*, 148–156.
28. Son, M.; Kang, H.; Lee, Y.; Lee, S. Abstract Line Drawings from 2D Images. In Proceedings of the 15th Pacific Conference on Computer Graphics and Applications (PG'07), Maui, HI, USA, 29 October–2 November 2007; pp. 333–342.
29. Cao, L.; Liu, J.; Tang, X. 3D object retrieval using 2D line drawing and graph based relevance reedback. In Proceedings of the 14th ACM International Conference on Multimedia (MM '06), New York, NY, USA, 14–18 October 2006; pp. 105–108.
30. Dey, N.; Mukherjee, A. *Embedded Systems and Robotics with Open Source Tools*; CRC Press: Boca Raton, FL, USA, 2016; pp. 1–185.
31. Angel, E.; Morrison, D. Speeding up Bresenham's algorithm. *IEEE Comput. Graph. Appl.* **1991**, *11*, 16–17. [CrossRef]
32. Reid-Green, K.S. Three early algorithms. *IEEE Ann. Hist. Comput.* **2002**, *24*, 10–13. [CrossRef]
33. Haque, A.; Rahman, M.S.; Bakht, M.; Kaykobad, M. Drawing lines by uniform packing. *Comput. Graph.* **2006**, *30*, 207–212. [CrossRef]

MDPI
St. Alban-Anlage 66
4052 Basel
Switzerland
Tel. +41 61 683 77 34
Fax +41 61 302 89 18
www.mdpi.com

Electronics Editorial Office
E-mail: electronics@mdpi.com
www.mdpi.com/journal/electronics

www.ingramcontent.com/pod-product-compliance
Lightning Source LLC
LaVergne TN
LVHW070705100526
838202LV00013B/1032